D0204627

The Political Economy of National Defense

About the Book and Authors

This timely and wide-ranging study covers both the economic and the political aspects of defense spending—first by providing a theoretical framework and then by explaining, in a political economy context, the results of decisions to allocate scarce resources to defense. In doing so, the authors provide a comprehensive picture of the interaction between defense spending and the economic and political structure of the United States, complementing their exploration of topical concerns such as SDI with analysis of long-term trends and issues of timeless importance in the defense debate.

Because of the politicizing of defense planning and procurement, there have been few significant applications of optimization techniques to high-level defense issues over the past decade. As a result, there has been a rapid decline in the importance of those techniques—historically the focus of books on defense economics. Like its predecessors, this book presents optimization techniques applicable to a wide variety of defense problems, but it also illustrates what happens in actual practice and why defense decisions are often not economically efficient. The authors discuss alternatives for cases when political constraints make efficient solutions unlikely and explore changes in the defense establishment and political structures that would make economically efficient resource allocations a reality.

William J. Weida is associate professor at The Colorado College, Colorado Springs, Colorado. **Frank L. Gertcher** is senior research specialist at R&D Associates, Colorado Springs, Colorado.

The Political Economy of National Defense

**William J. Weida
and Frank L. Gertcher**

Westview Press / Boulder and London

WIDENER UNIVERSITY
WOLFGRAM
LIBRARY
CHESTER, PA.

All rights reserved. No part of this publication may be reproduced or transmitted in any form or by any means, electronic or mechanical, including photocopy, recording, or any information storage and retrieval system, without permission in writing from the publisher.

Copyright © 1987 by Westview Press, Inc.

Published in 1987 in the United States of America by Westview Press, Inc.; Frederick A. Praeger, Publisher; 5500 Central Avenue, Boulder, Colorado 80301

Library of Congress Cataloging-in-Publication Data
Weida, William J.
  The political economy of national defense.
  Bibliography: p.
  Includes index.
  1. United States—Armed Forces—Appropriations and
expenditures.   2. Munitions—United States.
3. Munitions—Economic aspects—United States.
4. Budget—United States.   5. United States—Military
policy.   6. United States—Politics and government—
1981–   .   I. Gertcher, Frank L.   II. Title.
UA23.W3694   1987   355.6′22′0973   86-19015
ISBN 0-8133-0432-6 (alk. paper)

Printed and bound in the United States of America

The paper used in this publication meets the requirements of the American National Standard for Permanence of Paper for Printed Library Materials Z39.48-1984.

10   9   8   7   6   5   4   3   2   1

Contents

Tables and Figures

Preface

We developed this book to cover both the economic and the political aspects of defense spending—first by providing a theoretical framework and then by explaining, in a political economy context, the results of decisions to allocate scarce resources to defense. In so doing, we attempted to provide a comprehensive picture of the interaction of defense spending with the economic and political structure of the United States.

Past defense economics books have generally confined themselves to explaining the applications of economic optimization techniques to defense problems. However, there have been few important applications of these techniques to high-level defense issues over the past ten years, mainly because of the politicizing of the defense planning and procurement processes. This politicized approach has been accompanied by increasing defense budgets and deep ideological differences on the relative value of key weapon systems. The result has been a decline in the importance of optimization techniques in the top-level management of today's defense establishment and in the planning of tomorrow's defense systems.

Following its predecessors, *The Political Economy of National Defense* presents applicable optimization techniques for a wide variety of defense problems, but it also shows what happens in actual practice and why defense decisions often are not economically efficient. In some cases, the book also points out possible solutions. In cases where efficient solutions are not possible, given the relevant political constraints, the book discusses possible alterations to defense establishment structures that would permit more efficient solutions.

This book is designed for serious students of defense economics, for defense planners, and for people who wish to increase their understanding of the political economy of defense. Students may wish to spend extra time on the theoretical discussions and may wish to seek additional

details in the references cited in the notes at the end of each chapter. The more casual reader may prefer to spend less time on the technical details in favor of a more general review of the analyses and the conclusions. In either case, this book should provide the reader with a bridge between the theoretical world of economic efficiency and the politically motivated world of high-level defense planning.

William J. Weida
Frank L. Gertcher

Acknowledgments

We are grateful to the many individuals who aided in the preparation of *The Political Economy of National Defense.* Dr. Donald C. Washburn and others at R&D Associates graciously provided useful information on defense programs. Major Terry Raney and others at the Air Force Academy provided insightful reviews and comments. Professors George Staller and Judith Reppy of Cornell University provided both guidance and helpful suggestions. We also want to thank Lisa Gertcher, who typed four chapters of the manuscript and put up with her father's many revisions, and Joyce DeMeyer, who did an excellent job on the tables and figures. Finally, we want to thank our wives, Betty and Judy, for their encouragement and for listening patiently over the past two years to periodic lectures on the importance of defense economics.

Although every effort was made to eliminate errors in the book, we recognize that some may have slipped through. For these we take full responsibility, and we encourage readers to correspond with us concerning corrections and suggestions for improvements.

W.J.W.
F.L.G.

Part 1
The Economics and Politics of National Defense

1
The Dual Nature of Defense

INTRODUCTION

The fundamental goals of U.S. national security policy have remained essentially unchanged since the end of World War II. These are to preserve the independence, institutions, territory, and interests of the United States and to shape an international order in which U.S. institutions and freedoms can survive and prosper.

U.S. political leaders have developed certain national security objectives to support national security policy. Some current objectives were established by previous administrations; others are new or have been modified in response to changes and emerging trends in the international situation. As the end of the twentieth century approaches, the objectives include:

- To deter military attack or coercion by the Soviet Union and its allies against the United States, its allies, and other friendly countries.
- In the event of an attack, to deny the enemy his objectives and to bring a rapid end to the conflict on terms favorable to U.S. interests.
- To promote meaningful and verifiable mutual reductions in nuclear and conventional forces through negotiations with the Soviet Union and the Warsaw Pact.
- To inhibit expansion of Soviet control and military presence and to induce the Soviet Union to withdraw from countries where it has imposed and maintains its presence by force of arms.
- To strengthen NATO and U.S. capabilities to deter or defeat the threat posed by Soviet and Warsaw Pact forces.
- To maintain the security of U.S. sea-lanes and the supply of essential resources from other countries.
- To foster the security of allies and friendly nations throughout the world.[1]

These broad policy objectives provide a basis for a defense establishment, but they do not specify the nature of the forces that must evolve to meet threats that change over time. For example, the United States could rely upon an improved strategic retaliatory force as a deterrent against Soviet nuclear attack, or it could rely upon new ballistic missile and air defenses to stop incoming Soviet nuclear warheads before they reach their intended targets. The choice of one, the other, or a mix of these or other alternatives involves both economic and political decision criteria. Further, decisionmakers operate in an environment of uncertainty regarding potential enemy intentions, the reliability of weapon systems, the nature, location, and timing of conventional conflicts and terrorist attacks, the economic impacts of defense spending, and so on.

Given these uncertainties, no defense establishment can be expected to always make the "right" decisions, even if the criteria for judging what is right were agreed upon by all of the players in the decision process. It is to the credit of the U.S. defense establishment that for the most part, national security has been preserved over the past forty years in an increasingly dangerous and uncertain world.

U.S. national defense can be viewed as both an economic and a political problem. On the economic side, scarce resources that are allocated to defense are not available for civilian use—although defense technologies often have civilian applications. Defense is also political, not only because of the political aspects of perceived threats but also because the U.S. defense budget—about $300 billion in fiscal year 1987—accounts for about 7 percent of the gross national product (GNP) and about 28 percent of total government spending.

The level of defense spending in any given year is determined through a complex political process that yields decisions that are often not economically efficient. For example, the regional allocation of billions in defense dollars is always a concern in Congress because of the effect of defense spending on jobs and other regional economic activities. This fact is not lost on the Pentagon, which has often allocated defense contracts to key congressional districts to gain support for expensive, high-priority programs.

DEFENSE AS AN ECONOMIC PROBLEM

To attain an efficient force structure, the conventional view of defense economic planners is to maximize some objective, such as strategic deterrence, subject to budget and other constraints. For example, one could combine limited quantities of missiles, bombers, submarines, crews, bases, and maintenance facilities to produce a strategic force that would maximize some probabilistic measure of "warheads on target" subject

to budget, timing, and survivability constraints.[2] This is essentially the same economic problem (although in many respects a more difficult one) as the problem of combining limited quantities of steel, plastics, rubber, paint, fabrics, labor, and production facilities to produce automobiles in such a way as to maximize long-run profits. In both cases, there is an objective, there are budgetary and other resource constraints, and there is a potential for economic efficiency.

Economy and efficiency are two different ways of looking at the same characteristic of an operation. If a business executive or a military commander has a fixed budget (or other fixed resources) and attempts to maximize long-run profits or the attainment of some other objective, the choices that maximize the objective for a given budget are the same choices that minimize the cost of attaining that objective. For example, if a given mix of land-based missiles, manned bombers, and missile equipped submarines is the system that provides maximum deterrence with a $100 billion annual budget, it is also the system that most economically achieves that level of deterrence. In other words, there is no conflict between the budgeteer who wants to economize and the military commander who wants to be efficient. Except in the determination of the overall size of the budget and the nature of the objective to be achieved, they should be able to agree on all the subsequent decisions.

Clearly, this view does not account for the larger issues of budget size and overall national objectives. For example, the size of the defense budget is regularly reviewed and modified by Congress and the Office of Management and Budget (OMB) to account for trade-offs between nondefense and defense programs. Thus, the economic problem of defense also involves deciding how much nondefense goods and services to sacrifice in the interests of national security.

The economic problem of national defense can be expanded as follows. A nation has certain resources—now and prospectively in the future—which are classified by economists as various types of land, labor, and capital. These resources can be used to satisfy many competing objectives: national defense, a high standard of living, social security, a rapid rate of economic growth, and so on. If there is full employment, the more resources the nation devotes to defense, the less it will have for social programs, and vice versa.

Some economists have suggested the use of a "social welfare function," which could be maximized by appropriately allocating the nations' resources among various activities. However, for reasons that will be explained in this book, this approach to the problem of determining the size of the defense budget is not practical. Alternatively, one could break the resource allocation problem into manageable pieces and determine efficient solutions to objectives that are subsets of some overall

objective. By knowing the efficient solutions to the pieces, the budgeteer could determine the overall budget by a bottom-up approach. However, even if efficient economic solutions are found, political realities may often force solutions that are economically inefficient.

As a reasonable economic framework, let us divide the problem of allocating resources to national defense into three levels. From the point of view of an economist, national defense may be said to depend on: (1) the quantity of national resources available now and in the future, (2) the proportion of these resources allocated to national defense, and (3) the efficiency with which the resources allocated to defense are used. Several agencies of the U.S. government, including the Council of Economic Advisers and various congressional committees, are concerned with the problem at the first and highest level. Of course, government policies cannot influence the quantity of present resources, but policies can affect the full and productive employment of resources, as well as their rate of growth, and therefore the quantity of resources that will be available in the future. (Present resources are the consequence of past economic policies.)

Problems at the second level are the responsibility of the Office of Management and Budget and the appropriations committees of Congress, although all executive departments are involved, and every member of Congress is interested. When a decision is made to devote a given amount of national resources to defense, the size of the defense budget has essentially been determined. In effect, the government is choosing between more defense and less of other things, or vice versa. For example, the cost of one B-1 bomber is equivalent to new schools in more than twenty cities; or two electric power plants, each serving a town of 60,000 people; or two fully equipped hospitals; or some thirty miles of interstate highway.

Problems at the third level—the efficient use of the resources allocated to defense—are primarily internal problems to be solved by the Department of Defense and its agencies, although for reasons that we will examine later in this book, the president, other departments, and Congress are concerned with the solutions to some of them. These problems consist of choosing efficiently, or economically, among the alternative methods of achieving defense objectives within the budget and other constraints. Alternative methods may include different strategies, different tactics, various forces, or different weapons.

It may not be apparent to those who are unfamiliar with military problems how wide the ranges of choice actually are. There are usually a large number of ways to attain a defense objective, some much more efficient than others. Consider the range of choices in the following three examples, taken from three different levels of defense decision-

making. To determine a course of action that will protect the U.S. population and economy against nuclear attack, the following three alternatives might be considered: (1) a survivable retaliatory nuclear strike force that deters a potential enemy from initiating a first strike, (2) ballistic missile and air defenses that could destroy incoming enemy warheads between the time of launch and the time they would reach their intended targets, or (3) widespread dispersal of population and industry before an impending attack. There are, of course, many ways to implementing each of these three alternatives, as well as many possible combinations of selected elements of the three.

Given a first-level decision in favor of the first alternative, a second-level problem might involve the following alternatives: (1) the development of highly survivable ballistic missile systems (example: a land-based ICBM force hardened against nuclear attack), (2) the development of sophisticated manned bombers (example: the B-1 and the Stealth), or (3) the deployment of highly survivable nuclear submarines equipped with sea-launched ballistic missiles (example: Trident missile submarines). Again, there are many possible mixes of selected elements of these three alternatives.

At the third level, one might be concerned with decisions between alternative basing modes for small, single-warhead ICBMs. These could include: (1) survivable mobile launchers, each capable of carrying a single missile, (2) superhard silos capable of surviving all but a direct nuclear hit, or (3) deploying missiles in cannisters under the sea on the continental shelf.

Dividing the big economic problem into subproblems at different levels has some disadvantages that will be considered later in this book. However, this division does make difficult analytical and decision problems tractable, which is an advantage not to be taken lightly.

DEFENSE AS A POLITICAL PROBLEM

Those who have tried to use economic efficiency criteria for decisions at various levels within the defense establishment over the past ten years have often encountered resistance that was not present in the previous decade. This resistance is due, in part, to increased political influence in the defense planning and weapons procurement processes. Politicized approaches have accompanied increases in the defense budget. In addition, deep ideological differences on weapon systems have become the norm since the late seventies. The result has been a significant decline in the importance of economic optimization techniques in managing today's defense establishment and in planning tomorrow's forces.

This book is filled with examples demonstrating that although efficient solutions to defense problems can still be found, these solutions are often not relevant to the political environment. This situation creates problems extending beyond the discouragement felt by the junior analyst who finds his "better way" has been dismissed by those in power. It places defense spending in an environment where efficiency conditions are not binding and where subjective political criteria become major determinants at increasingly lower levels within the Department of Defense.

The reader may protest that what we are describing is merely the result of normal political actions and that one has no right to expect more from the defense process in terms of efficiency than one expects from any other political process. There are several reasons why we do not believe that this is a correct view. First, although they are often not important contributors to high-level defense decisions, economic optimization techniques are often incorrectly used to rationalize those decisions, particularly in explanations to the U.S. public. Second, defense budgeting is advertised as being based on efficient practices. Third, economic optimization techniques are often extremely useful in making decisions in weapons procurement, force management, and support functions. Fourth, economic optimization techniques are helpful in identifying the perverse incentives that so often cause apparent suboptimal solutions to be selected. Fifth (clearly the most important reason), defense is different than other government activities because of the types of goods purchased and what the decision to purchase those goods means for the rest of society.

THE DEFENSE PROCUREMENT PROCESS

Let us briefly consider the environment in which defense purchases take place. First, there is no free market at work at the defense industry prime contractor level because the federal government is usually the single initial buyer of defense goods. The combination of a single buyer, a few very large firms in each segment of the industry, and the production of relatively small numbers of extremely expensive weapon systems constitutes a unique structure in U.S. business.[3]

Prior to price negotiations with the Department of Defense, a prime contractor has a unique product and has some control over price. However, once negotiations are completed, the price of the system is fixed according to the terms of the contract. This price to the Department of Defense often sets the standard if there are future negotiations with subsequent potential buyers (foreign governments and, in some cases, private industry). In practice, fixed-price contracts for complex systems are usually

subject to some variance due to uncertainties: for example, variations in contractor costs, the division between contractor- and government-furnished equipment, allowances for government-proposed modifications, the variable costs associated with work done on the system by other contractors.

As in other industries within a competitive economy, market forces compel defense firms to attempt to maximize the present value of expected future profits. If a firm finds itself in a competitive market, its very corporate survival depends on its ability to do so. Even in noncompetitive defense markets, there are factors at work that promote long-run profit-maximizing behavior. For example, managers typically seek to maximize the value of the firm's stock because they often receive stock options and profit-related bonuses. Also, if the firm does not select the optimum stream of profits, the existence of suboptimal profits provides an incentive for stockholders, which may include other corporations, to install new managers to rectify profit performance.

Long-run profit-maximizing behavior by defense firms is entirely consistent with the behavior of U.S. business firms in general. However, because there is usually a single major buyer of weapon systems and because the firm is essentially a monopoly producer for follow-on contracts, competition is limited and contract controls are often difficult to enforce in practice. Given this structure, it should be no surprise to the government when problems occur in contract charges, cost accounting, and other profit-related activities.

Fluctuations in available funding, as well as changes in performance requirements and delivery schedules, have enormous impacts on the production costs of weapon systems. Consider the increases in weapon production costs due to variations from the optimal, or lowest cost, rate of production. The experience of past weapon system acquisition programs demonstrates a strong relationship between rate of production and program costs. This relationship has been documented time and again by the cost histories of programs that experience a production stretch-out. A stretch-out reduces the monthly rate of production and increases the number of months the system is in production, holding the number of weapon systems produced constant. For example, historical cost data on C-141A, RF-4C, F-111, C-5A, and F-15 aircraft show that schedule changes were one of the most significant factors in cost growth.[4]

Stretch-outs are usually directed by Pentagon resource managers to accommodate limited fiscal year funding, although in some cases, such as the F-111, frequent changes in performance requirements was also a major driver. In general, stretch-outs result in excess plant capacity, higher overhead charges allocated to each unit produced, wasted tooling capacity, and a compounding of the effects of inflation.

Although operational and budget constraints should be considered in the course of defining a production schedule for a weapon system, it seems logical that annual budget limitations for particular weapons, rather than being absolutes, should be evaluated in the context of an optimal, lowest-cost production rate. Yet, although the Department of Defense is aware of the sensitivity of program costs to production rates, political decisions on budgets often dominate efficiency criteria.

THE DEFENSE BUDGET PROCESS

Both economic and political factors combine to form the defense budget. In a sense, this is as it should be because the overall size of the defense budget cannot be determined only according to economic criteria. However, the political influence in the budget process often takes the place of legitimate economic analysis. This can be illustrated by describing the relationships among the executive budget, the congressional budget, and finally, the defense budget.

The Executive Budget. The budget prepared by the Office of Management and Budget (OMB) for submission by the president to Congress each January is a legislative proposal. It includes both revenues and expenditures, but these two halves are separated both in the process of development within the executive branch and in the subsequent review by Congress. Revenues are the result of tax laws, which are subject to infrequent changes relative to changes in spending. Revenues can therefore be forecast based on the structure of the tax laws and the expected economic activity over the next fiscal year. Although many nondefense expenditures are fixed by law and cannot be changed without legislation, a portion of both defense and nondefense expenditures may be altered each year. The budget process is therefore dominated by analysis of the appropriate level of variable government expenditures and the composition of those expenditures.[5]

In the executive branch, the budget process begins in the spring before the budget submission to Congress. At this time, the director of the OMB, the secretary of the treasury, and the chairman of the Council of Economic Advisers recommend initial overall budget guidelines to the president. Simultaneously, budget examiners in the OMB begin to evaluate programs in their areas of responsibility. In the summer before budget submission, the president announces his preliminary fiscal policy appraisal and sets general budget guidelines. As fall approaches, the budget review process escalates to a level at which department and agency heads deal with associate directors in the OMB. In December, the final decisions on economic policy are made by the president and the final changes in agency budgets are made so as to bring the level

of government expenditures in line with updated fiscal policies. On the fifteenth day after Congress convenes in January, the president submits his budget proposal for the following fiscal year.

The Congressional Budget. The Budget Control Act of 1974 established a congressional committee structure, revised the budget timetable, and provided for ceilings on overall spending, revenue, and deficits through a process of joint budget resolutions. In addition, the act prohibited presidential impoundment of budgeted funds. Money appropriated by Congress had to be spent unless Congress voted to confirm a presidential request not to spend appropriated funds. The act also established a budget committee in each house and a Congressional Budget Office (CBO). The committees were designed to guide each house in its consideration of the appropriate level of fiscal stimulus that should be provided by the budget, based on an analysis of current and projected economic conditions.

The newly created Congressional Budget Office provides economic analyses in support of the budgetary process. The CBO monitors the forecasts of the major computer models of the economy, reviews the projections made by the executive branch, and provides its own estimates of future economic performance. As a result, the CBO plays much the same role in congressional budget review process as the Council of Economic Advisers plays in the formation of the executive budget. It also provides budget analyses similar to those provided by the Office of Management and Budget in the executive branch. However, the CBO does not coordinate the budgetary process as does the OMB. This function is performed by the budget committee in each house.

By April 15 each year, the budget committees analyze the initial reports of other congressional committees and the CBO and report the first concurrent budget resolution, which proposes levels of government expenditures, receipts, and deficits. At the same time, the legislative committees report out the new "budget authority," or ceilings, for each program. The process of deciding on specific levels of spending authority takes place in the appropriations committees, or more specifically, in the subcommittees that consider each area of spending. The first concurrent resolution on the budget is approved by the full committees in both houses around May 15.

By the first week in September, Congress authorizes the funding of approved programs and appropriates specific spending authority to those programs. By the middle of September, Congress acts on the second concurrent budget resolution, which may revise fiscal targets, based on an updated analysis of economic conditions. By the end of September, Congress completes action, reconciling approved levels of spending and receipts with the fiscal limits set by the second concurrent resolution.

Table 1.1
Department of Defense Budget by Appropriation Category, 1982–1984
(millions of current dollars)

Line Item	FY 1982	FY 1983	FY 1984
Military personnel	42,829	45,485	47,946
Retired pay	14,940	16,155	16,806
Operation & maintenance	62,011	66,817	74,005
Procurement	64,106	81,879	94,088
Research, development, test & evaluation	20,103	22,805	29,622
Special foreign currency program	3	4	3
Military construction	4,881	4,487	5,973
Family housing & homeowners assistance program	2,219	2,564	2,836
Revolving & management funds	347	909	2,799
Undistributed		- 650	
Total direct program (total obligated authority)	211,439	240,455	274,078

Source: Weinberger, Caspar W., _Department of Defense Annual Report, Fiscal
Year 1984_, February 1, 1985.

On October 1, the new fiscal year begins, and assuming that the
appropriations bills are signed by the president, spending begins at the
new authorized levels.

After October 1, the process of implementing the budget and controlling
the level of expenditures reverts to the executive branch. Annual congressional approval to the executive branch to commit funds, or "obligational
authority," extends over several fiscal years. For example, funds for 1982
were obligated by congressional actions going back to 1976. About one-
third of annual defense expenditures are based on the authorizations
of earlier fiscal years, and two-thirds are based on authorizations passed
in the same fiscal year. Thus, in any given year, defense outlays are
different from the "obligational authority" appropriated by Congress
that year.[6]

The Defense Budget. The congressional budgeting process tends to
submerge the linkages between defense outlays and objectives. It centers
the budget debate on appropriation categories such as personnel and
procurement rather than on the expected outputs of defense programs.
For example, if we examine the defense budget from the congressional
perspective of line items, we quickly discover that appropriation category
line item entries tell us very little about defense programs.

Table 1.1 describes the levels of defense appropriation for 1982, 1983,
and 1984 by appropriation category. Note that each category represents
an input of personnel, equipment, research, or maintenance, rather than
an output of some defense program. In the early 1960s, Secretary of
Defense Robert McNamara introduced a Planning, Programming and
Budgeting System (PPBS), which was designed to emphasize the link

Table 1.2
Department of Defense Budget by Major Program, 1982-1984
(millions of current dollars)

Major Program	FY 1982	FY 1983	FY 1984
Strategic forces	15,339	20,649	28,132
General purpose forces	88,058	100,850	109,587
Intelligence and communications	13,939	17,057	20,842
Airlift and sealift	3,954	4,189	5,194
Guard and reserve forces	10,358	11,363	11,597
Research & development	16,921	18,683	23,481
Central supply and maintenance	18,717	21,290	24,122
Training, medical, other general personnel activity	39,602	42,530	45,605
Administration	3,643	3,081	4,833
Support of other nations	908	763	685
Total direct program (total obligated authority)	211,439	240,455	274,078

Source: Weinberger, Caspar W., <u>Department of Defense Annual Report, Fiscal</u>
<u>Year 1984</u>, February 1, 1985.

between resource inputs and defense outputs. With minor changes, the PPBS introduced by McNamara is still in use in the Department of Defense today.

Within the Department of Defense, the budgeting process is designed to show how increments in spending will move the nation closer to its defense objectives. Table 1.2 outlines the defense budget for fiscal years 1982 through 1984 in terms of ten output-oriented major programs. These programs allocate defense funds by function and provide a clear link to defense output objectives. About 10 percent of the defense budget is allocated to strategic forces (ICBMs, Trident submarines, intercontinental bombers), and about 40 percent goes to general purpose forces (fighter wings, naval forces, army and navy divisions). Each program is divided into subprograms (e.g., army forces—divisions, brigades, combat support forces—under general purpose forces) and subprograms are further divided into program elements (e.g., army battalions).[7]

The Five Year Defense Program. The Department of Defense's Five Year Defense Program (FYDP) spells out the projected levels of forces, weapons, and expenditures for each major program and program element over the next five fiscal years. The annual planning and programming debate within the Department of Defense centers around how program elements relate to current defense objectives and how defense funds should be allocated to the different elements. These decisions, made in the context of the FYDP, become the basis for the annual budget negotiated between the Department of Defense and the Office of Management and Budget and ultimately for the executive branch budget submission to Congress. The FYDP is updated three times each year: in January to reflect the president's budget, in May to reflect program proposals by

the services, and in September to reflect the service budget estimates resulting from decisions by the secretary of defense on service program proposals.

Under the FYDP, individual program elements receive detailed attention by the various services and agencies within the Department of Defense. Within each program element, the budget process expands into a variety of micro activities tailored to the specific nature of the services involved and the subelements themselves.

Defense Budgeting at the Micro Level. Below the program element level, economic optimization techniques tend to dominate political considerations. Budget-forecasting models that account for the life cycle costs of individual projects have been developed. For example, budget models exist for research and development (R&D) projects, computer software development projects, and weapon manufacturing projects.

SUMMARY: IS THE TOTAL EFFORT RIGHT OR WRONG?

This book provides a current view of selected aspects of the political economy of defense. In each area, it provides the applicable economic theory and optimization techniques; however, it also shows what happens in actual practice and why decisions were made in the way they were.

In addition to describing the problems involved with funding and managing defense, this book also points out possible solutions. The reader should be aware, however, that many of these problems have no generally acceptable solutions, and this may lead one to the conclusion that there are structural difficulties in the defense arena that must be attacked on fundamental levels. For this reason, solutions are often suggested that are clearly not compatible with current political constraints.[8] These solutions are not advanced to demonstrate our naiveté, but rather to suggest to the reader the magnitude of the changes that would be required to attack a particular problem and perhaps, to demonstrate why the problem remains unsolved.

In sum, this book describes a situation where a group of government and industry people are trying to deal with problems of an extremely complicated nature. There are few heroes or villains in this group—just ordinary people dealing with huge sums of money and extraordinary political pressures. What this has created is the subject of the pages that follow.

NOTES

1. Weinberger, Caspar W., *Annual Report to Congress, Fiscal Year 1984*, U.S. Government Printing Office, Washington, D.C., January 31, 1983.

2. Implicitly, we assume that weapons effectiveness can be related to levels of deterrence. For example, the greater the probability of "bombs on target," the greater the level of deterrence to a potential enemy attack. This approach was originally developed for defense by Hitch, C., and McKean, R., *The Economics of Defense in the Nuclear Age*, Harvard University Press, Cambridge, Mass., 1960. However, any good microeconomics text would provide the same theoretical framework. For example, see Layard, P., and Walters, A., *Microeconomic Theory*, McGraw-Hill Book Company, New York, 1978.

3. See Gansler, J., *The Defense Industry*, MIT Press, Cambridge, Mass., 1981.

4. See ibid., and Gansler, J., "Let's Change the Way the Pentagon Does Business," *Harvard Business Review* 55 (May-June 1977); Lorette, R., "Cost Estimate Growth in Air Force Weapon System Acquisition, unpublished Ph.D. Dissertation, Harvard University, 1967; and Comptroller of the Air Force, *An Analysis of Weapon System Contract Cost Growth*, Management Analysis Report 69-10, U.S. Government Printing Office, Washington, D.C., 1969.

5. See Olvey, L. D., Golden, J. R., and Kelly, R. C., *The Economics of National Security*, Avery Publishing Group, Wayne, N.J., 1984, and numerous Department of Defense Annual Reports, 1980–1984, U.S. Government Printing Office, Washington, D.C.

6. Korb, L., "The Price of Preparedness: The 1978–1982 Defense Program," *AEI Review*, no. 3, June 1977.

7. Weinberger, Caspar W., Department of Defense Annual Reports, Fiscal Years 1981–1985, U.S. Government Printing Office, Washington, D.C.

8. For example, one way to encourage burden sharing by U.S. allies might be to withdraw U.S. troop support from areas such as Japan and Europe so that foreign governments would have to fund more fully their own defense. The political impact of such a move has been unacceptable to date.

2
The Politics of National Defense Spending

As we look beyond the cessation of hostilities in Vietnam, we . . . need to recognize that the scale of defense expenditures has, to a significant degree, become a self-reinforcing process. Its momentum derives not only from the energy of military planners, contractors, scientists, and engineers. To some degree it is abetted also by the practical interests and anxieties of ordinary citizens. Any announcement that a particular defense installation will be shut down, or that a particular defense contract will be phased out, naturally causes concern among men and women who, however much they abhor war and its trappings, have become dependent for their livelihood on the activity whose continuance is threatened.

—Arthur F. Burns, 1968

THE EVOLUTION OF PHILOSOPHY, 1950–1985

Through most of its history, the United States has wrestled with the conflict between having a standing army that was an apparent waste of peacetime resources and the realization that a competent army could not be created overnight during an emergency.[1] In the 1950s, the security the United States had enjoyed from outside attack began to disappear. This, coupled with the lessons learned in World War II, left the country for the first time with large standing offensive and defensive forces.

Noting this change in his landmark speech of 1968, Arthur F. Burns pointed out that the age of nuclear weapons fundamentally changed the way the United States viewed defense. No longer could the nation maintain a posture of virtual disarmament until the start of a conflict—in an age of potential nuclear attack, there is no time to marshall the forces necessary to fight a war. In response to this threat, the United

States has maintained its military establishment in a state of constant readiness since 1950.[2]

The need for forces in readiness was emphasized by two factors: the U.S. pursuit of the philosophy of deterrence and the pace with which the Soviet Union acquired arms. The United States elected to pursue deterrence without a civil defense program because in the 1950s defense experts such as Charles J. Hitch and Roland N. McKean were stating that "The enemy could interpret preparations of this sort as steps toward a first-strike posture that would leave us vulnerable for several hours whenever brought into play. Instead of deterring the enemy, this policy might make a preemptive attack by him more likely."[3] Instead, the United States decided to rely on technological superiority over the Soviets to shield U.S. citizens from a potential attack—a decision that has provided the rationale for innumerable weapons.

Meanwhile, the Soviet Union developed weapons and accumulated forces in a manner that seemed to disregard totally conditions external to its borders. In times of poor relations with the United States and in times when relations were better, under economic conditions that varied from austere to relatively more affluent, the pace of Soviet building continued unabated. This behavior provided a continuing impetus for U.S. defense efforts, particularly after 1978 when the United States renewed efforts to modernize and expand its forces.

During the 1960s, the rationale behind the development and manufacture of U.S. weapons began to change. Arms were developed to fight wars of uncertain location and type, not in response to a conflict of known parameters. The indefinite character of potential conflicts, coupled with the rapidly expanding menu of possibilities provided by an accelerating level of technology, resulted in new, expensive weapons typified by vague purpose, unknown capability, and questionable reliability. Improvements were made in many areas, but the level of uncertainty surrounding the need for and potential use of many weapons remained. As a result, the benchmarks once used to make judgments about weapons were lost.

The impact of this situation on the budgeting process was profound. Weapons built for probabilistic encounters are difficult to explain and hard to justify because a present need is not evident. One is forced instead to rely on presumed scenarios in which the weapons will be employed. Of course, these scenarios are subject to the ideological persuasion of the forecaster.

In the 1960s another complicating factor was added to this process. For the previous fifty years, there had been popular support for military actions taken by the United States. This support had manifested itself in a willingness of the populace to pay for armed forces at the time

that those forces were required (for example, buying bonds to pay for World War II). The Vietnam War changed all that. It lacked the support of a large part of the U.S. public, and its financing requirements conflicted directly with the Great Society programs of the Johnson administration. As Burns noted, "at the very stage of history when demographic, technological and political trends [had] been releasing powerful forces to raise the costs of government, the defense sector likewise became an increasing burden on the Treasury."[4]

The lack of public support for the activities in which the military establishment was engaged after 1964 might at first be assumed to have severely constrained the defense budget. But successive administrations proceeded without public support by paying the defense bill with bonds and new money, and the result was just the reverse. The military was funded without immediate public sacrifice in a "credit card" philosophy—because the public did not pay promptly for the military goods that were purchased, initially it seemed as if no one had to pay at all.

This situation was further complicated by the increasing polarization between the two political parties regarding the largest and most expensive weapon systems. The systems supported by one faction were opposed by the other, and each time a party regained political control, it cancelled the programs favored by the other. The B-1 bomber is a classic example of this process: "The B-1's advocates helped Rockwell's [the manufacturer] bomber programs survive the production vetoes of John F. Kennedy, Lyndon B. Johnson and Jimmy Carter, and they pushed for research money from Richard M. Nixon and Gerald R. Ford, neither of whom had to decide about actual production. They held on until finally a president came along—Ronald Reagan—who thought manned bombers were great."[5]

This polarization had two unfortunate consequences. First, it contributed to the boom and bust atmosphere already prevalent among industries that provide weapons to the military. And second, the adoption of weapons for which the rationale had always been tenuous became an element of faith for one group or the other. As these views hardened into political positions on national defense, weapon purchases moved even further from the realm of rational processes.

One common view originated in the budget conflicts between expanding social programs and the defense spending required by the Vietnam War. Instead of attempting to allocate defense and social needs within a limited budget, the adherents of this view advocated ever-increasing spending for both defense and social goods—but without raising tax revenues to cover these expenditures. After the Vietnam War ended and after a number of the social programs had become insti-

tutionalized, the growth rate of the defense budget slowed substantially, but the adherents of this view never did address the fundamental issue that there was not enough money to fund both military and social programs on the scale envisioned by the advocates of each.

A second view originated as a backlash against the U.S. defeat in Vietnam. Adherents of this view saw the Soviet invasion of Afghanistan and the other events that occurred in the Carter years as a sign that U.S. military power had deteriorated to the point where the United States was being "pushed around" by the Soviet Union. To these individuals, the reason for this decline was clear: From the very beginning, the United States had not had enough national will to expend the resources necessary to win in Vietnam. Too little was being spent on defense, both in an absolute sense and compared to what was being spent on nondefense programs. When defense budget growth slowed in the 1970s, the adherents of this view became convinced that the actual survival of the United States was threatened.

Initially, these two points of view were neither mutually exclusive nor firmly situated in either political party. But by the 1980 presidential election, the view that defense and social programs could both be funded in spite of budgetary conflicts became clearly associated with the Democratic party. This was demonstrated by Carter's large increase of the defense budget in 1979 while maintaining or slowly increasing the prevailing level of social programs. Meanwhile, the Republican party adopted the philosophy that the nation was not allocating enough resources to defense to display a level of national will sufficient to deter the Soviets. This point of view gained substantial public support as the Iranian hostage situation unfolded.

In retrospect, it is clear that neither view could prevail without eventually cutting social or defense programs or without raising taxes. For the purpose of this chapter we need to recognize only one point: Although the two views became more and more opposed to one another over the issue of what would happen to social expenditures, neither view recognized that there were limited resources for defense spending.

The fact that two schools of thought that were so different both contained the same fundamental weakness set the stage for the defense budgeting experience that followed. And it destroyed that would have been a normal checks-and-balances relationship between the administration and the Congress—creating instead a mutual reinforcement by the two groups where defense spending was concerned. This resulted in the approach to budgeting for defense that will be discussed in the following sections, first from the standpoint of the administration and then from that of Congress.

THE REAGAN ADMINISTRATION
AND DEFENSE BUDGETING

Backwards Budgeting

The Reagan administration entered office committed to increased defense spending and to supply-side economics. Its legislative initiatives reflected this approach; increased production was stressed and increased taxes were avoided. However, as later statements by the director of the Office of Management and Budget (OMB) revealed, the administration did not anticipate that its entire program would pass through the Congress unscathed. The passage of the entire Reagan budget, which resulted, in part, from Congress's recognition of public support for defense, implied potential deficits that were of immediate concern.

The OMB contacted the civilian contractor that provided data analysis services for the OMB with a request, not for forecasts of the impact of the administration's budget on the performance of the U.S. economy, but for the contractor to run his models *backward*, given the budget passed by Congress and the desired deficit level, to discover one or more macroeconomic scenarios that would generate this outcome. The contractor protested that this was bad economics and a misuse of his models, and a compromise solution was developed that allowed the runs to be made, but removed the contractor's name from any product used by the OMB.[6] The same approach was attempted in the Department of Defense when it became apparent in late 1984 that budget cuts would have to be made. An economist who worked for the secretary of defense was sent to another civilian contractor to ask him to "massage" his models and to determine if there were any way that the deficit could be halved over a two-year period without defense cuts. The answer was "no."[7]

The Theological Approach to Defense Spending

The defense spending philosophy of the Reagan Administration seems inconsistent with its pronouncements about the need to reduce government spending and balance the budget. An analysis of this philosophy indicates that the Reagan administration's view of defense spending is closer to a theology than it is to a decision process based on an efficient allocation of resources. The theological approach to defense spending can be illustrated by investigating the attitude of an individual who supports a church. When asked what he or she expects in return when giving to such an organization, most would say "Nothing—I give to show commitment." This approach differs from that of an economist who seeks an efficient allocation of resources. The efficient allocator is

primarily concerned with *how much* each dollar buys relative to potential purchases elsewhere, while a person who spends to show commitment is only concerned with the amount spent.

A theological approach to defense spending is illustrated by the following examples:

1. Describing the initial meeting to determine the defense budget following President Reagan's election, Nicholas Lemann related that

> the Administration [decided to] immediately request a total increase of $32.6 billion, the largest and swiftest rise in defense spending during peacetime history. Now that there was a figure, the first question was not "Given our budget, what should our military strategy be and what programs will help us achieve it?" Instead it was *"What can we think of to spend all that money on?"*[8] (Author's emphasis)

2. In early 1984, a conversation between a high official in the Defense Department and a visiting economist went as follows:

> *Economist:* The F-16 program with Europe is a good example of how cooperation in building weapons can benefit all the nations involved.
> *Defense Official:* No. We should never have gotten involved with that program.
> *Economist:* But, by building the F-16 this way, all countries were able to get the aircraft cheaper than if any one had built it alone.
> *Defense Official:* That's the point. We should not have allowed the Europeans to participate even if that meant they paid more for another, inferior aircraft. *By paying more they would have shown more commitment.*

3. In September 1984, a decision had to be made on whether or not to close in (no longer pump oil from) the Elk Hills Petroleum Reserve in California. This reserve had already been depleted to the point where extraction rates were too low to be of any benefit during a national crisis. It seemed logical, therefore, to remove and sell the rest of the oil as quickly as possible and then to use the funds from this exchange to build the stock a reserve in the Louisiana salt domes. This new reserve could be pumped out quickly in an emergency, and it would be located where the oil would be needed (close to refining and distribution facilities).

However, high Department of Defense (DoD) officials, having been told that the low extraction rate from Elk Hills would render it useless during a crisis, still supported closing in the reserve to preserve the oil for defense needs. *The fact that the oil could not be used was incidental— closing the reserve showed commitment and resolve.* (A compromise solution,

calling for one year of continued pumping during which time the problem would be studied further, was later reached.)

These examples illustrate that a theological approach to defense creates an atmosphere where the amount of defense gained for a dollar spent is not important. What is important is the willingness to spend the dollar. When an administration elects to take this approach, the effect on the national budget (and the size of the deficit) will depend almost solely on the response of Congress.

THE CONGRESS AND DEFENSE BUDGETING

Since the late 1970s, Congress has shown little or no inclination to control the size of the defense budget. There are several reasons for this. First, Congress did not have to accept this role during most of the Carter administration, which itself constrained defense spending and was responsible for canceling major procurements like the B-1. Second, as the backlash to Iran and Afghanistan developed, it was clear that public support for defense was increasing. Congress, which had already approved defense budgets larger than those requested by the administration, continued to do so. And Congress became even more unwilling to stop defense spending in the late 1970s for fear of being labeled weak on defense—an argument that also affected the Carter administration in its last year. By the second Reagan administration, the fear of being labeled weak on defense had become so great that, even in a period of difficult budget cuts, Democrats and Republicans in Congress actively criticized each other's proposed defense cuts.[9] Third, and most important, defense spending became the dominant vehicle for regional allocation of federal spending. This meant that defense programs could no longer be cut with impunity: There were regional economic benefits in every decision to spend defense money, and the larger the program, the more regions affected.

Deployment Spending

A base or port located in a congressional district means jobs and stable federal spending. Bases and ports are viewed as being permanent, and in areas that are geographically isolated, they may be the sole support for the communities that spring up around their perimeters. For these reasons, bases and ports are ardently sought, and the proposed closure of a facility is always a major political decision.

It is not surprising that the Department of Defense may use base closings to reward or punish members of Congress for their stands on defense issues. By letting the equipment assigned to a base become obsolete and by not deploying modern systems to that facility, the

Department of Defense can make an excellent case for closing a base or port. The experience of Michigan is a good example of this process. Michigan senators Carl Levin and Donald Riegle, Jr., were well known for their hostility to the Department of Defense (and, in the case of Senator Riegle, to Secretary of Defense Caspar Weinberger). In 1983 the 87th Fighter Interceptor Squadron at K.I. Sawyer Air Force Base was deactiviated, costing Marquette and the Upper Michigan peninsula 599 military and 29 civilian jobs with an economic value of $15 million per year. Michigan, which was already severely affected by the economic recession, had lost three bases, 12,821 jobs, and $59.6 million in federal spending over the previous fifteen years. K.I. Sawyer Air Force Base was left with only a wing of obsolete B-52s, making it a prime candidate for complete closure. The B-52s might have been replaced by the B-1 (which Senator Levin vehemently opposed).[10] The connection between the Senator's voting records and the treatment given Michigan by the Department of Defense was not missed by the Michigan press, which relayed this message to the voters.

Base closings are often necessary to accommodate changes in defense plans. However, how bases are selected for closure may or may not be related to military requirements. In 1985, Senator Barry Goldwater of Arizona, in his role as chairman of the Senate Armed Services Committee, proposed closing twenty-two bases "around the country." Although thirteen states were represented on the list, five of the twenty-two bases were in one congressional district in Pennsylvania, that of Representative William Gray (D–Pa.), the chairman of the House Budget Committee and no friend of the Pentagon. Not surprisingly, no Arizona installations were listed in the Goldwater proposal and no bases in districts with Republican supporters of the defense budget were included.[11]

Similar rewards or punishments are also possible when new base locations are chosen. Democratic Representative Joseph Addabbo, chairman of the House Defense Appropriations Subcommittee, occupied a position that had a major say over navy appropriations. Therefore, he was able to have the battleship *Iowa* and its five-ship support group assigned to New York as its home port. The consequence was estimated to be approximately $80 million in payroll for 900 civilian and 4,800 military jobs.[12] However, when Congressman Addabbo became more vocal in his criticism of defense spending, and when some other members of the New York delegation expressed concern about the possibility of nuclear weapons being on the ships, Secretary of Defense Weinberger withdrew the money from the 1986 budget that would have gone to build the port, engaging "in a bit of budget gamesmanship against a Congressional delegation that included many opponents of President Reagan's military buildup."[13]

These actions represent simple pork-barrel politics, but the amounts of money involved make the economic consequences very serious. The attempt to use the allocation and manipulation of the military base and port structure to influence congressional voting patterns on defense has had a great effect in disciplining members of Congress and assuring appropriate support for other, unrelated defense projects. In fact, bases are so important to members of Congress that they attached a rider to the 1985 Gramm-Rudman bill to prohibit any base closings for one year, thereby stopping any attempt to make defense budget cuts by getting rid of unnecessary facilities.[14]

Politics and the Large Defense Contractor

There is a separation between prime defense contractors (those who bid directly for projects with the U.S. government) and defense subcontractors (those who bid on projects offered by the primes and work for the primes). Although a prime contractor for one contract may be a subcontractor on another, subcontractors are generally smaller than prime contractors and are usually more subject to the working of a competitive marketplace. These factors, coupled with the tendency of prime contractors to seek the cheapest sources for their subcontract work, create a fluid environment in the subcontractor field.

The environment of the large prime contractor is different. Here a few firms dominate in a curious mix of oligopolistic and monopolistic behavior. Prior to selection as a producer for a large weapon system, two or three of these companies compete for the contract, the complexity and production capacity requirements of the project ruling out other sources. This initial competition is, in the best sense, a demonstration of oligopolistic behavior: very few firms, virtually standardized products, rigid pricing, formidable obstacles to market entry, and the channeling of considerable resources to advertising and promotional activities. However, after a contract has been awarded, the situation becomes monopolistic. The prime contractor both develops and produces the weapon, and thus it has a huge advantage in competing for future contracts for weapons of the same type. At this point, the politics change considerably. A vote for a weapon becomes a vote for a company and for the region in which that company is located.

This is fundamentally different from the process that typifies other government procurement. For example, a congressional appropriation to buy more office furniture for the U.S. government results in a bidding competition, after which the contract is let to the lowest qualifying bidder. That bidder could be any one of a number of companies, and it could be located in any of a number of regions. But a congressional appropriation to buy intercontinental ballistic missiles was, in 1985, an

appropriation to buy MX missiles made by Martin Marietta in Denver, Colorado, and to employ subcontractors who were located in specific parts of the United States. Thus, a vote for missiles is a vote to allocate federal funds to specific regions of the country, but a vote for furniture has none of the certainty about where the money will be spent. For members of Congress looking for federal spending in their districts, it is clear which procurement involves the greatest risk.

Congressional Benefits

Even when a routine decision to buy a generic product has been made by the Department of Defense, members of Congress can benefit by manipulating this procurement to alter the regional economic impact. This is easier to do for small procurements than on major weapons. For example, Senator Ted Stevens of Alaska used his position as chairman of the Appropriations Subcommittee on Defense to require the military to buy coal from Pennsylvania for use in Germany. As a result, the army and air force must ship coal from the United States at an extra cost of $6 million per year instead of buying locally produced German coal.[15] Senator Stevens also got a special clause put in military regulations that exempts Alaskan moving companies from competing with lower-priced firms in the lower forty-eight states on military moves.[16] In addition, in 1984 Senator Stevens refused to hold hearings on the air force budget until the air force agreed to drop a plan to save $200,000 by purchasing milk for Alaskan military bases in the state of Washington.[17]

These actions cost the Department of Defense millions of dollars. It was therefore surprising when, one year later, Senator Stevens claimed that it was Congress's fault that the defense bill was so high. Pointing to the problems created by other members of Congress (and omitting mention of his own contributions) Senator Stevens claimed that "Congress has made the defense bill a jobs bill. We can cut, if *they* are willing to do the things you have to do."[18] (author's emphasis)

A reluctance to take responsibility for the problems Congress has created in defense budgeting is not limited to Senator Stevens. In the fiscal year 1984 defense budget, Congress changed about 65 percent of the individual appropriation line items (a total of 1,476 changes).[19] Each of these changes altered a procurement decision originally made by a knowledgeable program manager. For example, an air force project to buy laser-guided bombs, although having minor problems, was proceeding on schedule and below budget. The unit cost of the bombs was decreasing (from $45,660 in 1984 to $30,143 in 1985) due to efficient production. When congressional tinkering with the program stretched out the procurement period, the resulting inefficient production rates created a potential overrun of 40 percent on the $2.4 billion program.

The air force canceled the program rather than fight the bad publicity that was sure to result.[20]

Decisions like this have long-term implications. Programs that were approved in the past but that must be funded each year are essentially "uncontrollable"—they must be continued or all of the initial investment will be lost. For example, when Congress approved two new aircraft carriers in 1983, only about 25 percent of the funds for the project was appropriated. The rest of the money had to be appropriated in the following years. In 1980, about 27 percent of the defense budget was uncontrollable, and this figure rose to 36 percent in 1985.[21] The consequence is an increasing amount of defense spending not susceptible to cuts and providing a safe haven for pork-barrel projects. Recent forecasts estimate that as much as 85 percent of the military budget may be uncontrollable by 1990 if current trends continue.[22] These trends, coupled with Congress's alteration of budget line items, may kill most short-run budget flexibility in the near future.

Buying Political Support—The PACs

Congressional support is the critical factor in a weapon's success or failure. The trend toward more congressional involvement in defense budgeting developed concurrently with a trend toward heavier contributions from Political Action Committees (PACs) and other political groups that channel funds from defense interests to the Congress. For obvious reasons, PACs are very selective and funnel their money to members of House and Senate committees in charge of armed services, appropriations, and science and technology. These gifts are meant to influence the votes of the recipients; therefore, the distribution of funds is distinctly nonpartisan, with most PACs giving to every member of each critical committee.[23]

Much of this giving is centered around specific weapon systems where selection of the weapon governs selection of the contractor. Thus, twelve of the thirteen biggest MX contractors doubled their campaign contributions to Senate and House incumbents prior to the 1982 elections to help ensure reelection of supporters of the weapon system.[24] And as soon as the Strategic Defense Initiative became an issue in 1983, a supporting PAC (the American Space Frontiers Committee) was formed to raise at least $1 million for the 1984 election.[25]

Even with large amounts of money being contributed to various candidates by the PACs, there remains the question of how much influence is actually gained. The recipient of the largest amount of PAC funds, Representative Joseph Addabbo, has also gained a perfect rating from arms-control groups for his voting record. He led floor fights to cut all funds for procurement of the MX missile and to kill the B-1 bomber,

and he voted to ban the Pershing II and to enact a nuclear freeze.[26] However, Representative Addabbo's position as chairman of the House Appropriations Subcommittee on Defense simply cannot be ignored by defense contractors. Obviously, if everyone to whom defense PACs gave funds acted like Representative Addabbo, the PACs would cut donations and question spending money to finance the opposition. In fact, just the opposite has happened. The largest defense contractors doubled their political contributions in the period 1980 to 1984, with the top twenty contributing $3.6 million to congressional and presidential campaigns. In the same period, government contracts to those companies grew 150 percent to $69 billion. Of twenty House members receiving more than $15,000 from defense PACs, seventeen voted for more MX missiles. Thirteen of fourteen senators who received more than $30,000 each from the defense PACs also backed the MX.[27] The individuals and groups who donate money to finance the PACs have alternative uses for those funds, but it is obvious that they feel they are getting an ample return on their investments.

ADDITIONAL PROBLEMS

> Under the internal pressure of civilians who know not war and think that it is reducible to economics, as well as of "demilitarized" military men who have lost sight of the essentials of their profession, our Defense Department and the armed forces themselves are not merely distracted from the large issues of strategy by the petty questions of micro-management, but they are, in addition, directed to pursue the wrong goal, namely civilian efficiency.[28]

In this statement, Edward Luttwak sums up the frustration of the military services about the manner in which civilian control of the Department of Defense is exercised. Almost all members of the military recognize the need for civilian control, but this control has created major problems over the way economics and other systems analysis techniques have been applied to the defense sector. Two additional minor factors have also created a fertile ground for conflict between the civilian and military sides of defense:

1. The office of the secretary of defense (OSD) is increasingly composed of individuals who sat out the various wars in universities and other safe havens. The military officers with whom these individuals must interact were involved in those wars (many times in multiple tours of duty), and they often feel that the civilians lack the experience to comment on tactics, strategy, and equipment.[29] Those officers who served

in Vietnam also remain convinced that the input of unqualified civilians was largely responsible for the defeat experienced there by the United States. To many of these people, it is unclear why those who chose not to participate in the previous conflict should be allowed to plan the military's role in the next one.

2. The second factor is more subtle but also quite prevalent. A military officer knows that decisions made by him on any given day may have to be implemented by him in the future. The civilian, in contrast, can make allocative or strategic decisions knowing full well that he or she is independent of the battlefield conditions those decisions may imply. This means that the two groups make their decisions from vastly differing perspectives.

For reasons such as these, some antagonism between the military and its civilian leaders has been present since civilian control over the Pentagon was first introduced. Two events that occurred in 1961 focused this antagonism on the concept of economic efficiency. Herschel Kanter has pointed out that in that year defense economics picked up several new and separate themes resulting from Dwight Eisenhower's farewell speech and the appointment of Robert McNamara as secretary of defense.[30] These two forces permanently altered the dialogue on defense and the manner in which the defense establishment was controlled.

President Eisenhower's warning was centered around the problem of continually spending large amounts of our gross national product for defense, whether or not we were at war:

> Until the latest of our world conflicts, the United States had no armaments industry. American makers of plowshares could, with time and as required, make swords as well. But now we can no longer risk emergency improvisation of national defense; we have been compelled to create a permanent armaments industry of vast proportions. Added to this, three and a half million men and women are directly engaged in the defense establishment. We annually spend on military security more than the net income of all United States corporations.
>
> This conjunction of an immense military establishment and a large arms industry is new in the American experience. The total influence—economic, political, even spiritual—is felt in every city, every State house, every office of the Federal government. We recognize the imperative need for this development. Yet we must not fail to comprehend its grave implications. Our toil, resources and livelihood are all involved; so is the very structure of our society.
>
> In the councils of government, we must guard against the acquisition of unwarranted influence, whether sought or unsought, by the military-industrial complex. The potential for the disastrous rise of misplaced power exists and will persist.[31]

This warning represented the charter for much of the defense economics work that was done over the next twenty years. That Eisenhower went on to recommend cooperation between the military and industry was overlooked by later authors who published numerous books on the evils of the "military-industrial complex." Eisenhower stated: "We must never let the weight of this combination endanger our liberties or democratic process. We should take nothing for granted. Only an alert and knowledgeable citizenry can compel the proper meshing of the huge industrial and military machinery of defense with our peaceful methods and goals, so that security and liberty may prosper together."[32]

The second event that changed defense economics was the naming of Robert McNamara as secretary of defense. McNamara brought with him Charles Hitch and a number of other economists from the RAND Corporation and set out to run the Pentagon using the concepts of systems analysis—the attempt to allocate resources efficiently through optimization techniques and mathematical modeling. "Instead of showing how much money was being spent on such 'artificial' categories as personnel and procurement, the budget would show how much was being spent on strategic forces and on other functional programs. Programs and program objectives would be devised before budgets were set, and resources would be allocated so as to achieve program goals at the least cost. This was the now familiar Planning, Programming, and Budgeting System—PPBS."[33]

The military suspected that the concept of economic efficiency was given too much weight in the PPBS system by the civilian leadership in the Pentagon, while the strategic and tactical aspects of weapons (those factors best understood by military planners) were shortchanged. At the same time, systems analysts, who were aware of the inefficiencies caused by interservice rivalries and an acquisition process built around "cost plus fixed-fee" contracts, were of the view that only civilians were capable of running an organization that allocated efficiently. As Charles Hitch put it in a lecture in 1965: "[The] consequences were precisely what could have been predicted. Each service tended to exercise its own priorities, favoring its own unique missions to the detriment of the joint missions, striving to lay the ground-work for an increased share of the budget in future years by concentrating on alluring new systems."[34]

It is difficult to describe the atmosphere that these attitudes brought to the Pentagon, but an example of the prevailing mood is provided by an experience shared in the early 1960s by two officers from the faculty at the Air Force Academy. The two officers (Lieutenant "O" and Captain "J") had been working on a project that was, in the best sense of the term, an application of systems analysis. Both officers had doctoral degrees in economics from excellent schools, and as a result of their

work, they were asked to explain their findings to several high Pentagon officials. The two traveled to the Pentagon and arrived, in uniform, at the office of one of the officials. Upon entering the waiting area of the office, they were confronted by an aide who denied them access because the official was not interested in discussing economic matters with military officers. The two officers, determined to present their views, returned to their rooms, changed into civilian clothes, and arranged an appointment for Dr. "O" and Dr. "J" by phone with the same official. Upon returning to the office, they were ushered in and, as civilians, had a cordial meeting with the official.

There have been claims that one of the problems with systems analysis (and by implication, with other forms of efficient allocation) is that it was "adopted by the officer corps itself partly in self defense, [and] partly because the tools of cost effectiveness analysis were easier to learn and apply than the more traditional approaches that draw on personal experience, military history, and other non-quantitative sources."[35] Although it is true that the military quickly found a knowledge of efficient allocation techniques necessary for survival in the Pentagon bureaucracy, it would be wrong to say that this new knowledge detracted from the military's ability to manage its affairs. Problems arose because the officer corps viewed these techniques as one of many tools (to be used in conjunction with the traditional approaches), while the civilians viewed these techniques as the only tool.

ORGANIZING FOR ALLOCATION

The use of allocative techniques in defense was initially handled by small organizations within each branch of the military and in the office of the secretary of defense. In the OSD, Charles Hitch moved his team into the comptroller's office in 1961. This group later gained its own assistant secretary for defense systems analysis—Alain Enthoven—and became a separate branch in 1965. Meanwhile, allocative methodologies assumed a different character in each of the services. The navy concentrated on the techniques of operations research and built a very strong capability in this area at the Naval Postgraduate School in Monterey, California. The army lagged behind the other services in all types of applications, while the air force, strongly influenced by its relationship with the RAND Corporation, tended toward a relatively larger use of economic techniques along with the standard operations research approaches.

Each systems analysis group experienced conflicts with other units in its own service because each attempted to allocate funds efficiently across all budget categories in its particular branch. Because systems

analysis groups were new, they were usually headed by a relatively junior officer, and the influence of each unit was based on its political relationship with the commander of the service. There was the prospect that junior people would be able to override decisions of senior commanders—a recipe for disaster in any military unit, and a weakness that could, in time, destroy any staff organization. Even when things worked smoothly, expenditures were allocated across only a single branch of the military—a solution that did not begin to attack the critical problem of spending the entire defense budget in the best manner.

Thus, as the services struggled to allocate subsets of military spending, the systems analysis group at OSD moved to fill the void and to allocate the total defense budget. Since an efficient allocation of an entire budget may or may not correspond to allocations of parts of that budget, the OSD group immediately came into conflict with the services, and the services' systems analysis groups now faced continual sniping from both outside and within their organizations.

It was obvious that someone had to compile an overall budget. It was similarly obvious that, even with their newly acquired allocative techniques, the services would not work together to accomplish this task. As the OSD unit proceeded, it was forced to reallocate within each service's budget, and the amount of work involved (and the size of the OSD systems analysis group) expanded rapidly. Unfortunately, so did the number of enemies created when pet programs, which had survived the service's budgeting process, were cut or delayed.

The inevitable result of this process was that the systems analysis units within each service began to shift their focus away from the areas where decisions were being overridden (the budgetary areas) and toward areas where the service could maintain autonomous power (the application of weapons). This left more budgetary decisions to the OSD unit, but it did not decrease political inputs or increase rational economic thought. The services were forced to surrender some of their political power, but even after the McNamara reforms, budget cuts were still made in an ad hoc manner in the last hours before submission, the services still submitted padded estimates, and political choices were still made—they were just made at a different level.[36] As a result, last-minute political inputs were increasingly made by people who had litle contact with the services and minimal military experience.

This trend, established by the end of McNamara's tenure, continued unabated through the Carter administration. Bright young officers who wanted to participate in the allocative process and who possessed enough economic or operations research training to make a contribution, tried to join PA&E (Program Analysis and Evaluation), as the OSD systems analysis unit later became known, instead of groups belonging to their

own services. Promotions were perceived to be better, the work was more interesting, and the impact was greater. Although there was a certain "if you can't beat them, join them and work from the inside" philosophy involved in this situation, military officers in PA&E were usually assigned as analysts in narrow fields having little to do with their prior military experience or their service's programs, and the final decisions were made by their civilian supervisors.

PA&E's power over the budgeting process expanded until, by the time of the Carter administration, it was essentially complete. Service budgets were submitted to PA&E, which critically reviewed every item requested, made the final cuts, and created the final product. The frustration of the military grew as it was more and more excluded from the decisions it felt were rightfully its own and when the new and more sympathetic Reagan administration came to power, the first order of business was to change the defense budgeting process.

PA&E lost its assistant secretary of defense position and was relegated to a reduced status in the OSD hierarchy. From this time forward it could criticize only a very narrow category of additions to a service's budget; its redefined role was one of defending budgets, not criticizing them. Unfortunately, the services, which now had a much greater role in deciding how much would be spent and what it would be spent for, had long ago lost most of their allocative expertise, and the Reagan budgets were generated in an atmosphere virtually devoid of internal criticism. When this was added to a theological approach to defense spending—spending to show commitment, not to generate specific results—the consequences were the defense budgets and problems that have typified the 1980s.

RELATIONS BETWEEN CONGRESS
AND THE DEPARTMENT OF DEFENSE

Economists and systems analysts consider defense expenditures from a perspective of efficiency, but an entirely different factor also helps to shape the budget. This factor is based on the relationship between Congress and the Department of Defense, and two attributes merit attention as background pressures on the defense budget.

The first is Congress's role as a critic. Since the 1950s, this role has become increasingly muted as members of Congress have discovered the economic benefit of having defense programs in their districts and states. It is now common to find defense contractors spreading their subcontractor base as widely as possible to take advantage of this factor. Thirty years ago a weapon system was usually produced in a small number of factories and in a limited geographical area, but now one

finds that "contractors capitalize on Congressional preoccupation with military pork-barrel by spreading projects over a wide geographic area . . . it is not coincidence that the controversial B-1 bomber program has subcontractors in 48 states."[37]

Congress's attitude is a natural outgrowth of three forces that coincided at the beginning of the 1980s: increases in defense spending, the depressed state of the national economy, and decreases in the growth of nondefense spending. The lack of congressional oversight that occurred at the same time as the Reagan administration increased the defense budget (and curtailed in-house criticism), allowed large increases in defense spending to go almost unchallenged.

The second attribute is the Department of Defense's inability to stop bad projects. This occurs because the formal budgeting process requires extensive justification, publicity, and background work to get a weapon accepted as a critical military requirement. This is particularly true when a weapon is justified by requirements that are divorced from a plan based on prioritization and efficiency. If the military later finds that the weapon will not work or is not needed, it cannot back away from the project without calling into question all other projects it has similarly justified. When the Department of Defense has a reasonably constrained budget, only high-priority projects are developed into weapons, and this problem is minimized. But when projects with third- or fourth-level priorities are chosen (as happened at the start of the Reagan administration),[38] the military can be encumbered with inoperable or poorly designed systems that probably will not work, are not really needed, are expensive to maintain, and yet cannot be canceled without calling other projects into question.

SELECTING THE SCENARIO FOR WAR

Nuclear weapons add another complicating factor to defense issues already raised in this chapter. Although the United States has prepared for a nuclear war, the probability of such a conflict is regarded by most national leaders as being quite low. The prevailing attitude of most U.S. administrations of either political party was expressed by the chairman of the Joint Chiefs of Staff in 1984:

> There have been those who believe that if there is a major war, the war going nuclear is inevitable—particularly if there is a war between the Soviet Union and the United States. I would submit to you that that statement defies common sense. First, it is not inevitable that the war would go nuclear if there is a major war. Second, if we prepare only for that short war, we may well guarantee that we have the nuclear war

we're trying to prevent. So, we as a Nation cannot be found lacking in the sustaining power for our conventional forces.[39]

This type of assessment has led the superpowers to choose other ways to press for their political objectives, and of the ways involving armed conflict, the limited war has become common.

Limited wars exist within the overall national policy environment, and they are often viewed as an extension of other national strategies. In the words of a recent national security adviser: "Our military leaders know that perhaps more than ever before, military activity must be integrated closely with our diplomatic and economic strategy toward the achievement of clear political objectives."[40] If this is the case, military activity can become a prisoner of current priorities, and it may be subjected to large changes in policy as various administrations take control. Somehow, the military must arm itself so that it can accommodate swings in policy like those that occurred when the United States shifted its attention from NATO readiness (which occupied the early Carter administration) to an emphasis on Southwest Asia following the fall of Shah Reza Pahlavi of Iran.

Bruce Powers suggested that the only way to design a flexible force to react to all types of limited nonnuclear wars is to take into account the economic, political, and military trends determining the mission that the force is likely to encounter. As an example, he points out the following trends, which will effect force usage in the 1980s.

Economic Trends

1. Growing economic interdependence
2. Heavy industries moving to newly industrialized countries (NICs)
3. The decaying economic position of the United States
4. Localized combat that continues or spills over to another country associated with U.S. interests
5. Increased U.S. dependence on international trade and its associated vulnerability to trade disruptions

Political Trends

1. Intercountry rivalries replaced to a large extent by horizontal disputes: i.e., industrialized countries vs. less developed country (LDC) debtors.
2. Military power increasing around the world
3. Population growth in many developing countries outstripping resources

4. More U.S. citizens living and traveling abroad, giving increased opportunity to international terrorists
5. The U.S. public's support for military activities declining rapidly as the length of the activity increases
6. Increasing economic interdependence among major U.S. allies being countered by increasingly serious rifts in policy

Military Trends

1. The Soviet Union achieving a rough parity with the United States in nuclear weapons
2. The superpowers increasingly turning to surrogate wars to lower the risk of direct confrontation.
3. Powerful states expected to act with restraint
4. The definition of winning no longer clear
5. The growing costs and risks of large wars discouraging military confrontations
6. Terrorists able to perform a wide range of violent acts
7. Public reaction to the seizure of U.S. citizens strong when the hostages appear to be in danger of physical harm
8. Any decision to commit U.S. forces to combat being preceeded by lengthy debate[41]

What does this mean for the types of forces the United States should develop and purchase? In every case, these trends indicate that the nuclear standoff has created an atmosphere in which military action must be rapid, flexible, precise, and self-sustaining. These trends require mobile, highly trained forces that can be quickly moved to the scene of a conflict, combined with other forces for larger conflicts, and maintained in a constant state of high readiness. A review of the recent evolution of most U.S. forces, particularly the army and marines, will show that the United States has attempted to move in this direction.

However, adopting this force structure is neither cheap nor easy. (Major struggles were required within the various armed services.) The economic implication of this shift of strategy has been equally difficult to manage. The United States, which once maintained forces to fight only conventional wars, assumed a second major role as a nuclear power, and then a third as it equipped to fight the limited, nonnuclear conflicts typifying the current military environment. Eliot Cohen notes "the likelihood of direct U.S.-Soviet conflict is low, but military bureaucracies suffer few political costs in publicly planning to meet such contingencies."[42] Whether needed or not, the expense is paid. The cost of maintaining three different types of military forces is high and will

be even higher in the future as more diverse military roles are assumed without dropping old missions and obligations.

CONCLUSIONS

This chapter started with a description of the philosophy of spending to show commitment and then provided a broad overview of many of the factors that help to determine what we pay for defense. Any attempt to allocate defense funds efficiently must be able to function within the environment these factors create. This produces a dilemma for the analyst who must convert a discipline of optimization into a medium from which useful results may be generated in a real-world political context. It is fitting to end this chapter by looking at the actions of the president and Congress during the MX missile vote in March 1985. In retrospect, this vote probably represented the high-water mark of the Reagan buildup.

The MX, which had been reduced in numbers and subjected to radical changes in basing plans—recall that the missile was originally going to be deployed underground in long tunnels, then it was going to be deployed in a "racetrack" mode, etc., etc.—finally ended up in the same Minuteman sites that the military had originally claimed were so susceptible to damage from Soviet missiles that a new missile and basing system was required. Although the MX did carry more warheads than the Minuteman and although it was more accurate, there were so many questions concerning its vulnerability, its few advantages over the Minuteman, and the implications of the MX's weaknesses for strategy that the MX was impossible to sell on its own merits.

But the MX had another problem. By the time of the vote for the MX in 1985, the move to curtail defense spending was gaining momentum. If the defense budget was not allowed to expand at the desired rate, the MX's $4 billion request could crowd out other weapon systems such as the proposed small, single-warhead missile, the Stealth bomber, and the Trident submarine.[43] Those economic losses could adversely affect more members of Congress and more regions of the country than building the MX would positively influence. Thus, neither the strategic logic nor the potential pork-barrel effects of the MX missile could be used to sell the system. Realizing this, the administration tied the MX to the just resumed arms negotiations, claiming that approval of the MX was necessary to show national resolve. And Congress, for the first time, voted for a weapon simply because such a vote would show commitment.[44]

NOTES

Epigraph: Burns, Arthur F., "The Defense Sector: An Evaluation of Its Economic and Social Impact," *The Charles C. Muskowitz Lectures,* no. 8, School of Commerce, New York University, New York University Press, New York, 1968, pp. 83–84.

1. "Why an Army?," *Fortune* 12, no. 3, September 1935, pp. 48–49, 138–144.

2. Burns, "The Defense Sector," pp. 59–60.

3. Hitch, Charles J., and McKean, Roland N., *The Economics of Defense in the Nuclear Age,* Harvard University Press, Cambridge, Mass., 1960, p. 324.

4. Burns, "The Defense Sector," p. 61.

5. Greve, Frank, "Is The B-1 A Plane Whose Time Has Come?," *Philadelphia Inquirer* (Magazine), March 18, 1984, p. 23.

6. Conversation with Bill Fallon, head of east coast sales for Chase Econometrics, held at Dominiques's Cafe, Washington, D.C., December 12, 1984.

7. Conversation with David Blond, economist for the secretary of defense, PA&E, December 5, 1984.

8. Lemann, Nicholas, "The Peacetime War," *Atlantic,* October 1984, p. 72.

9. Dewar, Helen, "GOP Plan on Defense Payroll Hit," *Washington Post,* April 1, 1985, p. 1.

10. "The Lost Squadron," *Detroit News,* June 22, 1983, p. 6.

11. "22 U.S. Bases Called Surplus," *New York Times,* March 6, 1985, p. B9; and Fitzgerald, Randy, "Holding Pentagon Savings Hostage," *Wall Street Journal,* April 4, 1985, p. 30.

12. "Staten Island's Big Payoff," *U.S. News and World Report,* January 28, 1985, p. 36.

13. Keller, Bill, "Port on Staten I. Is Dropped Out in Budget Plan," *New York Times,* January 18, 1985, p. B4.

14. "New Law Forbids Base Closures," *Gazette Telegraph* (Colorado Springs, Colo.), December 14, 1985, p. A5.

15. Mossberg, Walter, "Some Congressmen Treat Military Budget as a Source for Patronage," *Wall Street Journal,* April 15, 1983, p. 1.

16. Ibid.

17. Hiatt, Fred, "Senator Voices Sour Opinion of Air Force Milk Purchase," *Washington Post,* February 1, 1984, p. 17.

18. "Senator Blames Congress for High Cost of Military," *New York Times,* January 11, 1985, p. 9.

19. Kyle, Deborah M., "Congress 'Meddled' With Over Half of DOD's FY84 Budget Line Items," *Armed Forces Journal International,* March 1984, p. 26.

20. Thompson, Mark, "Military Faulting Congress," *Fort Worth Star-Telegram,* February 24, 1985, p. 33.

21. "Why Congress Won't Freeze Defense Funds," *U.S. News and World Report,* February 11, 1985, p. 31.

22. "Defense Budget Seen Becoming Uncontrollable," *Washington Post,* April 4, 1985, p. 7.

23. Adams, Bob, "Congressmen Who Can Help Get Helped," *St. Louis Post Dispatch*, April 18, 1983, p. 1.

24. "PACs of MX Missile Contractors Doubling Campaign Contributions," *Washington Post*, October 14, 1982, p. 16.

25. Jacoby, Edmond, "New PAC To Finance 'Umbrella' Supporters," *Washington Times*, September 30, 1983, p. 2.

26. Mapes, Lynda V., "For PACs It's The Gift, Not The Thought, That Counts," *Wall Street Journal*, November 1, 1984, p. 30.

27. Parry, Robert, "Defense PAC Money Skyrockets," *Washington Post*, April 1, 1985, p. 7.

28. Luttwak, Edward N., "Why We Need More 'Waste, Fraud, and Mismanagement' in the Pentagon," *Commentary*, February 1982.

29. For a concise explanation of this argument in relation to political appointees see Goldwater, Barry, "Let's End Defense's Political Appointees," *Washington Times*, March 22, 1984, p. 1c. The same argument can be made for any civil servant in the Department of Defense who lacks military experience.

30. Kanter, Herschel, "Defense Economics: 1776 to 1983," *Armed Forces and Society* 10, no. 3, Spring 1984, pp. 426–448.

31. *Public Papers of the Presidents of the United States: Dwight D. Eisenhower, 1960–1961*, Government Printing Office, Washington, D.C., 1961, p. 1038.

32. Ibid.

33. Rosen, Stephen, "Systems Analysis and the Quest for a Rational Defense," *The Public Interest*, no. 76, Summer 1984, p. 7.

34. Tucker, Samuel A., ed., *A Modern Design for Defense Decision: A McNamara-Hitch-Enthoven Anthology*, prepublication edition, Government Printing Office, Washington, D.C., 1966, pp. 68–69.

35. Rosen, "Systems Analysis," p. 3.

36. Ibid., p. 8.

37. Rovner, Mark, "We Need a Strong Military, But Not Necessarily an Expensive One," *Norfolk Virginia–Pilot*, April 30, 1984, p. 8.

38. See Lemann, "The Peacetime War," pp. 71–82.

39. Vessey, John W., chairman of the Joint Chiefs of Staff, address to the Nineteenth Annual International Logistics Symposium, Minneapolis, Minn., August 21, 1984.

40. MacFarlane, Robert, assistant for national security affairs, remarks before the Commonwealth Club, San Francisco, Cal., August 3, 1984.

41. Powers, Bruce F., *Is the United States Prepared for Its Most Likely Conflicts?*, P-6592, RAND Corp., Santa Monica, California, February 1981, pp. 5–10.

42. Cohen, Eliot A., "Constraints on America's Conduct of Small Wars," *International Security* 9, no. 2, Fall 1984, pp. 153–154.

43. Keller, Bill, "MX Debate: It's Not Over," *New York Times*, March 30, 1985, p. 1.

44. Ibid.

3
The Economics of Production, Distribution, and Defense

INTRODUCTION

Every nation has various resources at its disposal to produce the goods and services that are wanted. If we define production in a way that does not confine it to what happens in a factory, we can say that resources (or factors of production) are used to make "products." So the first question facing all economic systems is (1) How should resources be allocated among products? This allocation will determine both the quantity of each product produced and the technologies available for production. The first question gives rise to another: (2) How should the products be distributed among the different entities within the system? This will be determined by the distribution rules set up by government. The process that leads to answers for these questions must be understood if the reader is to perceive the true nature of the political economy of defense.

In this chapter, we describe alternative economic systems—ranging from a competitive, free-enterprise system to a command economy. We then narrow our focus to the free-enterprise economic system of the United States, which is characterized by private ownership and control of the means of production and by freedom of consumer and job choice. We then discuss market failure—the real-world cases for which optimization in a free-enterprise economy does not occur. For these cases, involvement of government in markets can be justified on the grounds of increasing efficiency in the allocation of resources. Finally, we expand on government involvement in the production of public goods: National defense is a classic example.

ALTERNATIVE ECONOMIC SYSTEMS

Economic systems can be categorized according to two characteristics: ownership of the means of production and control over the means of production. For example, in the United States, individuals own most of the means of production. Individuals enjoy freedom of consumer choice and job choice. Firms are free to determine their own outputs and techniques of production. The government exercises some control by providing a legal framework, by resolving the problems of market failure, by influencing the stability of the system through taxation and expenditure policies, and by regulating certain processes and products that are either harmful to health or contrary to public moral and social conscience.

Command economic systems are the antitheses to free enterprise systems. The central government plans major economic activities, determines the pace and direction of growth, and in so doing, determines the output of goods and services. For example, in the Soviet Union, the state owns and controls the means of production. Soviet citizens enjoy consumer choice and some freedom of job choice, but government preferences dominate the system.

The systems between free enterprise and command can be described as "mixed systems." These systems have both private and state ownership of property and private and state control over economic processes. Along this spectrum, there is a significant group of countries with a strong tradition of private property and individual freedom that for various reasons have nationalized selected defense and other industries. The nationalized industries normally function as private corporations in markets, but their ultimate responsibility is to the state rather than to private stockholders. Government planning exists in terms of targeted aggregate goals of output, employment, prices, and growth. For example, Britain and France, two major competitors of the United States in international arms markets, have nationalized certain defense industries.

EVALUATING ECONOMIC SYSTEMS

In order to evaluate an economic system, it is necessary to establish a set of criteria. Consider the following:

1. *Wealth and Rate of Growth:* The wealth of a country reflects its past economic performance. Gross national product (GNP) indicates the production of the economy in a given year, and GNP per capita tells how much each individual would receive if the output per year were distributed equally to people within the country. National governments have attempted to design economic policies that promote growth in GNP. A rising GNP increases the economic alternatives available to a

country. Growth has the potential to raise the standard of living of citizens and to enhance the economic, political, and military power of the state.

2. *Stability:* Economic stability provides a constant base that allows consistency in social and defense programs. Typical stability objectives include the promotion of growth without generating wide and frequent cyclical movements in employment, output, and prices. A critical question is whether wide fluctuations are inherent in the system. If so, policies have often been designed to neutralize fluctuations, sometimes with success, sometimes not.

3. *Efficiency:* Each economy attempts to maximize the output of desired goods and services per unit of time, given the level of technology and the available factors of production. At the efficient level, the system cannot increase the output of any one product without reducing the output of another. The efficiency criterion is difficult to apply because the production technologies of a system are continuously changing. Thus, an economy must constantly adjust its economic allocations to achieve efficient production.

4. *Security:* How well an economic system provides for the defense of the whole and for the security of individual citizens is a critical concern of government. People are concerned about the security of the country from outside dominance, security of jobs, security from the burden of medical bills, and so on. There are trade-offs. For example, too much defense spending may decrease economic security.

5. *Economic Freedom:* This criterion measures the extent to which individual consumers and firms are free to make basic economic decisions concerning the choice of goods and services and the use of private resources. Such freedoms include consumer choice, job choice, and the freedom of firms to make allocation and production decisions.

6. *Equity:* A country can be evaluated on the extent of economic and social discrimination within the system. Discrimination based on sex, race, age, national origin, and so on, occurs. For example, discrimination may take the form of different wage levels for the same job or use of criteria other than personal capabilities for filling a position. Clearly, the nature of what is considered discrimination changes from country to country and over time. In general, equity criteria are normative and provide fertile ground for political decisions regarding all forms of national spending.

An analysis of an economic system requires certain normative cautions. For example, theoretical models should be compared to real-world relationships, and assumptions should be subjected to criticism of their relevance. Also, evaluation criteria require a value framework for judgments. For instance, if personal freedom is considered a basic right of

man, then within this value framework, authoritarian systems would seem to be inferior to more liberal systems. Finally, countries should be evaluated within the context of their own set of objectives. If growth is the goal of a society, then to say it does not achieve static equilibrium is to make an observation but not a relevant evaluation.

FOUR TYPES OF MARKET FAILURE

Beginning with Adam Smith in the eighteenth century, economists have developed sophisticated models proving that under perfectly competitive conditions, free-enterprise economies are highly efficient in the allocation of resources and in production of goods and services to meet a society's wants.[1] However, perfectly competitive conditions do not exist in the markets for many resources, goods, and services. In economists' jargon, noncompetitive conditions often lead to market failure i.e., the market is no longer efficient. In this section, we consider the conditions that can cause market failure. By identifying these conditions, we can also identify the situations where government intervention is justified to promote economic efficiency. A discussion of market failure is particularly relevant as prelude to discussions on defense as a public good.

Externalities

Even if markets are highly competitive, optimal resource allocation may not occur because of differences between social and private benefits and costs. In a free-market economy, private valuations are reflected in market prices, which, in turn, determine the output of goods produced and the allocation of resources. If private and social valuations differ, from society's point of view, nonoptimum output levels will result in the marketplace. Externalities can occur in both production and consumption.

Consider a munitions plant that pollutes the air with toxic emissions near a major city. While the private cost of production, as measured by the firms's cost, may be $100 per artillery shell, the social cost per unit of production may be higher, perhaps $120 per shell. Included in the social cost are the private costs to the firm and the health costs imposed on the city's inhabitants due to increased toxic emission concentrations in the air. As shown in Figure 3.1, the socially optimal output of artillery shells (and pollution) is Q_s, where marginal social benefit (MSB) equals marginal social cost (MSC). Unfortunately, because the private cost is $100 per shell, this leads to an output of Q_p.

There are also situations where production externalities confer positive attributes. For example, the marginal social benefits of residual em-

Figure 3.1: A Production Externality

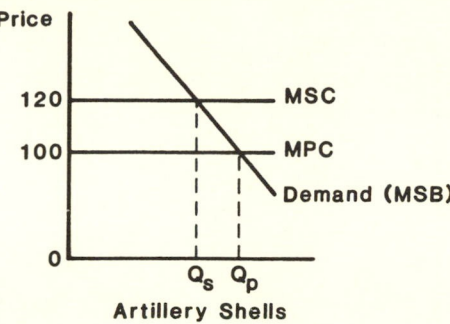

ployment caused by the movement of a new defense plant to a small community may exceed the private benefits to the plant's parent firm. In this case, the local government may choose to subsidize the relocation of the plant to the community.[2]

Decreasing Cost Production

If a firm's long-run average cost function declines continuously over a broad range of plant sizes, the industry is vulnerable to the development of an oligopoly or a natural monopoly. Decreasing cost functions are typical of many defense-related industries, including those that produce aircraft, trucks, tanks, specialized computers, and certain kinds of electronics systems. With economies of scale persisting over a complete output range, perfect competition is neither feasible nor efficient. Large firms can displace other small competitors by simply increasing production and at the same time lowering price and average costs. Production from fewer, larger firms results in efficiency benefits to society since economies of scale allow larger firms to produce at lower real resource costs.

Monopoly and Oligopoly

Perfect competition assures that the optimal combination of private goods and services are produced. Consider the effect of a monopoly in the production of B. According to Figure 3.2, a monopolist in the production of B would face the market demand curve, a horizontal long-run average cost curve (LRAC) and marginal cost curve (LRMC). The profit-maximizing monopolist would produce only the output for which the marginal cost of production equals its marginal revenue (MR). Contrasted to the competitive outcome where price equals marginal cost (output Q_c and price P_c), the monopolistic outcome is lower production Q_m and a higher price P_m. This outcome depicts a long-run equilibrium

Figure 3.2: The Effects of Monopoly on Resource Allocation

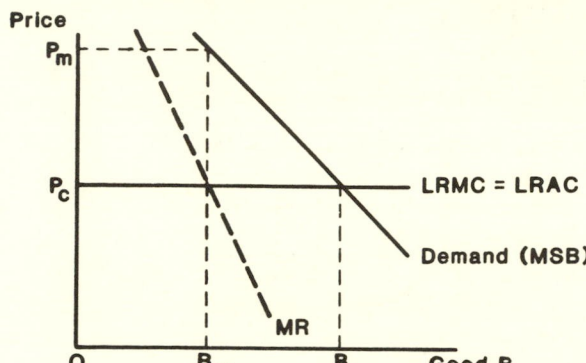

Figure 3.3: Monopolistic Production and the Production Possibilities Frontier

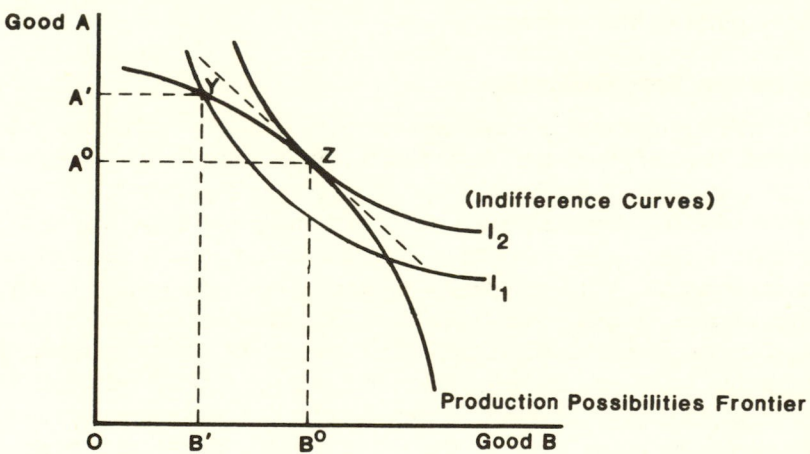

with a corresponding misallocation of resources, because for the Q_mth
output, price (P_m) exceeds LRMC.

The effect of monopoly on resource allocation can be seen in Figure
3.3. With production at Point Y on the production possibilities frontier,
the monopolist in the production of B has succeeded in raising the price
of B above its marginal cost. Assuming that A is supplied competitively,
the price of B relative to A has risen. Consumers react by choosing
combination Y, entailing less B and more A. Thus even though point
Y is on the production possibilities frontier, resources are misallocated
because resources could have been diverted from the production of A
to the production of B, thereby raising consumer welfare.

Oligopoly arises when there is more than one producer, yet the number of producers is small enough that they recognize their mutual interdependence. Pricing and output decisions by any one firm are likely to have repercussions on the pricing and output decisions of other firms. Unlike pure competition and monopoly, oligopolies do not lead to well-defined predictions as to market prices and quantities. In practice, the behavior of oligopolies varies dramatically from one industry to the next, depending on entry conditions, the number and size of the firms, and so on. In cases with high barriers to entry and only a few firms, oligopoly can lead to the same price-quantity outcome as monopoly. However, if the number of firms is larger, the industry may be "workably competitive." Over the long run, price will equal long-run marginal costs, and profit levels will tend to be normal.

For example, oligopoly and monopoly conditions are typical at the prime contractor level for military aircraft. Under the "fly before buy" philosophy, two or three firms build prototype aircraft and engage in fierce competition for a single Department of Defense contract. This is a classic oligopoly situation. However, once the Department of Defense selects a particular aircraft, that firm is usually the sole producer for subsequent production runs, spare parts, and contracts with foreign governments. This, of course, is a classic monopoly situation.

Public Goods

Public goods are a special case of a consumption externality in which one person's consumption of the public good does not preclude others from enjoying similar benefits. Once produced, a public good can be made available to additional consumers at zero cost. Examples of public goods include television signals, lighthouses, and national defense. A new television watcher can tune into a particular channel without weakening the signal received by other viewers of that channel. Similarly, ships entering a dark harbor can all benefit from the light beams from the lighthouse. Finally, new immigrants and newborn babies can benefit from the level of national defense at essentially zero additional cost.

If public goods are only purchased by individuals, the amounts purchased will either be zero or very small compared to the optimal levels for society as a whole. Since the private benefits accruing to any one individual are small compared to the cost of the item, the public good will be severely underproduced. Thus, if national defense were supplied privately, some citizens might acquire handguns, others might hire bodyguards, but most citizens would not have the resources to outfit an army capable of defending the country (or themselves) from external attack.

DEFENSE AND THE THEORY OF THE PUBLIC GOOD

National defense is often regarded as a pure public good because once a defense capability is established, every citizen benefits from that capability. The consumption of defense benefits by one citizen does not reduce the benefits available to another citizen. Also, it is not necessary that all citizens agree that a public good, such as defense, should be provided for it to be regarded as a public good. It only requires that once provided, it can be consumed by everyone and anyone without limiting the supply of it to a single individual.[3]

It is necessary to qualify the view that defense is a pure public good. Suppose we use defense to cover all aspects of military provision, including war. Insofar as we think of defense as a deterrent, it fulfills the criterion of a public good. All members of the society gain from the deterrent effect of defense expenditures. This is not necessarily true when hostilities break out.

The war situation is analogous to that of congestion on a public road. The community gains from having a road, but when congestion occurs, it can hardly be argued that one motorist's consumption of the road is having no effect on the consumption by other motorists. Similarly, in an attack on the territory of a country, the consumption of defense resources by one region could conceivably be at the expense of another region. Indeed, the contingency plans of the military may involve the abandonment of some parts of the country to the enemy in order to defend more strategic parts. Some parts of a country are prime target areas, and these may receive a relatively greater amount of military attention. In the nuclear age, a government may have some ideas about "acceptable damage," which it is likely to regard as a military secret. One of the reasons for secrecy is that broadcasting the levels of acceptable damage may prove to be totally unacceptable to those likely to be damaged. Information about the likely effects of war damage may cause some regions of the country to vote for higher defense expenditures to increase the deterrence value of military capability; it could just as easily cause other regionss to prefer "safe" foreign policies, even at the risk of surrender—a "better red than dead" outlook.

Thus, deterrence is the public good provided by defense. It is unambiguously indivisible in its nature. In the event of war, the situation is not so clearly defined. It is possible to make defense during war a public good by introducing ethical values about the nature of the society in which every individual is a part and in which unequal sacrifices for the common good are regarded as contributions toward the privilege of living in the society. For example, young men typically have become the "cannon fodder" of past conventional wars. Governments during

Figure 3.4: Marginal Benefits of Deterrence

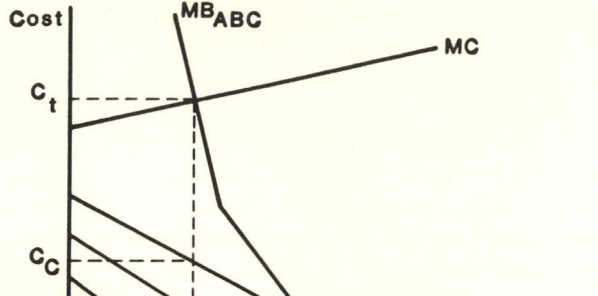

wars, revolutionaries during their struggles, and fanatics fired by their own certainties have voiced some version of the equalization-of-sacrifice doctrine. They are in fact merely attempting to make a public good out of their convictions and the consequences of their actions.

Let us accept for the moment the idea of deterrence being a public good without qualification. This enables us to examine a possible means of assessing individual contributions toward providing the good. We have established that individual consumers of a public good can consume as much of it as is provided without reducing the consumption of others. The marginal cost of extra consumption is zero, but the marginal benefit to the individual is positive. However, different consumers can put different amounts of value on the benefit to themselves. Conceivably some citizens could value the benefit to themselves as being zero, or even negative. A pacifist, for example, might hold that defense expenditures are completely worthless; a supporter of a potential enemy may regard them as negative.

According to Adam Smith, the cost of providing the public good could be met by the citizens on the benefits-received principle.[4] We can use this principle to construct a model of the implications of such an arrangement. We ignore for the present the ability-to-pay approach. Ignoring it has the advantage of bringing out the inadequacies of the benefit approach. As with all economic models, we take liberties with reality, not in order to misrepresent reality, but to isolate certain aspects of it. Thus, the model in Figure 3.4 is a means to an end and not an end itself.

In the figure, we measure the cost of providing defense capability along the vertical axis and the "amount of deterrence" purchased along

the horizontal axis. We leave aside the problem of how to measure deterrence, except to assume that as the distance from the origin increases horizontally, deterrence increases. Next we assume, for simplicity, that there are only three individuals in this society—this saves cluttering up the diagram. Individual A receives benefits from defense expenditures, and he values the marginal benefits of deterrence as shown by the downward sloping line MB_A. This is in accord with the economic theory of diminishing marginal utility, which asserts that the more we have of a particular thing the less we value additional amounts of it up to the point of satiation. It is also consistent with an economist's view of diminishing returns, and in this case it could be that the increment in deterrence for additional amounts of expenditure will fall.

Suppose also that individuals B and C estimate their marginal benefits from increasing deterrence as shown by MB_B and MB_C. We assume that each of the three individuals estimates his marginal benefit separately, and that it is in each case different. For the society as a whole—i.e., A, B, and C—the marginal benefit of additional deterrence is the sum of the individual benefits. We therefore add vertically the marginal benefits and produce the line MB_{ABC}. We assume that the cost of providing additional deterrence is an increasing function, but it could be a constant function without altering the argument that follows. Our marginal cost line is upward-sloping and marked MC. It cuts the MB_{ABC} line, which gives the cost of providing the appropriate level of deterrence as C_t. We now have a point of intersection of the combined marginal benefit of a given level of deterrence and its cost; thus we know how much deterrence is needed and how much it costs.

The next problem is to decide, on the basis of individual benefits, how much of the cost to assign to each member of the society. If we assign costs proportional to benefits, we must arrive at a position that, on the benefit principle, is fair and that completely pays the costs to the society. This we can read from the diagram by the vertical heights of C_A, C_B, and C_C. These will add up to C_t. Each individual pays a contribution to the total cost of producing the desired level of deterrence. This contribution equals the marginal benefit each believes he gets from the total level of deterrence. If any or all individuals changed their minds about the marginal value of deterrence, let us say by deciding it was worth less to them, the total MB_{ABC} line would move to the left, giving a smaller amount of deterrence than before and reducing the individual amounts that had to be paid. The converse would happen if they increased their valuations.

The diagram seems to exhaust the problem of allocating the costs of providing a public good like deterrence. Based on its assumptions, the model is quite sound. But this qualification is the giveaway: The as-

sumptions are not realistic, particularly the essential one that each individual tells the truth about his valuation. Consider individual A, who values deterrence along the line MB_A. The other two members of the community have marginal valuations that fall entirely above MB_A. As the combination of MB_B and MB_C must clearly be in excess of MB_A, in these circumstances at all levels—the sum of two numbers larger than a third number must be greater than the third number—individual A must realize, in the real world, that if he opts out of declaring an interest by pretending to be a pacifist or, to avoid offense to those pacifists who are sincere people, by claiming to value the marginal amount of defense at a lower rate, nearer zero—he can get B and C to pay for the deterrence level that still protects him. He could become a free rider, which is someone who gets the benefits of other people's activity without contributing to the costs. As long as the other individuals continue to reveal their interests candidly, and their combined interests amount to more than individual A's, he can continue to free ride. His only problem is if the other two figure out what he is doing and, by force of law, insist that he pay his fair share.

Thus, individuals have an interest in concealing their marginal benefit from the provision of a public good. Once the service is provided, the externalities ensure that everybody gains whether they contribute or not. If the cost allotted to each person depends on what he declared regarding his marginal benefit, there is an incentive to cheat and become a free rider. If, as one of the three individuals in our model society, a person declared he had no interest in defense, he would be excluded from payment though there is no way he could be excluded from the benefits. Thus the benefit principle would prove to be unworkable in the real world because of the inability of the society to be sure that individuals were declaring their true interests.

Even apart from this, there would be serious problems devising a scheme by which the society could determine the real marginal benefits believed to be appropriate by the individuals themselves. Even if they were all honest, can we can be sure that they were accurate? The society could still end up with too little or too much deterrence.

There is another flaw in the model as applied to deterrence. Even if we assume that individuals are blessed with absolute integrity, they would still need to have perfect information. Without knowing the amount of deterrence purchased for each level of cost, it would not be possible to derive an accurate marginal benefit schedule. Unfortunately, perfect information in defense discussions is not a normal condition of the real world. Indeed, elaborate and expensive efforts are made to surround defense activity with secrecy by every government. The argument used in support of secrecy is that information about defense

Figure 3.5: Defense and Civilian Goods Production Possibilities Frontier

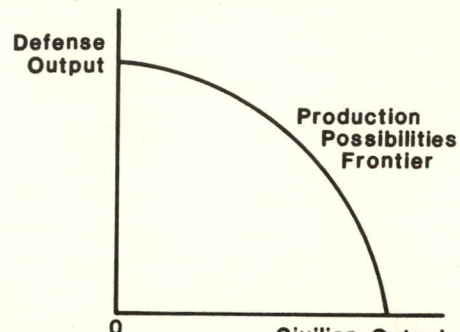

activities is of use to potential enemies. Secrecy is one of the weapons of defense, though total secrecy is not always imposed—it would be pointless in a strategy of deterrence to keep information about everything secure—for how would the enemy know enough to be deterred?

Each country invests resources in finding out about other countries and their defense capabilities, but these resources are not available to individual citizens. It is illegal in most countries for citizens to acquire, or attempt to acquire, details of the defense capability of their own country, even though they are paying for it. Thus, citizens who try to discover their marginal benefits from defense expenditures place themselves in legal jeopardy by seeking the information they need to derive this model.

Although aggregate U.S. defense expenditures are known, this information is of little use to the average citizen in determining the efficiency of the expenditures. Because citizens are not able to know what actual "defense" the expenditures purchase, they are unable either to lie about their interests or to tell the truth about it. As they do not know what they are getting, they cannot evaluate its efficiency. They can only compare different levels of defense expenditures with other headings such as education, health, welfare, making crude estimates of the opportunity costs.

We could redraw the production possibilities curve as in Figure 3.5 to indicate possible trade-offs between the production of defense goods and of civilian goods. This concept could then be used to indicate the nature of the opportunity costs of defense spending. In practice, however, the lack of detail on the shape of the curve and quantity measurements, among other problems, cause this approach to be useful only in a broad conceptual context. This leaves us with the question of how to decide upon the appropriate relative levels of defense and other public (and

private) goods to be provided by government. To gain insight, we resort to a different type of model.

A MODEL OF U.S.
FEDERAL GOVERNMENT EXPENDITURES

First, we assume that federal programs are approved or rejected according to economic criteria. To be considered for approval (and funding), a program must exhibit a net social benefit. Initially, we also assume that all federal programs are independent and all benefits and costs can be measured in dollars. Later, we relax both of these assumptions. For this simple case, a rational decision process would include a rank-ordering of programs. The program with the greatest net social benefit would be ranked first, the next greatest, second, and so on, for all programs with net social benefits. Under a fixed-budget scenario, programs would be funded beginning at the top of the list and continuing down until all programs on the list are funded or the budget limit is reached, whichever comes first. If budget deficits are allowed, the more programs can be funded, depending on the size of an "acceptable" deficit.

Under these assumptions, the net benefit for a given program can be measured using standard present-value techniques. Essentially, this technique discounts dollar estimates of the benefits and costs that accrue over the life of a program at an appropriate social discount rate. In simple terms, the net present value of a program is the algebraic sum of its discounted future benefit and costs. The present value of a future benefit or cost from year i is directly proportional to the dollar amount and inversely proportional to one plus the discount rate raised to the ith power. Of course, factors for inflation and future risk can easily be incorporated into the model. Using this method, future dollar benefits and costs for a given program can be converted to a single dollar amount in the present time period. As a result, the net present values of alternative programs can be compared directly. The program with the greatest net present value is the program with the greatest net social benefit. This technique, or one of its legitimate variants, always provides consistent rank-orders of alternative independent programs. Again, depending on their relative position on the rank-ordered list of alternatives, programs would be funded or not funded.

Now let us relax the assumption of independent programs. Essentially, related programs can be grouped according to categories. These categories of programs can then be compared using the present-value technique, and rank-ordering of these categories can be achieved. Ostensibly, this technique is used by the Department of Defense (DoD) to rank-order

categories during the DoD budget process. Other government agencies (especially the Army Corps of Engineers) have long used this technique. Implicitly at least, members of Congress who are concerned with funding programs that exhibit net social benefits use a similar rational thought process in their budget deliberations.

Let us look at some practical problems that make the actual present-value decision process more difficult. Two problems come to mind immediately: the selection of appropriate social discount rates and the estimation of expected future benefits and costs. One theoretically sound method of estimating a social discount rate is to measure the opportunity cost of funds diverted from the private economy to government use. The government diverts funds in two ways: by selling bonds and by levying taxes. The opportunity cost of bonds is simply a weighted average of market rates for various types of government bonds. The opportunity cost of taxes is a weighted average of the rates of return taxpayers could have received if they had used their money in the private sector.

The problem with this is that the opportunity cost of diverted funds is likely to change from year to year. Thus, forecasts of weighted-average, expected social discount rates for each year over the life of a program are necessary. Unfortunately, the independent variables that determine discount rates are subject to a wide variety of political as well as economic shocks. Reasonable people may therefore come up with different discount rates, depending on their assessment of future political and economic events. This problem is of considerable importance, since net present-value estimates are highly sensitive to variations in the discount rate. Different discount rate estimates might result in different rank-orders of programs. Currently, different rank-orders inevitably lead to debates over which programs have precedence for funding.

Net present-value estimates are also sensitive to variations in estimates of future benefits and costs. Again, reasonable people may assess future expected amounts differently and as a result, have different rank-orders of programs. Even for those benefits and costs that are quantifiable, it is difficult to identify all of the dollar benefits and costs associated with a given program. For example, politicians have long been aware that many defense contracts result in multiplier effects on regional economies (see Chapter 5 for details). Should the "benefits" from this multiplier effect be included in the net present-value calculation? The answer to that depends on which district or state will benefit from the multiplier! On the cost side, externalities such as environmental pollution associated with certain production might be considered relevant by some deci-sionmakers and not by others. Other examples could be given.

Initially, we assumed that all benefits and costs could be measured in terms of dollars. This assumption is usually valid for costs, but not for benefits. For example, what is the dollar benefit of an F-15 aircraft? In a larger sense, what are the dollar benefits of deterrence? As stated earlier, benefits can theoretically be measured in terms of marginal dollar benefit curves, but in practice, these curves are extremely difficult to estimate.

In the United States, the resolution of the problem begins in Congress, which implicitly at least, sets some loose, overall budget constraints for broad categories of programs (e.g., the DoD budget). The responsible executive agency (e.g., the DoD) then compares alternative programs with similar benefits but different costs. For a particular benefit, the alternative with the least present-value cost is selected. A list of these "best alternative" programs is then compiled. Finally, the appropriate agency rank-orders these selected programs according to nonquantitative estimates of their relative benefits. Of course, related programs can be grouped, and rank-ordering of these groups within the broad DoD category can be obtained. The crunch comes at the margin: those programs toward the bottom of the list and close to a somewhat flexible budget constraint.

All of the above analysis is entirely consistent with the politicized process we currently have for rank-ordering federal programs, groups of programs, and categories. Reasonable people may simply hold different views with regard to future discount rates and benefits and costs associated with the programs available. It is important to note that a fixed budget (without a deficit) would not solve these problems. In practice, it may even make the decision process more politicized and perhaps more acrimonious than in the past. Also, certain programs with long-term net benefits to society may not be started because high initial costs exceed inflexible budget constraints. Indeed, in a microeconomic sense, an annually balanced budget may result in an inefficient allocation of society's resources. The "gaming" aspects of net present-value estimates are obvious from the previous discussion and need no further elaboration. A second source of inefficiency would be the elimination of programs with substantial net social benefits. Other programs, even if approved, might be forced into nonoptimum production schedules to satisfy a no-deficit budget.

CONCLUSIONS

All economic systems, from free-enterprise economies to Soviet-style command economies, must solve two basic economic questions: (1) How should resources be allocated to products? and (2) How should products

be distributed among citizens? For market economies with private ownership of the means of production, the perfectly competitive, free-enterprise model breaks down in the face of market failures: externalities, decreasing cost production, monopolies and oligopolies, and public goods. In all four cases, government intervention in the free market can be justified on the grounds of efficiency.

The economic concept of a pure public good has some utility in understanding the nature of defense expenditures. However, there are limitations. Deterrence at the national level is a pure public good, but this cannot be extended to defense expenditures when deterrence fails without imposing ethical values about the survival of the state. The criterion suggested by Adam Smith, payments according to benefits, although analytically sound, fails when applied to the real world. Some version of the ability-to-pay principle appears to be an acceptable alternative. Indeed, this approach is inherent in the U.S. progressive tax system and is even more pronounced in the tax systems of Western European countries.

In the end however, we are left with the problem of how a free-enterprise system determines the appropriate levels of public goods, defense in particular. Individual citizens are simply not in a position to know the appropriate level of defense expenditure, let alone the degree of efficiency inherent in alternative defense systems. In the United States and other countries with democratic institutions, citizens do have some voice in major defense issues (level of aggregate expenditures, the desirability of certain major weapon systems such as MX), and this collective "voice" is heard through the democratic political process. Command economies such as the USSR provide even less opportunity for individual citizens to participate in defense decisions. However, even in the United States, details of defense are normally left to experts, who are given general guidance by the political administration in power and the specific budget constraints imposed by Congress.

NOTES

1. For example, see Layard, P., and Walters, A., *Microeconomic Theory*, McGraw-Hill Book Company, New York, 1978, pp. 4–42 and 52–78.

2. See Musgrave, R., *The Theory of Public Finance*, McGraw-Hill Book Company, New York, 1959.

3. For a more complete treatment of defense as a public good, see Kennedy, G., *The Economics of Defense*, Faber and Faber Publishers, London, 1976, pp. 40–57.

4. See Millward, R., *Public Expenditure Economics*, McGraw-Hill Book Company, London, 1971, pp. 131–140. Also see Kennedy, *The Economics of Defense*. The individual lines in Figure 3.4 are added vertically because individual consumption is not at the expense of other consumers. If we were concerned with a private good, we would add horizontally.

4
Making and Controlling the Defense Budget

The worst thing that could happen is for the nation to go on a defense spending binge that will create economic havoc at home and confusion abroad, and that cannot be dealt with wisely by the Pentagon.
—Former Defense Secretary Melvin R. Laird, 1980

Every penny we spend on defense is for one sacred purpose: to keep young Americans from having to shed their blood in a war that could have been prevented.
—President Ronald Reagan, 1982

[The overestimated inflation in the 1986 defense budget] . . . exceeds the $7.7 billion the president says we could save by terminating 18 federal programs, including Amtrack support, the Job Corps, the Small Business Administration, postal subsidies, rural electrification, urban development action grants and others. It matches the $8.2 billion we would save by eliminating all federal COLAs. It dwarfs the $5.6 billion we could save by eliminating Social Security COLAs. To paraphrase the late Senator Everett Dirksen, this is real money we're talking about.
—Congressman Les Aspin, 1985

The spending side of the budget is not the place where adjustments in fiscal policy should be made.
—William H. Taft IV, 1984

INTRODUCTION

There are two ways to view the budgeting process in the Department of Defense. The first could be labeled the "accounting" view. This view concentrates on the mechanics of the budgeting process. It concerns itself with the manner in which the budget is derived, how the budget

deals with competing needs for defense funds, and how money is accounted for and apportioned within the defense establishment.

The second view of the budgeting process concentrates, instead, on the philosophy and assumptions that underlie the budgeting process. Because these factors drive the mechanical process, it is accurate to say that the second view is far more important in determining the allocations in any particular budget and thus, this view deserves more careful attention than the first when the economics of the defense budget are considered.

BUDGET AUTHORITY AND OUTLAYS

One difficulty of discussing the defense budget is that at any given time, different figures may be properly quoted as representing the size of the defense budget. One figure is the *budget authority*. This figure represents the legal authority to enter into obligations that will result in immediate or future outlays. For the Department of Defense, this could be expressed as a"congressional appropriation" for a given fiscal year or as "contract authority" to enter contracts or incur obligations in advance of an appropriation.[1] A second figure is the *budget outlay*. This figure represents the amount of money actually spent in a given fiscal year. This figure will be less than the budget authority in a period of rising defense expenditures.

Budget outlays are composed of money from several previous fiscal year appropriations. Figure 4.1 shows that each year's budget authority (the total spending represented by each fiscal year's "S" curve) is spent over a period of four to five years. Thus, the real expenditure for defense in any year—the outlay—is the sum of several incremental expenditures, each of which is based on a budget authority from a different budget.[2] In a period of rising defense expenditures the budget authority for each budget will be higher than that for the previous budget. In this situation, the outlay for each fiscal year (the sum of the incremental expenditures that were authorized under previous, lower budget authorities) will always be lower than the budget authority for that fiscal year.

The difference between budget authority and outlays has been substantial in the 1980s. Table 4.1 shows the figures for budgets in fiscal years 1981 through 1985. Outlays, which lagged behind budget authority by as much as 14.5 percent in fiscal years 1982 and 1983, gradually approached the amounts in the budget authority as the growth of the defense budget slowed. In fiscal year 1985, outlays were 10 percent less than budget authority.

Figure 4.1: Fiscal Year Outlay Patterns and Actual Defense Budget Expenditures

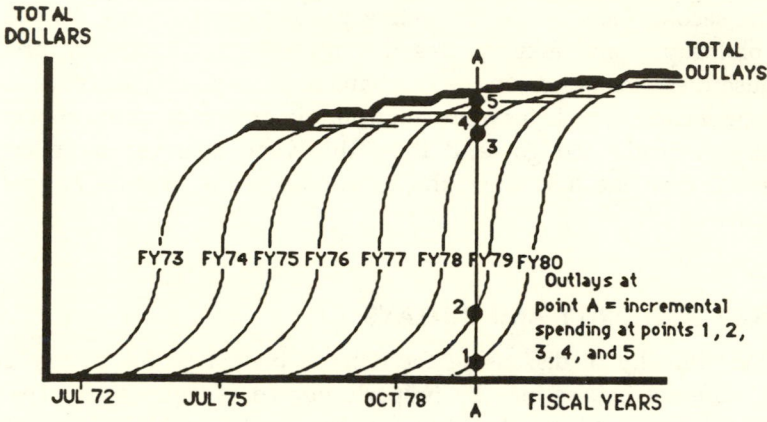

Source: Weida, William J., "Some Fundamental Properties of Governmental Expenditure Patterns—Theory and Evidence Based on Military Expenditures," *Journal of Technology Transfer,* 5(2), 1981, pp. 64–76.

Table 4.1
Defense Budget Authority vs. Outlays (billions of dollars)

	1981	1982	1983	1984	1985
Budget authority	$178.4	$213.8	$239.5	$258.2	$292.9
Outlays	$156.1	$182.9	$205.0	$231.0	$264.4

Source: "Defense Department Looks for Double-Digit Growth in 1985," National Review, February 4, 1984, p. 206.

THE PROCESS:
HOW THE DEFENSE BUDGET IS MADE

The Technical Procedure

The methodology used in budgeting in the Pentagon is known as PPBS. This is an acronym for the *P*lanning, *P*rogramming, and *B*udgeting steps that make up the complete *S*ystem.[3] The process starts with a paper known as the Defense Guidance. This document is reviewed by senior DoD officials who are members of the Defense Resources Board (DRB) as a culmination of more than two years of intensive planning within the Defense Department. The Defense Guidance contains the secretary of defense's direction concerning military objectives and planning, and it gives Fiscal Guidance, which the military services uses to constrain their budgets over the next five years. (This is the Fiscal Guidance shown in Figure 4.2.) These events all take place within the *planning* part of the cycle.

Figure 4.2: The Growing Defense Dollar Mismatch: Fiscal Guidance vs. the Defense Budget and Appropriated Dollars

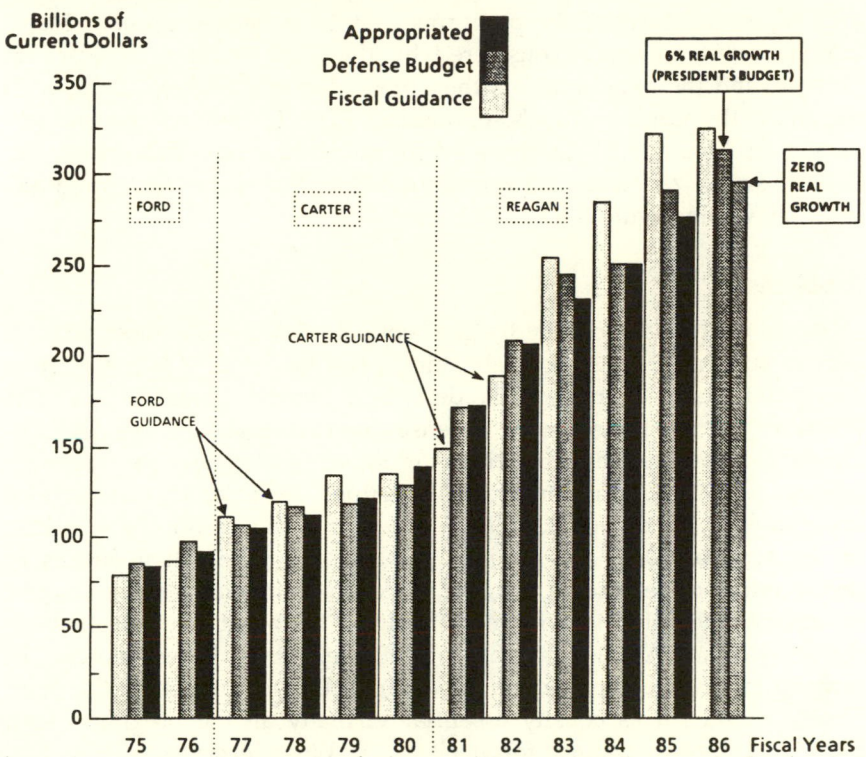

Source: Department of Defense, Washington, D.C., 1985.

The *programming* part of the budget cycle starts with the submission of a Program Objective Memorandum (POM) for each branch of the military service. This formal document prioritizes the programs of each military service within the constraints established by the Defense Guidance. In this process, trade-offs between new and old programs are established, as are trade-offs between goals such as readiness, increased force structure, people programs. The POMs are also subjected to a DRB review during which specific issue papers are presented by the staff of the secretary of defense. These papers present alternative solutions to the more contentious allocation decisions that must be made by the DRB. By the end of this process, the service POMs have been amended and combined into a Program Decision Memorandum, ready to be put into the president's budget along with the requests of other government agencies.

At this point, the actual *budgeting* process begins. The staff of the secretary of defense and the Office of Management and Budget verify and adjust the costs of the programs that have been proposed. Major budget issues are again considered by the DRB and the secretary of defense, and the final budget is then presented to Congress, along with the rest of the administration's submission. (This is the "Defense Budget" shown in Figure 4.2.) Congress then holds hearings and enacts the defense authorization and appropriation bills. (This is the "Appropriated" level shown in Figure 4.2.)

Problems

Anyone who has done budgeting work knows that the most difficult part of such an exercise is establishing priorities. And it is precisely at this point that the process just described tends to break down. The priorities of the secretary of defense are expressed in the Defense Guidance. However, these priorities are loosely stated, and the hierarchy among them has been very loosely defined in order to gain service acceptance of the Defense Guidance document. As a result, the priorities in the service POMs may or may not represent the actual desires of the secretary of defense. In fact, the POMs contain such a small amount of prioritization that it is often difficult to tell what the objectives of the services are. As past secretary of defense, Harold Brown, noted: "In making [a] five-year projection of defense budget priorities, the Joint Chiefs would list as equally essential virtually all the programs each individual service wanted for itself. . . . When everything has 'top' priority, nothing has."[4]

To add to the confusion, the commanders in chief (CINCs) of the various services also have priorities that they feel are necessary to accomplish the war-fighting tasks assigned to them. These preferences may not match either those of the secretary of defense, or those of their own service. As a consequence of these conflicts, the military budgeting process is short on overall priorities, factual justification, and a unified approach to defense, and long on political maneuvering as each service attempts to gain benefits for itself at the expense of the rest of the military establishment.

When the budget gets to Congress, it is not considered as a unified program (i.e., whether or not it is justified, based on the actions of the Department of Defense), and the armed services and appropriations committees make line item decisions on each of the 1,100-plus catagories. These decisions are made in an environment essentially free of the priorities expressed in the PPBS process and heavily weighted in favor of the political implications of continuing or curtailing certain kinds of

spending. The inevitable result of this process is a compromise document that is not linked to a unified set of defense priorities.

REQUESTS AND APPROPRIATIONS

Throughout the budgeting process just described, the dollar amounts involved are constantly changed. However, the past few years have shown a tremendous inconsistency in the direction of this change. Figure 4.2 shows what has happened in the budgeting process since 1975. In this chart, "Fiscal Guidance" is the size of the defense budget that was recommended by the secretary of defense (and hence, by the administration) at the start of the budget cycle. The "Defense Budget" is the number generated by the Department of Defense after the entire in-house budget cycle ran its course and the services made their inputs. The "Appropriation" number reflects what Congress actually provided for the military budget.

As the notations on the Figure 4.2 indicate, the lag in the budgeting system (the budget for FY 86 was considered during CY 1984) results in the first two budgets of any administration being decided by the previous administration. The experience of the Ford administration in 1975–1976 is typical of what one would expect from this process. The administration's initial request was raised during Pentagon review and then reduced by Congress. However, after the Carter administration came to power, this pattern changed. First, in a reflection of the prevailing political mood in the late 1970s, administration requests were decreased both by the Pentagon and by Congress. Then, as public opinion began to shift in 1979, Congress actually incrased the requests made by the Pentagon, and finally, by 1982, both Congress and the Department of Defense proposed higher figures than those recommended by the administration. The Reagan administration's emphasis is shown clearly in the budgets from 1983 forward. Here, guidance from the administration outstripped both the ability to acquire weapons and the willingness of the Congress to fund them.

ACCOUNTING FOR INFLATION

The Moot Factors

To understand the relationship between the military budget and the methods used to account for inflation, it is first necessary to look at the historical evolution of the process of calculating inflation in the price of military goods. In the late 1960s, the Department of Defense used inflation indices that were closely aligned with the GNP deflator.

However, as the military budget grew (due to both the accelerating cost of weapons and the increasingly expensive Vietnam War), a theory developed that the money spent for military goods was causing higher inflation because the Department of Defense bid up the price of scarce resources and granted defense contractors overly generous adjustments for inflation.

When the rate of inflation grew to the 6 percent level in 1971, the adherents of this philosophy argued that if the Department of Defense would only forecast smaller amounts for future inflation, and if military procurement contracts could be written to reflect these reduced amounts, national inflation would be lowered in the long run. In response to the political pressures generated by this group and in spite of the dubious logic behind their argument, the Department of Defense agreed to publish a mandatory inflation index to be used for all future defense contracting.

This list, published under the signature of Assistant Secretary Charles Moot, became known as the "Moot Factors." It specified future rates of inflation in the range of 1.5 percent to 2.5 percent—figures that military planners dutifully cranked into all estimates of future weapons cost, even though it was obvious to everyone involved that real cost escalation would actually be much higher. As inflation accelerated past 10 percent, contracts for weapons carrying prices based on the mandatory 2 percent inflation rates encountered serious cost overruns. Defense contractors were protected from financial loss by inflation adjustment clauses (IACs) in their contracts, but the Department of Defense was condemned for the poor management that allowed such overruns to occur, even though sizable portions of many of these overruns were due to the use of low, politically mandated inflation indices.

DoD-Specific Inflation Indices

The Department of Defense reacted to this criticism by reevaluating the entire inflation forecasting situation. Cost Analysis Advisory Groups (CAAGs) had been formed in the services and in the office of the secretary of defense to develop better ways to forecast costs, and from these groups and the leadership in the Department of Defense a second theory evolved. This theory claimed the rate of inflation in military goods was higher than that for the economy as a whole. Although this theory had a certain commonsense appeal (defense goods were limited in supply, of high quality, and so specific in nature that military demand, coupled with that of the general economy, caused greater supply problems and hence, greater inflation), there was little evidence to support it. Instead, the theory was the result of frustration with rapidly growing prices in defense procurement and a conviction that these price increases

had to be due to exogenous factors, not factors that the Department of Defense could control.

Based on this impression, the Department of Defense asked the Bureau of Economic Analysis (BEA) to develop specific inflation indices for all major defense goods. These indices were first constructed for components of weapon systems. Component indices were then combined using a weighted average to develop an inflation index for a whole class of weapons (e.g., aircraft, ships). From this point, it was only a small step to develop an index for the hardware side of the entire defense budget. This was done, and the BEA index was presented to Congress by the Department of Defense for the first time in 1981 as part of the rationale for the size of the FY 1983 defense budget.

The BEA work purported to show that the inflation rate for military hardware purchases in four major catagories (ships, aircraft, missiles, and combat vehicles) was roughly twice that of the GNP. Congress was unwilling to accept this figure, and a compromise inflation rate for military goods of 1.4 times the GNP inflator was adopted for the FY 1983 and FY 1984 budgets. (For example, if the GNP inflator had been forecast to be 5 percent, the defense inflator was assumed to be 5% $\times$ 1.4 = 7%.) For FY 1985 and FY 1986 this compromise resulted in a rate of 1.3 times the GNP inflator being applied to the defense budget.

Problems with Defense Inflation Estimates

There were two serious problems with this attempt by the Department of Defense to deal with inflation. The first was the BEA index itself. The BEA had used the output costs of weapons in a manner similar to that used to develop the Producer Price Index. No attempt had been made to correct for the quantity produced (the lower the number produced, the higher the per unit cost), and the BEA data also included overhead, profit, contracting anomalies, and changes in the prices of factor inputs— all mixed together and then adjusted (quite subjectively) for changes in quality by comparing each weapon with a predecessor system. The result was an index that imperfectly charted one aspect of the increase in prices of weapons but that said very little about the actual inflation caused by the price of the materials used to make the weapon.

The BEA itself stated that this index was not appropriate for calculating the rate of inflation in weapons, but the Department of Defense used the BEA figures anyway. And because the index included all payments to defense contractors, an overpayment in one period became part of the index forecasting allowable increases in price in future periods. This created a feedback loop in the calculation, driving the estimates of inflation in weapon prices even higher. Thus, the BEA index, which

was initially too generous, also resulted in these overly generous rates being compounded in each succeeding year.

The second problem came from the method used to calculate future weapon prices prior to an inflation adjustment. This was accomplished through the use of a "baseline" estimate derived from the prior cost experience associated with the weapon system. Unfortunately, the costs used to develop this baseline were not deflated, and thus, future expectations were directly influenced by the inflation already experienced in the production of a system. If, as occurred in the first half of the 1980s, one was in a period of decreasing inflation, this methodology caused prices of weapons to be greatly overstated even before an inflation adjustment was applied.

These two problems, coupled with the low rate of industrial capacity utilization (and hence, even lower rate of actual inflation) associated with the recession of 1981–1983, meant that the inflation indices applied to the defense budget starting in FY 1983 greatly overcompensated for whatever real inflation was present. For example, in 1981–1982, in the depths of a major recession, the BEA index called for a 14.3 percent rate of inflation in major weapon systems.[5] In 1982–1983 and in 1983–1984, the BEA index called for 9 percent and 8 percent inflation respectively.[6] Each of these indices was approximately twice the GNP deflator and also approximately twice the actual rate of inflation in major weapon systems. In the first four years in which this method was used to overinflate weapon prices (which were already overstated), the defense budget was granted an unwarranted increase for inflation of almost $50 billion ($9–10 billion in FY 1983, $11 billion in FY 1984, $12–13 billion in FY 1985, and $15 billion in FY 1986).

There is considerable speculation about where all this extra money has gone. Approximately $2 billion of the $32 billion in unwarranted inflation reimbursement for fiscal years 1983, 1984, and 1985 had been reprogrammed (redirected to other projects). Another $10 billion was unspent. However, approximately $20 billion has still not been accounted for, although the Department of Defense undoubtedly has records of these funds. This money may have gone into increased contractor payments, "black" (classified) programs, or it may have been transferred into other accounts.

SPENDING CHOICES

Readiness and Sustainability

During past periods of fiscal austerity, the Department of Defense has shown a propensity to cut spending for "readiness and sustainability"

Figure 4.3: Progress Toward Sustainability in Munitions

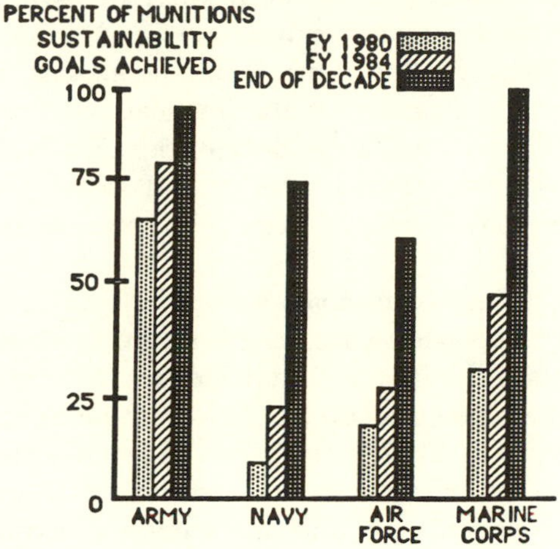

PERCENT OF MUNITIONS
SUSTAINABILITY   FY 1980
GOALS ACHIEVED   FY 1984
END OF DECADE

Source: Weinberger, Caspar W., *FY 1986 Annual Defense Report*, Department of Defense, Washington, D.C., p. 1-D-6.

programs—those expenditures necessary to have enough stockpiled munitions and spare parts on hand to fight and live off internal resources—and to preserve spending for weapon systems. This approach leads to a "hollow army" of soldiers who are not properly trained and equipment that is not properly maintained, an army whose supplies are so limited that military effectiveness is greatly reduced. In the military services, funds for these purposes are contained in the operations and maintenance (O&M) accounts, and it is axiomatic among service members that cuts in the defense budget are usually taken in the O&M area.

Figure 4.3 is representative of the level of progress made in the entire readiness and sustainability area, and it demonstrates why the recent defense buildup has generated mixed signals about the ability to solve this problem. The goal of munitions sustainability is to have sixty days supply of all the munitions required to carry out a full-scale war. Note that the most progress toward this goal has been made in the branches of the service with the fewest expensive weapon systems. The army is clearly the best off, the marines have a long way to go, but the navy and the air force, which have spent massive amounts in modernizing their forces, have an almost impossible task to accomplish by the end of the decade.

Evaluating progress made after four years of increased military spending, Lt. Col. David Evans, a marine staff analyst, concluded in 1984 that readiness and sustainability had actually declined in recent years

because "the services marched to the drumbeats of their own agencies" and "spent more money buying additional hardware. Modernization (new systems with improved technology) and force expansion took precedence." To illustrate this point, Evans noted that Air Force General Wilbur L. Creech, commander of the Tactical Air Command, outlined a list of "high priority" readiness deficiencies that had to be corrected for his command to function properly, and then "Creech cited force structure growth from 35 to 40 Tactical Fighter Wings as 'our number one priority.' "[7]

The budget numbers themselves show the level of priority devoted to readiness. As new systems are added to the inventory, the spending on maintenance, spare parts, and munitions must rise to accommodate the weapons that are being acquired. However, the Congressional Budget Office found that, in fiscal years 1981 to 1984, while the average annual rate of real growth in defense procurement was 17.2 percent, the annual rate of growth in operations and maintenance accounts was only 6 percent. And the General Accounting Office concluded that the Defense Department's record over the three-year period "points to an imbalance among the four functional areas which comprise military modernization. Progress made in the force structure, modernization, and personnel readiness areas is not matched by progress in other readiness areas and in sustainability."[8]

Part of the reason for the lack of emphasis on readiness and sustainabilty is a feeling among the military that new weapons must be bought while funds are available—readiness can always be improved later when the equipment is in hand. However, this view underestimates the growth required in O&M just to keep up as new weapons are added to the inventory. For example, the air force seriously erred in estimating the demand for spare parts in the early 1980s. As new weapons entered service, this demand grew rapidly, and the air force found that it had underestimated its requirement for peacetime spares by $873.5 million in 1982 alone. The same faulty process was used in the 1983 and 1984 budgets, resulting in a total shortfall of about $4 billion in spare parts.[9]

Thus, the Reagan buildup has produced a fighting force that will have higher quality weapons but insufficient readiness. In early 1984, 25 percent fewer army units were certified as combat ready than in 1980. The mission-ready status of navy aircraft had fallen from 86 to 83 percent. Battalion field training days, aircraft flying hours, and ship steaming time were all well below the level cited as necessary by military commanders.[10] Some of these problems are measurement anomalies— for example, when the army designates a unit to receive a new tank model, the unit immediately becomes noncombat ready until the deliveries

are made—but most of the problems stem from the simple fact that, in spite of the rhetoric, readiness is not of high enough priority to receive proper funding.

Force Structure and Modernization

Although there is little hard evidence that readiness is a high-priority item in the Reagan defense buildup, there is ample evidence that force structure (the acquisition of men and weapons) and modernization (the development of new weapons) are both top-priority items. However, there is a big difference between awarding contracts and actually taking delivery on weapon systems. By the end of 1984, most of the hardware ordered by the Reagan administration had yet to be delivered. The pipeline was full of back-ordered weapons, but as Table 4.2 shows, the actual changes in the armed forces between the years 1980 and 1984 were quite small considering the amounts of money spent, and most of those changes were the result of actions taken by the Carter administration. For example, of the ninety-three ships received by the navy in the four-year period, eighty-six had been authorized by the Carter administration and the remaining seven were used vessels that were brought out of mothballs by the Reagan administration.[11]

Even the critics of the Reagan buildup concede that military strength has risen due to the huge increases in defense spending in the 1980s. These increases, however, have not been so large as the spending changes would seem to indicate, and a major question remains concerning the actual equipment acquisitions resulting from these expenditures. The failure of new equipment to appear in spite of the massive defense spending during the first four years of the Reagan buildup can be traced to two causes. First, many of the new systems are more expensive and time consuming to develop than had been anticipated. Second, the delivery schedule for new weapons has been very slow. Consider, for example, the Navy shipbuilding program shown in Table 4.3.

The slowness with which the new shipbuilding program has gotten underway is apparent from this table. Similar delays have also affected the navy's acquisition of the F-18 fighter (84 in 1984, 84 in 1985, 84 in 1986, and 102 in 1987), the air force acquisition of the B-1 bomber (10 in 1984, 34 and 1985, and 48 in 1986) and the F-16 (144 in 1984, 150 in 1985, 180 in 1986, and 180 in 1987), as well as the acquisition of most other major systems.[12] This pattern of delayed acquisitions occurs because the major systems involved are extremely expensive and increasingly complicated to build. Companies that construct the systems have limited capacity, and the defense budget has limited funds available. As a result, the United States can only afford to purchase a small number

Table 4.2
Changes in the Armed Forces, 1980-1984

Category	1980	1984
Military personnel	2,036,287	2,143,823
Battle force ships	479	524
Air Force active primary tactical aircraft	1,680	1,752
Navy active primary tactical aircraft	894	939
Marine active primary tactical aircraft	422	401
Land-based ballistic missiles	1,052	1,031
Sea-based ballistic missiles	576	616

Source: Weinberger, Caspar W., Secretary's Annual Report to Congress, FY 1985, Department of Defense, Washington, D.C., 1985.

Table 4.3
U.S. Navy Five-Year Shipbuilding Programs (new ships only)

Five-Year Plan	1982[a]	1983	1984	Ships Per Year 1985	1986	1987	1988	1989	1990
FY 1983-1987	17[a]	18	21	24	32	38			
FY 1984-1988			17	21	28	28	30		
FY 1985-1989				23	27	22	24	25	
FY 1986-1990					23	20	24	22	18

Note: [a]From 1981 Carter budget
Source: Schemmer, Benjamin F., "When Reagan Promised You a 600-ship Navy, Why is Lehmen Building You a 700-ship Fleet?," Armed Forces Journal International, April 1985, pp. 78-81.

Table 4.4
Changes in Unit Costs of Selected Weapons (in millions of 1984 dollars)

Weapon	Initial Year	Initial Cost	1984 Cost	% Change
M1 tank	1972	$ 2.0	$ 2.8	+ 42.4
F-15 fighter	1970	$23.6	$27.7	+ 17.5
DIVAD gun	1978	$ 5.2	$ 6.7	+ 29.7
Bradley IFV	1979	$ .7	$ 1.5	+113.5[a]
F-18 fighter	1975	$19.3	$29.0	+ 50.0

Note: [a]Canceled in 1985
Source: "How the Pentagon Spends Its Billions," Newsweek, February 11, 1985, pp. 26-28.

of weapons each year, and the numbers of each system purchased drop even more when there is an attempt to acquire a large number of different weapons simultaneously. To make matters worse, the unit cost of the weapons purchased continues to increase faster than the rate of inflation. Table 4.4 shows the cost increases incurred over the past decade by some representative systems.

What conclusion can be drawn from the difficulties encountered by the Reagan administration in building force structure? The main point is that weapon systems have become so expensive and so difficult to develop that even the United States cannot successfully engage in an all-out buildup of its armed forces. The Reagan buildup has devoted an unprecedented amount of resources (at least, by the standards of the 1970s and 1980s) to building and modernizing the force structure, but

even these resources have been insufficient—after spending over $1 trillion on defense, sustainability has increased by only two weeks and force structure has been only slightly altered.[13] This does not mean that force structure will never increase; it simply means that weapon deliveries now lag defense plans by such a length of time that the new weapons, when they do arrive, can become a disruptive influence.

Readiness and sustainability can be achieved in a reasonable period of time, but they have been sacrificed to allow expenditures for equipment. And when the equipment is finally delivered, it will consume so much of the O&M budget that there will still be no money left for readiness and sustainability. In addition, the large expenses and long delivery times associated with major systems cause an unfortunate cycling effect in defense acquisitions, driving up the price of weapons further. In short, this is a process of chasing one's tail. The answer to this dilemma is to introduce a level of consistency in defense spending that allows new weapons to be procured at a constant rate, thus facilitating planning and funding for readiness and sustainability needs.

THE STRATEGY BEHIND THE DEFENSE BUILDUP

Ideally, spending for any endeavor should closely follow the overall strategy for the success of that endeavor. Various competing projects should be evaluated by how well they contribute to the strategy, and money should be allocated accordingly. However, the strategy associated with the Reagan buildup has never been completely clear. Chapter 2 covers what appears to be one aspect of this strategy—spending to show commitment. But because such a strategy indicates merely that one ought to spend as much as possible, it provides little indication of priorities. Another aspect of the Reagan strategy appears to be the perception that the danger posed by the threat is so great that any amount of spending is justified. In other words, there are no constraints in this problem—it has an unbounded solution that requires infinite resources. Again, this type of strategy is useless in determining priorities.

An analysis of the budgets presented by the secretary of defense casts doubt on the existence of well-defined, guiding strategy. Upon reviewing the 1985 budget, a prodefense magazine, the *Armed Forces Journal International*, noted that:

> Secretary of Defense Caspar W. Weinberger's Fiscal Year 1985 *Annual Report to the Congress* . . . exposes a serious paradox. On the one hand, it indicates that we are buying strength without any clear strategy. On the other hand, [it] suggests that the programs that make up that strength

will not affect the balance—that we are buying programs without power. . . . If we have a strategy anywhere in the world, the Secretary's Annual Report fails to present it.[14]

However, within this paradox there is an indication that an extremely broad strategy does exist: namely, that U.S. military forces should be able to meet and defeat any enemy force (or combination of forces) at any point on the globe. Less ambitious aspects of this strategy have been discussed starting from the one-and-one-half war (one major and one limited war) and the two-and-one-half war (two major conflicts and one limited war) on up to the three-and-one-half war scenario, with the military services planning to build and support their forces accordingly. However, the actual statement of this strategy implies an even larger commitment. In 1983, Caspar Weinberger claimed that "Our long-term goal is to be able to meet the demands of a worldwide war, including concurrent reinforcement of Europe, deployments to Southwest Asia and the Pacific, and support for other areas."[15]

If this is indeed the strategy, the amount of military force required to pursue successfully such ends is virtually unlimited and clearly well beyond the current capacity of the U.S. armed forces. As a result, U.S. forces are in a position of being constantly overcommitted—something that can only be attacked through the acquisition of more force structure. And since this strategy is broadly framed and without specific guidance (i.e., "be prepared to fight anything, anywhere"), the result during the first four years of the Reagan buildup was predictable and observable: As many weapons as possible, of every type available, were acquired on the theory that some situation would be encountered where each weapon would be the key to victory. This type of strategy fits nicely with the effort to spend resources to show commitment and the feeling that the threat is infinite. In addition, because the threat and the mission are so ill defined, the concepts of readiness and sustainability are difficult to quantify and easy to overlook in the rush to purchase weapons.

The defense budgets themselves give credence to the existence of the general strategy outlined above. In the period 1982 through 1984, investment in procurement, construction, and research and development rose 86 percent, while expenses associated with the operations and support of the defense establishment increased by only 30 percent.[16] Thus, a very general strategy of total U.S. involvement in a complete, worldwide conflict has provided the rationale for defense spending without giving any specifics on how the results of that spending should be used. As Senator Sam Nunn has noted, "Our current military strategy as set forth in Weinberger's defense posture statements has little relationship to our present capability or to foreseeable resources."[17]

Figure 4.4: Federal Budget Outlays (1985 approved; others estimated)

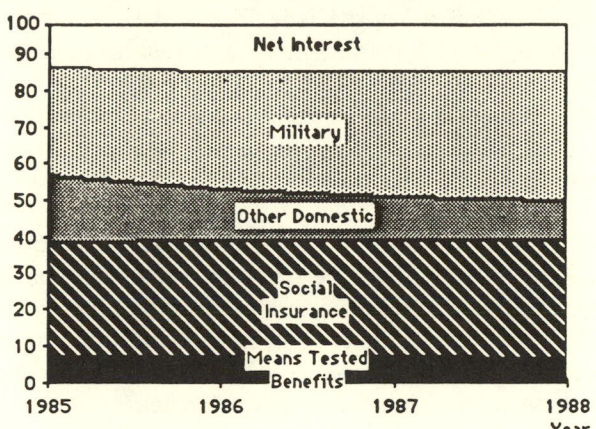

Source: Weinraub, Bernard, "President Depicts Budget as Change for a New Course," *New York Times,* February 5, 1985, p. 1.

THE DEFENSE BUDGET IN THE CONTEXT OF THE NATIONAL BUDGET

The increased spending associated with the Reagan defense buildup came at an extremely fortuitous time. While an economic slump of major proportions in all other sectors of the economy kept bottlenecks from developing in production facilities, high values for the dollar and record imports of consumer goods kept inflation down. Virtually the only adverse effect of the large increases in defense spending (combined with other government expenditures) was a huge budget deficit arising from the government's decision not to raise taxes.

However, during this period defense spending played a critical role in allocating the discretionary part of the federal budget. Figure 4.4 shows that in FY 1985, 38.2 percent of the federal budget was composed of entitlements (Social Security and means-tested benefits), 29.5 percent was defense spending, and 13.6 percent was interest payments. This left only 18.7 percent of the budget for everything else. This breakdown means that the potential for nonmilitary discretionary spending exists in only 18.7 percent of the budget—interest and entitlements are essentially fixed. Using this method of calculation, by 1988 the discretionary part of the budget will have shrunk to only 11.3 percent.

Thus, major discretionary changes in the federal budget (such as cuts) must either involve the defense budget or risk increasing the deficit unless taxes are raised. However, this creates a second problem because a large proportion of millitary expenditures are also nondiscretionary.

Figure 4.5 shows that because of the spending patterns associated with each year's defense budget (see Figure 4.1), only 13 percent of the defense outlays for procurement in a fiscal year actually occur in that year. Therefore, 87 percent of the procurement spending is non-discretionary—it comes from obligations made in previous years' budgets. This behavior is representative of the entire military investment part of the defense budget—an amount equal to 43 percent of all defense spending.[18]

Figure 4.6 shows the discretionary/nondiscretionary breakdown for the entire federal budget when the parts of the defense budget that are discretionary and nondiscretionary are separated. When viewed in this manner, the pivotal role of defense spending in adjusting the amount of the federal budget is obvious. One-half of all discretionary federal spending is done in the defense sector. This leads to two inescapable conclusions: First, if major adjustments to the federal budget must be made, it is mandatory that the defense sector be involved in those changes; and second, because 87 percent of the investment side of the defense budget is nondiscretionary, cuts or other adjustments in the federal budget will always have a disproportionate effect on the operations and maintenance part of the military budget. Both of these realizations lead one to the conclusion that budget cuts will always cause serious deterioration in the readiness of U.S. military forces. It is interesting to note that the reverse of this rule does not hold. Increases in the budget may not increase readiness if the additional money is spent for investment in major weapons—in general, this is the story of the Reagan defense buildup.

This situation is further complicated by arguments about the choice of cutting defense or nondefense expenditures to lower the budget deficit. The multiplier for military spending appears to be higher than that for transfer payments or for interest payments. Therefore, cuts in military spending actually contribute less toward deficit reduction than cuts in the other two categories. For example, a 1984 Data Resources, Inc., study found that a cut of $1.00 in either military spending, transfer payments, or interst payments would affect the budget deficit as shown in Table 4.5.[19] The multiplier argument has been used to justify the continuation of defense expenditures and the cutting of social expenditures in order to arrive at a faster solution to the deficit problem. However, this line of reasoning misses two important points. First, in order to claim that cuts should be based on calculations such as those presented in Table 4.5 (assuming the calculations are correct) one must assume that the marginal benefits of the last dollar spent in defense and nondefense areas are equal. Given the lack of efficiency and direction that has typified the current defense buildup, such an argument would

Figure 4.5: FY 1984 Procurement Outlays: Discretionary vs. Nondiscretionary

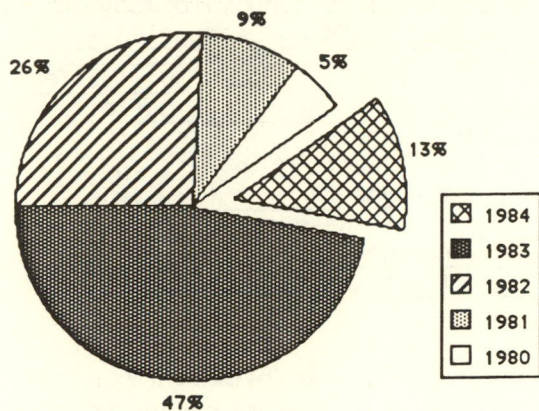

Source: Korb, Lawrence, "Points of Confusion in Forecasting Defense Expenditures," Conference on Forecasting the Impact of Defense Expenditures, Washington, D.C., May 8, 1984.

Figure 4.6: Discretionary and Nondiscretionary Parts of the Federal Budget

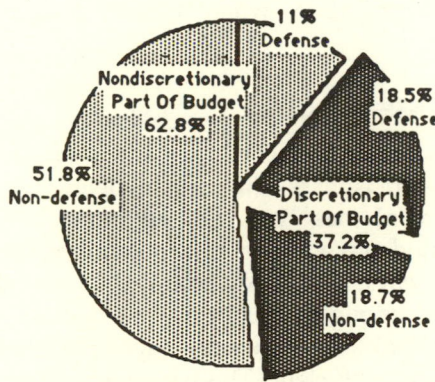

Source: Budget of the United States, 1985, Office of Management and Budget, Washington, D.C.

be very difficult to make, even in the face of similar inefficiencies in the nondefense areas. And second, this line of reasoning is another attempt to justify the use of defense expenditures to gain economic ends. As we have previously indicated, this can never be considered to be an adequate rationale for defense spending.

However, the basic paradox remains. The only time that the military can hope to improve readiness is during periods of increased defense budgets. But this is also the only time at which investment purchases

Table 4.5
The Effect of Cutting $1 of Government Expenditure
in Various Spending Categories

A $1 cut in:	Will Effect Reduction of	
	Deficit	GNP
Military spending	.50	2.00
Transfer payments	.63	1.50
Interest payments	.93	.30

Source: Data Resources, Inc./McGraw-Hill,
Conference on Forecasting the Impact of Defense
Expenditures, Washington, D.C., May 8, 1984.

can be made. And if large investment purchases are made, they will obligate so much of the military budget for future years that spending cuts, when they do come, will be at the expense of readiness.

There are two ways out of this paradox. The first is to keep defense spending consistent enough that there is no longer a need to spend quickly when funds are available. The second is for the military to have enough budget discipline that it will spend heavily for readiness instead of major weapons during times when military budgets are fat.

CUTTING THE DEFENSE BUDGET

By mid-1985 the reality of the budget and trade deficits had finally created a political atmosphere that made defense cuts more likely. Estimates of the size of these cuts ranged from $300 to $400 billion over a five-year period. Faced with this possibility, the armed services reacted in different ways. The army planned to abandon its objective to buy and stockpile enough ammunition to fight in Europe for sixty days, electing instead to keep a twenty-day supply level, which it had stated in the past was insufficient. The navy considered canceling orders for two destroyers, the air force contemplated canceling two aircraft programs (the T-46 trainer and the Sikorsky HH60 helicopter), and the marines reconsidered buying a new fleet of tilt-rotor assault aircraft.[20]

These decisions demonstrate once again the inability of the Defense Department to consider and prioritize all programs across all services. For example, there is no reason to believe that each of the programs retained by the services was more critical than *any* of the programs that was canceled. Similarly, there is no reason to believe that these types of budget reduction are even appropriate, given the size of the cutback that will have to be taken over the next few years. If this is the case, what alternatives are available for cutting the budget?

Table 4.6
Discretionary Budget Balance Changes for the United States and its Allies

| | Discretionary Budget Changes as a Percent of Nominal GDP/GNP | | |
	1983	1984	1985
United States	− .5	− .2	1.3
Japan	.7	.8	.6
Germany	1.5	1.1	.6
France	0	.6	.4
United Kingdom	−1.7	.4	.2
Italy	2.3	.3	− .4
Canada	− .7	− .2	− .3

Source: Chase Econometrics Conference, Washington, D.C., September 18, 1984.

Alternatives for Cutting the Defense Budget

1. *Get Help from Our Allies.* One obvious alternative to spending the amounts we dedicate to defense would be to cut back and to have our allies pick up the slack. However, as the section on burden sharing (in Chapter 10) explains, our allies do not have the same view of spending for defense and social requirements that we have. It is probable that our allies would be unwilling to change these fundamental spending patterns and would, instead, have to rely on available discretionary income to pick up the slack. Table 4.6 shows that this is also unlikely to happen. As Table 4.6 demonstrates, the amounts of discretionary income available to the United States and to its allies have been generally stagnant or declining, not the type of situation likely to give rise to additional defense spending in any Western nation. It therefore appears that the United States will have to proceed on its own if it desires to cut back on defense spending.

2. *Reduce the Worldwide Defense Commitments of the United States.* The United States could maintain essential security with approximately eight land divisions (six army and two marine), twenty tactical air wings (eleven air force, four marine, and five navy), and six carrier battle groups. With a strategic nuclear force of submarines, missiles, and bombers, this would require a manpower strength of about 1.185 million people, and after all adjustments were made over a period of ten years, the cost of this force would be about $154 billion in 1985 dollars. By contrast, the Reagan administration is requesting seventeen army and three marine divisions, forty-four tactical air wings, and thirteen carrier battle groups. This force requires 2.166 million people and will cost $305 billion. Over ten years, a policy of "disengagement" as outlined here would save about $2.2 trillion[21]—all that would be required is a national political decision to decrease dramatically U.S. military presence in the world. As Earl Ravenal has noted: "[This] involves nothing less than the dilemma of a mature 'imperial' power, facing multiple challenges

but unable to generate sufficient resources for the defense of its extensive perimeter. The question is 'Will U.S. leaders have the vision and courage to go beyond minor and superficial adjustments and confront questions of national strategy?' "[22]

3. *Cutting and Stretching the Procurement of Defense Systems.* This approach is represented by the alternative budget prepared for the Committee for National Security by William Kauffman of MIT in 1984. Suggested cuts included the MX, the B-1, one hundred F-15 interceptor aircraft, binary chemical weapons, and land-attack submarine-launched cruise missiles. "Star Wars" research funds would be reduced, two carrier battle groups and two navy wings would be cut, new procurement of F-14 and F-15 aircraft would be traded for lowered procurements of F-16 and F-18 aircraft, and the Patriot and Bradley army programs would be stretched. For fiscal year 1985, this program would have saved $28.1 billion in budget authority and $5.4 billion in outlays, and over the next five years $196 billion in budget authority savings and $80 million in outlay savings would be realized.[23] These suggestions, however, contain several weaknesses that would make their adoption difficult. First, they concentrate so heavily on strategic systems that many would consider they "gut" the strategic forces. Whether or not such strategic force cuts are warranted, they are unlikely to generate a political consensus. Second, the trades suggested for the aircraft purchases demonstrate a lack of understanding of the different missions for which aircraft are designed and are thus impractical. And last, stretching programs provides only illusory savings and almost always costs more in the long run. Other suggestions made for these cuts would also require a change in national policy similar to that outlined in the previous section on worldwide commitments.

4. *Cutting the Costs that Arise from Waste, Fraud, and Abuse.* Cuts in these categories center around the defense money wasted by shoddy military goods, lack of coordination among the armed services, and general malfeasance in government and in the defense industries. Further savings may be possible through the introduction of greater competition for defense contracts and through a reduction in the use of defense contracts for regional economic gain.[24] Each of these suggestions is appropriate, but even if all the problems associated with waste, fraud, and abuse were corrected, the relatively small amounts of money associated with these items would still make further defense cuts necessary. The point is that it does no good to produce a weapon as cheaply as possible if that weapon is not needed in the first place. However, it is obvious that if cuts in defense are going to be made, as much as possible must be done in this area.

5. *Freezing or Capping the Defense Budget.* This philosophy of cutting the defense budget caps the amount that may be spent for defense and, by so doing, forces the Department of Defense to allocate its remaining funds more efficiently. This route might provide the most satisfactory way to ensure that limited defense funds are allocated appropriately if one can assume that the Department of Defense is capable of efficiently managing its own resources (and has unambiguous instructions from the executive branch concerning the use of U.S. forces). In most cases, the Department of Defense is capable of allocating its resources, but the mere fact that it would begin to spend defense money without concern for either pork-barrel politics or the regional economic impacts of its actions is enough to guarantee that Congress would never allow this type of cut to be used.

6. *Cutting Operations, Maintenance, and Personnel Costs.* These types of cuts are often attractive to Congress because they are felt immediately and do not affect the weapon programs that transfer large amounts of money into the congressional districts. For example, Senator Lowell Weicker, Jr., proposed cutting the defense budget by, among other things, denying military pay raises, limiting military personnel moves, freezing the civilian work force, and making other reductions in the operations and maintenance accounts.[25] Although it is obvious that cuts in the military retirement system are needed, other cuts in operations, maintenance, and personnel can have disastrous results. Paying people less, particularly when there is no draft, guarantees that military people will be those who cannot find employment elsewhere. Cutting operations and maintenance funds guantees that the ability of the military force to operate effectively is reduced. Both of these results are a terrible price to pay so that a member of Congress can continue the pork-barrel military projects in his district.

This list of possible cuts demonstrates clearly that there is no simple solution to the problem of defense spending. Simplistic solutions will lead to more problems than we now have—but so will inaction. What is required now is action by Congress, based on national needs, not regional desires, and action by the executive branch, based on rational choices, not ideology.

CONCLUSIONS: DEFENSE AND COMPETITION
FOR THE FEDERAL BUDGET

The amount of defense spending that occurred during the first five years of the Reagan admininstration was extremely large. That fact is obvious to everyone. A number of the elements leading to this spending have been discussed in this chapter; others are covered in the remainder

of this book. However, the most interesting question, given that so much spending has occurred, is what will happen following a slowdown in arms spending. This question is complicated by the fact that large portions of the defense budget are nondiscretionary. Thus, slowdowns in defense spending have a much narrower impact than increases in defense spending.

During the period 1980 to 1984, defense spending increased by 55 percent, Social Security and Medicare spending by 31 percent, and spending for other government programs decreased by 17 percent. During this same period, net interest on government debt increased by 98 percent.[26] Among these spending categories, defense was very different in one major respect: Spending for defense was in response to a perception of the military threat to the United States. This perception was held, in different forms, by a majority of the people in the United States during the first Reagan administration. But spending for defense lacked a valid measure of success. And as a result, it has become difficult to sustain. Public support for defense spending eroded continuously from a high point in January 1981 (when 61 percent of the population favored increased defense spending) to January 1984 (when 24 percent favored such increased spending).[27] In a sense, the absolute size of the defense budget was of secondary importance compared to the political problems with fraud and waste and to the fact that the measures of success (and damage) in other areas of government spending were more readily apparent.

The result of these factors was that the military finds itself locked into the very part of the defense budget that has been losing public support—the purchase of major equipment items—while it may be forced to cut operations and maintenance expenditures, which everyone agrees are important. At the same time, the Strategic Defense Initiative has created even more competition for the military budget—competition that funnels more money into investment and leaves even less for readiness.

It is reasonable to assume that barring an actual war, there will never be an appropriate measure of success for defense spending. As a result, it is probably also reasonable to assume that defense spending will continue to be justified on the basis of perceptions and to be driven by the factors discussed in this chapter. Given these considerations, it is unlikely that a period of growth in defense spending will ever be sustained. This adds further impetus to the idea that defense spending must be restructured to occur in a manner that avoids the cycles of the past twenty years. And it also further confirms the point that the military establishment must do a better job of balancing its investment and operations spending.

NOTES

Epigraphs: Reagan, Ronald, "Address to the Nation," April 24, 1982; Aspin quote in Dewar, Helen, "Aspin Says Deficit's Size Overstated," *Washington Post,* May 14, 1985, p. 7; Taft, William H. IV, "The Economic Effects of Defense Spending," Forecasting the Impact of Defense Spending, a conference sponsored by the Institute for Defense Analysis, Washington, D.C., May 8, 1984.

1. *The United States Budget In Brief—FY1985,* Office of Management and Budget, Washington, D.C., February 1, 1984, p. 85.

2. For a detailed study of forecasting the effects of this type of outlay pattern on the size of budget outlays see: Weida, William J., "Some Fundamental Properties of Governmental Expenditure Patterns—Theory and Evidence Based on Military Expenditures," *Journal of Technology Transfer,* 5(2), 1981, pp. 61–76.

3. *The Planning, Programming and Budgeting System,* Directorate of Programs and Evaluation—AF/PRP, Department of the Air Force, Washington, D.C., December 1983, pp. 1–40.

4. "Reorganizing the Top Brass at the Pentagon," *Long Island Newsday,* April 29, 1985, p. 30.

5. Memo from the Comptroller (Program/Budget), Ofice of the Assistant Secretary of Defense, "FY 1984 Revised and FY 1985 Budget Estimates Guidance," July 27, 1983.

6. Helm, Robert W., "Price Escalation Indices," memo from the comptroller, Office of the Assistant Secretary of Defense, January 14, 1985.

7. Burgess, Tom, "Readiness an 'Illusive Goal,' Analyst Charges," *Navy Times,* February 4, 1985, p. 19.

8. Nunn, Sam, "U.S. Military Readiness: Its Measure Is Muddled," *Miami Herald,* August 5, 1984, p. 1E.

9. Correll, John T., "Why Spares Are Short," *Air Force Magazine,* September 1983, pp. 56–58, 61–62.

10. Hiatt, Fred, "Since Reagan Buildup, Number of Combat-ready Units is Down," *Washington Post,* March 5, 1984, p. 1.

11. Seib, Gerald F., "Arms Buildup Ordered by Reagan Could be Less Than Meets the Eye," *Wall Street Journal,* October 29, 1984, p. 1.

12. Ganley, Michael, "Dod Asks 5.9% Real Growth for FY86, But Deficit Threatens Dubious Digits," *Armed Forces Journal International,* March 1985, pp. 54–64.

13. Wilson, George C., and Atkinson, Rick, "U.S. Gambles on Peacetime Military," *Washington Post,* August 19, 1984, p. 1.

14. Cordesman, Anthony H., "Strength Without Strategy, Programs Without Purpose?," *Armed Forces Journal International,* March 1984, p. 54.

15. Weinberger, Caspar W., quoted in Doe, Charles, "Analyst Urges Radical Defense Shifts," *Air Force Times,* October 8, 1984, p. 23.

16. "Buying defense—or just weapons?," *Baltimore Sun,* April 22, 1984, p. B3.

17. Nunn, Sam, "It's Not What We Spend on Defense," *Washington Post,* June 4, 1985, p. 17.

18. Korb, Lawrence, "Points of Confusion in Forecasting Defense Expenditures," Conference on Forecasting the Impact of Defense Expenditures, Washington, D.C., May 8, 1984.

19. Data Resources, Inc., Conference on Forecasting the Impact of Defense Expenditures, Washington, D.C., May 8, 1984. Calculations: A cut of $1.00 in military spending (multiplier of 2) will reduce the deficit by [$1.00 − ($2.00 × .25 average tax rate) = $.50] 50 cents but will reduce the GNP by $2.00. A cut of $1.00 in transfer payments (multiplier of 1.5) will reduce the deficit by [$1.00 − ($1.50 × .25 tax rate = $.375) = $.63] 63 cents and the GNP by $1.50. Interest payments have a multiplier of approximately .3. Thus, a cut of $1.00 in interest payments will reduce the deficit by [$1.00 − ($.30 × .25 = .075) = $.93] 93 cents and the GNP by only 30 cents.

20. Wilson, George C., "Reagan's Rearmament Plan Meets the Reality of Budget Cuts," *Washington Post National Weekly Edition*, September 30, 1985, p. 29.

21. Ravenal, Earl C., "On Scaling Down Defense Ambitions," *New York Times*, February 16, 1984, p. 27.

22. Ravenal, Earl C., "Defense Budget: Where is the Bottom Line," *Oakland Tribune*, April 16, 1984, p. B-6.

23. Kauffman, William W., "Spending for a Sound Defense: Alternatives to the Reagan Military Budget," *The Committee for National Security*, March 22, 1984.

24. Halloran, Richard, "Trimming the Budget: The 7 Places to Look," *New York Times*, April 9, 1984, p. 16; and "How to Cut the Deficit," *Business Week*, March 26, 1984, pp. 49–106.

25. Weicker, Lowell, Jr., "Cap, You're Wrong: Defense Can Be Cut," *Washington Post*, February 26, 1985, pp. C1–C4.

26. "Cap on a Hot Tin Roof," *Time*, February 11, 1985, p. 26.

27. Keller, Bill, "As Arms Buildup Eases, U.S. Tries to Take Stock," *New York Times*, May 14, 1985, p. 1.

5
Regional Defense Spending

The combination of domestic spending cuts, military spending increases and tax cuts will widen disparities between the affluent Sun Belt states and the poorer Frost Belt regions, with Texas and California as the major gainers.
—Thomas B. Edsall, 1982

Jobs, jobs, jobs!
—Senator Alphonse M. D'Amato

I don't think we should spend money on defense because it is a good jobs-producing program, but the simple fact of the matter is that it is.
—Caspar W. Weinberger, 1982

Aside from one or two extremely capital-intensive activities, defense spending generates fewer jobs than almost any other industry where similar amounts of money are spent.
—Professor John E. Ullman, 1984

BUDGETING FOR REGIONAL GAIN

Successful budgeting requires, among other things, that the allocation of resources be firmly controlled by some entity possessing an overall or "god's eye" view. This entity must ensure that a country's resources are distributed in the manner most likely to achieve national goals. Unfortunately, this is not the way the U.S. budgeting process functions. Since the end of the Roosevelt administration, the executive branch of the government has been increasingly subject to wide fluctuations in philosophy and short periods of control. These conditions have made long-term budgeting almost meaningless and they have relegated the executive branch (which is the only agency suited to provide the overall guidance on resource allocation) to short-term fixes of the efforts of previous administrations. This situation has been further complicated as administration policies became polarized and lost the centralist theme

that at one time was able to give general budgetary guidance independent of the administration in power.

Without consistent, long-range plans, short-run budgeting loses its sense of direction and becomes increasingly subject to the political whims of special interest groups. Almost all of these groups are linked, either directly or indirectly, to specific geographic regions of the United States.

The Changing Mix of Federal Spending

In the early 1980s, the change to a conservative philosophy resulted in reduced growth in social funding and rapid growth in defense spending. These generic programs are like two spigots that pour money into various regions of the United States, and in the 1980s every region was faced with reduced flows from one spigot and the potential of increased flows from the other. The Congressional Budget Office described the process this way:

> Defense spending would grow by an average of 17.1 percent annually between 1980 and 1984 [under the Administration plan], while non-defense spending would be held to an increase of about one percent a year after 1981. In real terms, adjusting for inflation, defense spending would grow by an average of over 8 percent per year between 1980 and 1984, but non-defense spending would fall to a level 15 percent lower in 1984 than in 1980.[1]

As nondefense spending dried up, the flow of money shifted more and more to the defense spigot. This was immediately felt in each region of the nation, and legislators actively tried to preserve or increase the total amount of federal money spent in their districts. Because defense projects represented the best chance of continued federal funding, Congress adopted a role of advocacy for these programs.

In muting its role as a critic, Congress acted in a manner that, although understandable, had the undesirable effect of further limiting nondefense spending. Because the size of the national budget was constrained by low-to-moderate growth and by revenue-limiting tax cuts, increased defense spending gave defense a growing proportion of the total budget and required, in turn, either more nondefense cuts or more deficit spending. Members of Congress saw that the growing defense budget was becoming the "only game in town" and fought harder for a share of defense funds for their regions. What resulted was more than simple pork-barrel activity: It was a reallocation of the federal budget, independent of priorities, putting Congress in such an active role that even

the Pentagon was forced to oppose congressional attempts to spend defense funds for unnecessary activities.

Examples of this congressional behavior abound. In the past the Department of Defense was forced to buy the A-7 fighter (which it did not want) and more A-10 fighters (which it did not need) to keep military procurement money flowing to specific regions. The 1980s had many more examples of this phenomenon. One of these was spawned by a 1983 decision to cancel the "Dense Pack" mode of MX basing, resulting in a cut of $400 million in the military construction budget. Members of Congress immediately allocated all $400 million to regional projects, a use of the funds that the Defense Department opposed. Rep. Ronald V. Dellums (D–Calif.), chairman of the House Armed Services Subcommittee on Military Facilities and Installations, responsible for this reallocation, summed up this budget philosophy by noting that "as long as 'powerful' members can get their projects through it would be discriminatory to vote against anyone else."[2]

THE MECHANICS OF REGIONAL DEFENSE SPENDING

Direct and Indirect Regional Impacts

Every regional impact has two parts. The first is a direct impact when the U.S. government buys from a local contractor. This transaction involves a direct payment from the government to a prime contractor. If the prime contractor buys products from someone else to satisfy part of the contract, an indirect impact also occurs. For example, a large cheese maker in Wisconsin may win a contract to supply cheese to military bases around the world. The cheese maker is a prime contractor who receives a direct payment from the Department of Defense. If the cheese maker buys his milk from Wisconsin farmers, the farmers are "sub" contractors who receive indirect payments.

When calculating the regional effect of defense (or nondefense) spending, one must include the sum of direct and indirect effects to get an accurate picture of total impact. Indirect expenditures are often overlooked in these calculations, but they are often larger than the original direct payment and sometimes determine most of the total impact of defense spending on a region. In 1981 Data Resources, Inc., (DRI) found that both direct and indirect defense expenditures had relatively large impacts in California, Texas, New York, Pennsylvania, and Florida. In most other states one type of impact was dominant. "Virginia, Connecticut, Washington, Missouri, and Massachusetts are all ranked within the largest ten direct suppliers, but rank lower in terms of indirect spending. Illinois,

Ohio, Michigan, New Jersey, and Indiana similarly rank among the largest ten indirect suppliers but are lower ranked in terms of direct spending."[3] DRI went on to note that "indirect spending impacts are frequently of considerable importance to overall state economic activity levels and are often more important within states not generally associated with defense production."[4]

Regional Multipliers

Defense money is spent over and over after it enters a region's economy. Each transaction diminishes the amount of money as some is siphoned off for savings, but the cumulative effect—called the effect of the spending multiplier—is to increase the amount of the gross regional product (similar to the gross national product) by an increment larger than the initial expenditure. The actual size of a regional multiplier for defense spending cannot be determined precisely because a region cannot be completely isolated from its neighbors and leakage or infusion can occur across its borders. However, estimates of the regional defense spending multiplier in the Colorado Springs, Colorado, area in the late 1970s were about 2.5.[5] This meant that a defense dollar spent in that area would create about $2.50 in gross regional product. Values of 2 to 2.5 were probably a reasonable guess for many regions during that time. Research also indicates that the GNP multiplier was about 2.0 in 1984, a value in the range in which regional multipliers can be expected to fall in most areas of the United States.[6]

THE EMPLOYMENT IMPACT OF DIRECT AND INDIRECT DEFENSE SPENDING

The employment multiplier is another measure of the regional impact caused by defense (or nondefense) expenditures. In this case the multiplier value indicates how many jobs will be created by a direct job (one created directly from military spending). In the Philadelphia area, this multiplier was calculated to be 2.4.[7] Thus, 5,000 direct jobs associated with a Philadelphia shipyard can be expected to generate about 7,000 indirect or secondary jobs, creating a total impact on Philadelphia employment of 12,000 (5,000 + 7,000) jobs.

Most debates about defense- and nondefense-based employment imply that job creation is a relevant factor in deciding on all federally funded programs.[8] But employment, like other economic effects that flow from defense spending, should never be a reason for acquiring new weapons or continuing to build old ones. However, even if one agrees that the employment effects of defense spending should not be of primary concern, two employment issues are still of major interest: (1) The difference

between the employment effects of defense and *government* nondefense spending, and (2) The difference between the employment effects of defense spending and *private* spending.

One reason that the debate over employment effects has been so lively is that both questions are hard to answer in a straightforward manner. Direct employment due to defense spending is fairly easy to determine, but indirect employment is difficult to calculate accurately. As a result, indirect effects are often discounted in studies of defense-created employment. For example, direct employment of aerospace workers hired to build F-16s for the U.S. Air Force is easy to identify. Indirect employment occurring when a fast-food restaurant builds a faciity outside the aircraft factory is almost impossible to specify with precision.

Direct and Indirect Defense Spending and Employment

The Department of Defense estimated 1983 direct defense expenditures by state to be those in Table 5.1. Questions have been raised about whether nondefense spending has a higher or lower multiplier than defense spending—the implication being that spending with the highest multiplier should be used for fiscal stimulation of the economy. However, recent research by Chase Econometrics shows that the multiplier for both defense and nondefense government spending is roughly the same, except for entitlements, which have a much lower multiplier (see section in Chapter 4, "The Defense Budget in the Context of the National Budget").[9] However, even with equal GNP multipliers, the direct effect of defense spending on employment is probably less than the direct effect of other types of spending. This lower direct employment occurs for two reasons. First, defense-related jobs tend to be more capital intensive, requiring the employment of fewer workers. And second, salaries paid in the defense sector reflect the high skill levels of the people employed, and hence, a given amount of money will hire fewer people.

These factors have inspired a series of studies, papers, and articles, all of which attempt to show that defense spending damages the economy by employing fewer people than other types of spending. A recent study by the Council on Economic Priorities (CEP) is representative of these arguments. According to the research on which this work was based, each $1 billion of defense expenditures creates 28,000 jobs while, alternatively, the same $1 billion could create 32,000 jobs in public transit, 57,000 jobs if the money were used for personal consumption, and 71,000 jobs in education.[10] (Note that as the occupations become more labor intensive, the employment rises.)

There are two serious problems with the argument stated by CEP. First, direct and indirect employment are not considered separately, and

Table 5.1
DOD Estimated Payroll and Prime Contracts by State, FY 1983 (thousands of dollars)

State	Civilian Pay	Military Active Duty Pay	Reserve & National Guard Pay	Retired Military Pay	Total Compen- sation	Civilian Functions Contracts	Military Functions Contracts	Total Contracts
Alabama	640,157	456,530	124,785	348,466	1,569,938	26,974	1,100,093	1,127,067
Alaska	155,052	354,132	14,092	48,605	571,881	18,634	367,795	386,429
Arizona	234,283	418,178	40,543	373,295	1,066,299	9,050	1,350,698	1,359,748
Arkansas	99,431	178,987	40,597	196,320	515,335	56,881	571,903	628,784
California	3,372,341	4,896,205	274,146	2,123,226	10,665,198	88,006	26,299,154	26,387,160
Colorado	322,888	623,938	58,562	406,345	1,411,733	6,942	999,992	1,006,934
Connecticut	120,821	211,690	29,026	98,072	459,609	6,178	5,126,170	5,132,348
Delaware	41,945	83,385	16,051	42,993	184,374	1,817	217,720	219,537
D.C.	468,460	321,107	41,514	148,652	979,733	4,972	1,128,445	1,133,417
Florida	716,738	1,654,602	81,332	1,443,509	3,896,181	52,741	4,597,446	4,650,187
Georgia	839,843	1,044,314	178,539	526,220	2,588,916	70,949	2,378,152	2,449,101
Hawaii	558,704	1,007,322	33,862	126,162	1,726,050	23,892	615,083	638,975
Idaho	25,940	99,386	15,612	68,559	209,497	14,640	34,651	49,291
Illinois	519,548	616,676	100,910	242,961	1,480,095	96,895	1,437,783	1,534,678
Indiana	335,790	115,803	100,504	143,565	695,662	1,765	2,115,396	2,117,161
Iowa	35,468	10,411	33,378	63,660	142,917	14,202	392,446	406,648
Kansas	137,327	430,443	57,946	142,927	768,643	10,242	1,564,331	1,574,573
Kentucky	304,588	614,575	70,852	158,375	1,147,990	21,505	398,070	419,575
Louisiana	204,099	433,375	67,629	244,972	950,075	272,592	1,211,693	1,484,285
Maine	46,671	138,050	19,362	79,997	284,080	1,683	403,079	404,762
Maryland	1,055,635	641,923	76,463	383,060	2,157,081	16,798	3,522,823	3,539,621
Massachusetts	301,187	204,741	103,220	197,004	806,152	12,209	6,315,296	6,327,505
Michigan	298,712	168,610	67,630	163,798	698,750	44,557	1,737,606	1,782,163
Minnesota	67,573	21,210	54,916	99,469	243,168	20,801	1,584,025	1,604,826
Mississippi	260,014	339,280	53,926	177,221	830,547	156,447	1,683,874	1,840,321
Missouri	878,444	267,380	109,135	240,195	1,095,154	76,690	5,560,829	5,637,519
Montana	22,001	70,923	14,954	44,042	151,920	10,741	106,060	116,801
Nebraska	92,177	264,051	20,923	92,332	469,483	10,370	152,411	162,781
Nevada	43,846	198,489	9,718	132,093	384,146	329	158,353	158,682
New Hampshire	246,344	84,639	13,960	80,410	425,353	478	540,263	540,741
New Jersey	698,553	320,014	86,151	229,631	1,343,349	17,570	2,622,405	2,639,975
New Mexico	240,212	306,308	17,319	162,837	726,676	15,683	447,272	462,955
New York	419,949	375,323	128,422	261,175	1,184,869	33,448	9,601,163	9,634,611

North Carolina	338,110	1,596,174	72,292	458,896	2,465,472	18,816	767,452	786,268
North Dakota	37,666	187,083	13,803	18,463	257,015	4,269	132,244	136,513
Ohio	844,692	267,943	94,903	281,320	1,488,858	39,742	3,325,167	3,364,909
Oklahoma	561,343	514,773	81,557	261,794	1,419,467	15,451	596,159	611,610
Oregon	81,658	15,620	34,405	161,164	292,847	41,800	138,944	180,744
Pennsylvania	1,249,202	221,431	252,462	352,683	2,075,778	39,935	3,288,771	3,328,706
Rhode Island	107,574	114,684	18,622	54,691	295,571	954	380,504	381,458
South Carolina	462,499	1,075,935	103,692	367,841	2,009,967	46,213	323,731	399,944
South Dakota	25,562	104,983	15,454	28,204	174,303	9,961	32,450	42,411
Tennessee	171,650	188,390	64,886	284,438	709,367	37,139	791,176	828,315
Texas	1,335,346	2,283,714	194,371	1,513,998	5,327,429	125,102	8,103,777	8,228,879
Utah	495,046	110,378	32,817	81,024	719,265	3,249	718,975	722,224
Vermont	13,084	2,120	12,240	23,159	50,603	93	179,763	179,856
Virginia	2,745,709	3,130,182	90,495	948,512	6,914,898	18,996	7,052,814	7,071,810
Washington	719,443	853,539	84,248	509,345	2,166,575	50,120	3,935,487	3,985,607
West Virginia	40,532	9,110	22,079	67,640	139,361	32,421	89,288	121,709
Wisconsin	62,469	22,055	88,817	96,330	269,671	5,716	769,642	775,358
Wyoming	20,028	62,955	7,930	28,293	119,206	131	38,868	38,999

Note: "Civilian Functions Contracts" are for utilities for military bases, food, and similar items. "Military Functions Contracts" cover weapon purchases, research, testing, etc.

Source: Atlas/State Data Abstract for the United States, FY 1983, Directorate for Information, Washington Headquarters Services, Department of Defense, 1983, p. 6.

second, sectoral employment differences are not accounted for. A complete analysis of the effects of defense and nondefense spending should include all types of employment, both direct and indirect. A research study done by Data Resources, Inc., using its model of the national economy showed that direct employment from defense spending was approximately 15,400 per $1 billion spent while direct employment from $1 billion spent in the economy as a whole was 17,400. Both of these employment figures would create further indirect jobs through the action of the employment multiplier.[11]

What conclusions can one reach about the total employment effects of defense spending? The large econometric models have not spoken with one voice on this subject. Chase Econometrics predicted in 1982–1983 that $1 billion in defense spending would create 70,000 direct and indirect jobs. Wharton EFI (Economic Forecasting, Inc.) predicted 50,000 jobs, and DRI called for 35,000. The Department of Defense, faced with a choice of which estimate to use, chose the most conservative, 35,000. If military employment were also considered, this would create a total of 57,000 new jobs per $1 billion (22,000 military and 35,000 nonmilitary jobs created). According to all three models, the employment results of nondefense government procurement spending were roughly the same as those noted for defense. For transfer payment–related expenditures (such as Social Security), fewer people would be employed.[12]

SECTORAL EMPLOYMENT AND DEFENSE

Taking solely the direct employment figures cited in the Data Resources study and assuming the national employment multiplier creates indirect jobs for both defense and nondefense spending at about the same rate, one would expect total nondefense employment to be slightly higher than that related to defense spending. But these differences are small relative to the vast differences in nondefense sectoral employment. In fact, wide variations in sectoral employment rates completely overwhelm the minor differences between total defense and nondefense employment. For example, Table 5.2 shows the number of jobs that Data Resources, Inc., calculated at $1 billion in spending would create in sectors of the U.S. economy.

Table 5.2 clearly demonstrates why employment effects of various types of spending must not influence a decisionmaker's choice of programs. If, alternatively, spending on defense and other government programs were done for employment reasons, not only would one reduce outlays for defense, one would also never spend money on mining, real estate, insurance, ultilities, and nondurable manufacturing. In fact, one would funnel all spending into services and trade—clearly a suboptimal

Table 5.2
Sectoral Employment (per $1 billion in output)

Sector	Number Employed
Construction	17,100
Finance, insurance, real estate	8,800
Mining	3,400
Transportation, utilities	9,400
Services	38,200
Wholesale and retail trade	28,300
Non-durable manufacturing	7,400
Durable manufacturing	12,400

Source: Data Resources, Inc./McGraw-Hill, "Defense Spending and Jobs," Defense Economics Research Report, Volume II, No. 11, November 1982, p. 4.

solution for the country as a whole. As George F. Brown, the vice president of Data Resources, Inc., noted in testimony before Congress:

The relative employment impacts of alternative spending programs depend upon the mix of sectors from which output is purchased. . . . More jobs can clearly be created if spending is transferred from Defense programs to programs which draw more heavily on labor intensive sectors of the economy (e.g., service sector oriented programs such as health care and education), and fewer jobs would be created if spending were transferred to less labor intense categories of production, once again underscoring the need to decide upon Defense programs from a national security perspective rather than from an economic one.[13]

Most arguments that attempt to show that defense spending creates fewer jobs only cite, by comparison, the jobs that would be created if comparable amounts were spent in the high employment sectors listed in Table 5.2. For example, Representative Les Aspin of Wisconsin claimed in 1982 that although defense spending created 48,000 jobs per $1 billion spent, that same $1 billion would create 76,000 sewer construction jobs, 76,000 public housing jobs, 77,000 nursing jobs, 100,000 teaching jobs or 151,000 Job Corps jobs.[14] (The source of Rep. Aspin's figures, which differ widely in all areas from others used in this debate, was not revealed.) Not only does this type of comparison ignore the difficulties involved in channeling massive government funding into these sectors, it also tends to disregard the fact that average total defense-created employment is not significantly different enough from average total nondefense-created employment to warrant any change in U.S. policy.

ACTUAL EXPERIENCE WITH DEFENSE EMPLOYMENT

Employment Multipliers—Why They Change

The employment multiplier used in the previous sections is not constant throughout a defense buildup. The multiplier for the defense sector was roughly 2.25 in 1983 when, early in the defense buildup, the construction of facilities and manufacture of components both involved very labor-intensive processes. By 1987, this multiplier is expected to fall to about 2.0 as facilities and weapons come on-line, starting a more capital-intensive period. As an example of this process, fewer people are needed to run a radar station than are needed to build it. Thus, the employment multiplier for a completed facility will be lower than that for a facility under construction.

Recent Employment Experience

The conjunction of two events, the recession of 1981–1983 and the long lag time between budgeting defense funds and spending those funds in the economy, means that employment effects of the first three years of the Reagan military buildup are very small. For example, the *Wall Street Journal* reported in 1983 that "production of military equipment hasn't increased fast enough to significantly accelerate the economic recovery. . . . Moreover, the beneficiaries of rising defense spending so far have been mainly high technology companies, many of which didn't suffer severely from the recession anyway."[15]

The growth in employment was well below that anticipated by many groups that had supported increased defense spending. But disappointment over lagging employment was often greater than necessary because the employment effects of defense programs had initially been oversold. For example, Senator Alphonse D'Amato claimed that stationing a battleship group at Stapelton Piers on Staten Island, New York, would mean 9,000 new jobs. Calculations by the Department of Defense showed that this project would generate only 1,500 to 2,000 temporary (eighteen-month) jobs during the construction phase of the project, and 300 to 400 local jobs thereafter.[16] Even accounting for the facts that the Department of Defense was talking about direct jobs and that Senator D'Amato may have been referring to total jobs, the 9,000 job figure was overstated.

Inflated employment estimates are also frequently encountered when there is local hesitancy about the effects of military programs. As a result, some local leaders have attempted to protect their areas against future employment problems. In Jefferson County, New York, local unemployment was 20 percent, but some residents still expressed res-

ervations about army plans to locate a new base in their county (as many or more were in favor of the plans). When army officials predicted that $1 billion "could be" spent in constructing new facilities to accommodate Fort Drum (and its 7,500 soldiers), county officials were concerned about the validity of the spending figures and were worried that there would be no long-term employment benefits once the construction was completed. To guard against this possibility, these officials demanded that the base not be self-contained, and that schools, health-care facilities, and housing be built in the local community.[17]

PROJECTED GROWTH IN DEFENSE EMPLOYMENT

Defense spending was almost the only area of the economy showing growth during the 1981–1983 recession, and the impact grew faster in 1984—four years after the start of the Reagan buildup and five years after the first Carter budget increase. By October 1984, a decline of over 80 percent in the durable goods sector was attributed solely to a temporary slowdown in defense and transportation orders.[18] And in the next month, an increase in defense business alone restored growth in durable goods.

The highly technological nature of the Reagan defense buildup means that employment growth will never match the expansion of employment generated in previous military buildups. Even so, the employment effects of defense spending are wide ranging: By 1987 about 1.2 million new jobs, or 16 percent of employment growth projected over the period 1981–1987 will have come from defense spending. Defense expenditures will be responsible for 65 percent of new factory jobs. About 50 percent of these new jobs will be blue-collar, and only 8.3 percent of the factory jobs created will be craft jobs, where employment was already high— the bulk will be in areas where unemployment was worst. By 1987 defense will employ about 40 percent of the new engineers and 13 percent of all new scientific and technical personnel. Defense's share of the total engineering pool will rise from 15 percent to 18 percent by 1987.[19]

DEFENSE AS A COMPETITOR FOR EMPLOYEES: SPENDING ON SCIENCE AND ENGINEERING

The Impact of Defense Hiring

Defense spending creates employment across the spectrum of skilled and unskilled workers. In each employment category, defense industries compete actively with other industries to hire workers. This competition is not a matter of concern when unemployment is high because there

are plenty of blue- and white-collar workers to go around. However, where scientific, technical, and engineering labor are concerned, this is not the case. Table 5.3 shows how defense's need for workers will alter its share of employment in various occupations by 1987. Note that in many critical high-skill areas, defense will employ between 25 and 60 percent of new workers by 1987. One effect of this absorption of talent is to deny skilled people to nondefense industries, and this in turn can damage the U.S. technological competitiveness. For example, in the semiconductor and electronics industries, a shortage of engineers, due in part to defense hiring, is one of the biggest impediments to the innovation needed to overtake foreign competition.[20] Although it is wrong to attribute all export and competitive problems to defense's absorption of skilled labor, devoting so much talent to defense industries represents a level of priority that puts defense well ahead of other types of government and private investments.

Research and Development Spending

An emphasis on defense-related science and engineering is further demonstrated by the U.S. government's spending on research and development (R&D). These outlays directly influence the output of U.S. engineers and scientists, and they are heavily weighted toward the defense sector. At present 60 percent of all federal money spent on R&D goes directly to projects of the Defense Department or to defense-related projects of the Energy Department. The 1985 budget increased defense R&D by $34 billion—most of which went for weapon system development.[21] Because of tight budgets, the increases for defense-related R&D came at the expense of other R&D funding. The Environmental Protection Agency was cut from $245 million in 1980 to $160 million in 1983. Funding for cancer research remained level, and social science research supported by the National Science Foundation was halved.[22]

Thus, the elements necessary to give defense an overwhelming influence in the science and engineering fields are in place. Both more money and more jobs allow an expanding defense sector to absorb a large proportion of new scientific, engineering, and technical graduates. More money and more jobs also make the defense sector increasingly competitive in hiring older scientists and engineers. And the ability to control a major part of the R&D budget allows the defense sector to employ scientific and engineering people throughout the academic and research communities. These factors suggest that the United States has established an industrial policy focused on the defense sector. Even if this has been unintentional, its effect is the same as a decision made after great planning and forethought.

Table 5.3
Employment From Defense Spending: Selected Occupations (thousands of persons)

	1982 Defense	1982 Total	1987 Defense	1987 Total	Average Annual % Growth Defense	Average Annual % Growth Total	1987 Defense Share (%) Total	1987 Defense Share (%) Net Growth
Engineers	129	1,159	196	1,346	8.8	3.0	14.5	35.9
Aero-astronautic engineers	28	68	47	91	10.7	6.0	51.5	81.7
Electrical engineers	41	329	62	398	8.9	3.9	15.7	31.4
Scientists, NEC	9	304	12	334	7.1	1.9	3.6	11.6
Engineering & science technicians	68	1,252	100	1,417	8.0	2.5	7.1	19.4
Electrical & electronic technicians	28	358	42	419	8.6	3.2	10.0	23.2
Technicians, NEC	10	280	14	303	6.2	1.6	4.6	15.7
Computer specialists	19	459	31	582	10.9	4.9	5.4	10.2
Social scientists & other professionals	150	9,492	200	10,086	5.9	1.2	2.0	8.4
Business professionals & staff	671	34,815	927	37,666	6.7	1.6	2.5	9.0
Craft & related workers	437	11,905	597	12,695	6.4	1.3	4.7	20.2
Construction crafts workers	104	3,218	141	3,406	6.3	1.1	4.1	19.6
Mechanics, repairers & installers	95	3,879	131	4,218	6.6	1.7	3.1	10.6
Metalworking craft workers excluding mechanics	61	863	84	911	6.6	1.1	9.2	47.3
Operatives	587	13,468	813	14,161	6.7	1.0	5.7	32.6
Assemblers	172	1,532	248	1,719	7.5	2.3	14.4	40.3
Metalworking operatives	125	1,506	174	1,622	6.9	1.5	10.7	42.5
Service workers	227	15,627	323	17,024	7.3	1.7	1.9	6.8
Laborers, except farm	141	5,657	189	5,963	5.9	1.1	3.2	15.4

Source: Data Resources Inc./McGraw-Hill, "Defense Spending and Jobs," Defense Economics Research Report, Volume II, No. 11, November 1982, p. 66.

REGIONAL SPENDING
AND MILITARY FORCE DEPLOYMENT

One of the obvious ways to get direct defense spending into a region is to have a military base located there. Although the location of new bases in the United States is dependent, to a large extent, on political pressure, this pressure is applied after most basic military requirements have been decided and thus, is unlikely to have a major detrimental effect on military capabilities. Locating the Consolidated Space Operations Center in Colorado Springs, Colorado, is an example of this process, as is the selection of a new navy base on the Gulf Coast. The latter process involved sixteen cities and illustrates why competition for new bases is so fierce. Each region was attempting to secure an "annual Navy payroll of $50 million to $60 million, a $100 million port construction project, $9 million annually in housing allowances for 3500 sailors, and up to 3500 civilian jobs."[23] The number of regions contending for this type of facility allows the Department of Defense to play competing political interests off against one another to minimize the political inputs to the decision.

Because only one region is involved, political pressure is more severe when a base closing is threatened. At least in the short term, an economic loss is almost certain. In these cases, the pressure for regional defense spending can adversely affect the ability of the military to deploy or to modernize its forces and facilities. Throughout history, U.S. military bases have been geared to the communication and transportation networks and to the technological levels that exist at a given time. For example, the air force originally had a number of large bases along the northern border of the United States. These bases were needed because during the post–World War II era, bomber and tanker aircraft had to be stationed as close to the Soviet Union as possible for both range and speed considerations.

Northern bases were not favorites with many military people because these bases were isolated and the winters were so severe (also a detrimental factor in aircraft maintenance). In addition, these facilities were hard to maintain. Later, new aircraft made it unnecessary to be located close to the potential enemy. For these and other reasons, the Department of Defense decided to close many of the northern bases (as well as many others). The reaction to these closings was, in virtually every case, tremendous resistance as each region's population viewed the removal of its base as an economic threat. The local groups were so successful in keeping the Department of Defense from closing bases that the military was forced to set up offices that dealt solely with the economic and political aspects of base closures. These offices became

heavily involved in regional economic planning, establishing, in many cases, alternative uses for the bases such as industrial parks and airports. (The bases were usually sold to local authorities for $1.00 after the military units moved out.)

However, a successful closing is still an exceptional event. Since the mid-1970s, the Department of Defense's military and civilian employee population has decreased from about 5 million to about 3 million people. During this same period, the number of military installations and bases has remained essentially constant—5,600 in the United States and overseas. The Grace Commission noted that of the 3,000 domestic military bases, all but 300 could be closed without harming defense needs. However, the commission went on to say that Congress has so restricted the Pentagon's control of facilities that it is virtually impossible to close any military installation in the United States.[24]

ALLOCATING REGIONAL DEFENSE EXPENDITURES

Regional Allocations Based on Tax Revenues

How should defense spending be allocated across geographic regions of the United States? Allocating defense spending to geographic regions, based on the proportion of total taxes generated in each region has been suggested, at least by implication, in a number of publications of which those by Employment Research Associates (ERA) of Lansing, Michigan, are an example.[25] According to the ERA study: "Military spending as it is now carried out, 'guarantees depletion and deprivation for large areas of the country and provides a parasitic stimulus for areas in which military contractors and installations are located' . . . 320 of the 435 Congressional districts recorded a net loss of tax money in the Pentagon budget."[26]

Allocating money to regions based on tax revenues is an overly simplified and unworkable solution. Carried to its logical extreme, this method mandates that spending in each region of the United States should follow exactly the proportions of the national budget because, theoretically, each tax collar is split among all the uses for which federal funds are expended. This type of approach would lead one to the following ridiculous conclusion: Tobacco subsidies generated from U.S. tax dollars are paid to U.S. tobacco farmers. This "depletes and deprives" areas where no tobacco is grown, so an amount of tobacco subsidy proportionate to the tax provided by, for example, Idaho should be paid to that state.

Regional Allocations Based on Employment Criteria

Another choice for a regional allocation strategy would be to try to target "labor-surplus areas" for defense expenditures. These areas are defined as jurisdictions with populations of 50,000 or more whose unemployment rate has exceeded the national average by 20 percent over the previous two years. However, if one assumes that such areas would have the required facilities for defense production and if one is willing to absorb the inefficiency inherent in using defense expenditures for this purpose, a third problem still remains. Since 1953, the Maybank Amendment has been part of every defense appropriations bill. This amendment exempts the Department of Defense from having to direct procurement to labor-surplus areas.[27] Why such an amendment has been passed each year by Congress leads to some interesting speculation. As has already been noted, using defense funds to implement a regional employment program implies a certain degree of inefficiency. However, it is unlikely that this concern caused congressional action. Instead, it was probably the realization that redirecting defense funds to areas of high unemployment would result in a reallocation of the very defense contracts for which each member of Congress had fought. Regions already having established defense industries and the economic benefits those industries generate can only lose if fixed defense funds are reallocated. This factor alone is enough to ensure that the Maybank Amendment will be a permanent fixture on future defense appropriations bills.

PROS AND CONS OF REGIONAL DEFENSE SPENDING

The Effects of Current Regional Allocations

Given the absence of a compelling reason to change the allocation of defense procurement funds, it is likely that the current situation will persist. As might be expected, the actual economic effects of the current method of doing business are quite variable. On the plus side, in the early 1980s defense spending represented the only positive growth in most of the regions of the United States. This occurred at a fairly measured rate, with defense increasing its share of the GNP by about 0.2 percent a year while nondefense outlays lost about 1 percent of GNP a year. The amount of defense spending in any given region was linked to two major factors: politics (already discussed) and "marketability" (established base of contractors and infrastructure).[28]

The growth in defense spending had a disproportionate effect on regions that already had major defense industries. The impact on these

companies was magnified even further by changes in government policy regarding defense contracts. In the past, payments for defense work were made as the work was completed, and many companies took out loans to tide them over until the first payment arrived. However, under a new policy, payments were made prior to the start-up of work on the contract. This reduced costs by cutting the interest payments made on loans, and it also gave the companies large pools of available cash. In addition, companies were able to pay taxes under the "completed contract" accounting method, which allowed them to defer income tax payments until the last item in a contract had been delivered. The effect of both changes was to give companies with defense contracts interest-free government loans.[29]

This money, along with the regular payrolls associated with defense work, was spread unevenly across the fifty states. Out of $187.5 billion in defense money spent in the United States in FY 1983 ($802 per person), $119 billion went for contracts, $27.7 billion for active duty pay, $22.7 billion for civilian pay, $14.8 billion for retired pay and $3.4 billion for the National Guard.[30] Table 5.4 shows that the total and per capita expenditure varied considerably from state to state. The difference in spending levels was heavily influenced in the short term by the political and regional marketability factors already mentioned. Unfortunately, the states at the low end of the scale were also big losers in the tax policy changes and nondefense spending cuts that occurred in the first half of the 1980s. The average per capita benefits of all government programs during this period was $65, but states with large defense programs fared much better ($145 in California and $127 in Texas) while states with little or no defense spending were considerably worse off (Arkansas lost $38, and New York gained only $33). On the whole, the combined effect of all programs was to redistribute wealth from the depressed frost-belt regions to the affluent sun-belt areas.[31]

Regional Defense Spending and Investment

One effect of the regional variation in defense spending is its impact on corporate investments and on the ability of regions (and companies) not receiving defense money to compete seriously for defense contracts in the future. The ten largest prime contractors dealing with the Defense Department in 1983 received about $44 billion in contracts. This was about one-half of the $90 billion that went to the hundred largest prime contractors. The major defense industries used this money to spend large amounts on research and development—General Electric alone spent about $100 million a year on engine research in the first half of the 1980s.[32] Thus, companies that could afford to spend enough to maintain their technological lead in the past are the same ones that

Table 5.4
FY 1983 Defense Spending, by State

State	Total Spending ($ billions)	Per Capita ($)	State	Total Spending ($ billions)	Per Capita ($)
D.C.	2.1	3392	Nevada	0.5	609
Virginia	14.0	2520	Maine	0.7	601
Hawaii	2.4	2312	North Dakota	0.4	579
Alaska	1.0	2001	Louisiana	2.4	549
Connecticut	5.6	1782	North Carolina	3.3	535
California	37.1	1472	New Jersey	4.0	533
Washington	6.2	1431	Indiana	2.8	513
Missouri	6.7	1355	Arkansas	1.1	491
Maryland	5.7	1324	Pennsylvania	5.4	454
Massachusetts	7.1	1237	Ohio	4.9	452
Mississippi	2.7	1032	Minnesota	1.8	446
New Hampshire	1.0	1007	Vermont	0.2	439
Kansas	2.3	966	Kentucky	1.6	422
Utah	1.4	890	Nebraska	0.6	395
Georgia	5.0	879	Montana	0.3	329
Texas	13.6	862	Tennessee	1.5	328
New Mexico	1.2	850	South Dakota	0.2	310
Arizona	2.4	819	Wyoming	0.2	308
Florida	8.5	800	Michigan	2.5	274
Colorado	2.4	771	Idaho	0.3	262
South Carolina	2.4	738	Illinois	3.0	262
Rhode Island	0.7	709	Wisconsin	1.0	220
Alabama	2.7	681	Iowa	0.5	189
Delaware	0.4	667	Oregon	0.5	178
Oklahoma	2.0	616	West Virginia	0.3	133
New York	10.8	612			

Source: "Defense Dollars, State By State," U.S. News and World Report, June 25, 1984, p. 10.

currently have excess funds for research, and the present imbalance in the allocation of defense spending is likely to remain.

Investment decisions such as this have many long-term regional implications. Industries and regions that have become more narrowly focused on defense work require increased political activity to ensure that defense contracts continue to flow. Alternatives to defense-related business decrease, and areas can become so dependent on defense spending that a regional economy may rise or fall based on the outcome of a single contract.

It is a common belief that regions with heavy military contracts will be technological leaders because most technological advances in the United States come as the result of research performed on defense contracts. Although this may be true, other profound technological developments would probably result from research in nondefense areas, if money were spent in the same quantities as now allocated to defense. The major issue concerning regional investment is that heavy military investment will have a substantial effect on the types of goods and services a region will be able to produce over the following twenty years. The present distribution of defense spending is essentially a proxy for a U.S. industrial policy where "the likely beneficiaries are defense-related R&D firms plus a few elements of the large scale manufacturing sector. A negative impact is [likely] in two areas: non-defense related R&D, which will be at a disadvantage in competing for science and engineering talent, and higher risk investments (such as lending for the start-up and expansion of new enterprises), which inevitably suffer when capital is tight."[33]

The lesson here is a simple one. The decision to invest is a decision about the type of goods or services that will be produced in the future. If this decision is made by one or two companies that comprise the bulk of a region's economy, the decision also predetermines the future of that region.

FUTURE IMPACTS
OF REGIONAL DEFENSE SPENDING

As we have noted, regions with large defense contracts usually have a defense production infrastructure already in place. It therefore seems reasonable that these same regions would be most affected by future growth in defense spending. Although this is true to some extent, there is no direct relationship between current defense spending in a region and the share of future growth in that region attributable to defense spending. There are several reasons for this: (1) The indirect effect of defense spending in a region can change due to expansion or contraction

of the subcontractor base. (2) If defense spending is the only government expenditure growing significantly, the effect of defense spending on all regional growth rates will be increased. (3) Defense's share of a region's growth is also dependent on how much that growth is influenced by other sources. Mainly as a result of (2) and (3), defense's share of growth for the period 1981–1984 is high in all regions of the United States. Data Resources, Inc., found that direct and indirect defense spending accounted for at least 10 percent of the growth in every state in the nation except for Montana (8.9 percent), Nevada (7.8 percent), and Wyoming (9.2 percent). In a number of states, defense's forecast share of growth for the 1981–1988 period is extremely high: Alaska (44.4 percent), Connecticut (32.5 percent), Indiana (23.9 percent), Missouri (24.2 percent), Vermont (27.1 percent), and Washington (25.4 percent).[34]

Based on the potential defense expenditures associated with planned purchases of weapons and other defense goods, the Department of Defense has forecast the total defense expenditures in each state for the period 1983 to 1989. This forecast, which assumes that each state's present share of defense activity will remain constant through 1989 (a risky assumption given the factors listed in the previous paragraph), is shown in Table 5.5. The Department of Defense stated that the data on which these results are based, when viewed on a per capita expenditure basis, do not support the hypothesis that defense expenditures were disproportionately allocated to states in the South and West.[35] However, it should be noted that per capita expenditures also tend to distort the regional defense expenditure situation because they overstate the importance of defense in the sparsely populated states of New England, and they unfairly elevate Connecticut, which for tax reasons contains the corporate headquarters of a number of defense contractors, to a position of being the leading state in defense expenditures. These statistics do not mean that defense spending is becoming more evenly distributed across all regions. Even if areas with healthy economies experience growth rates from defense equal to or slightly less than those in areas where the economy is weak, growth in the healthy areas is usually occurring on a much larger base. Thus, the difference between the "haves" and the "have nots" is actually widening.

As areas rely more heavily on defense funding, the spending involved can cause large changes in regional economic stability. For example, funding for federal employment is normally very stable, and growth in this sector should result in a larger, very consistent economic injection into an area. However, areas such as Washington, D.C., and northern Virginia found that growth in federal employment stopped during the Reagan administration and that it was replaced by growth in government contracting.[36] The change to contracting greatly decreases economic

Table 5.5
Estimates of Total Defense Expenditures (millions of 1983 dollars)

State	1983	1984	1985	1986	1987	1988	1989
Alabama	4,902	5,252	5,620	6,101	6,509	6,774	6,996
Alaska	1,164	1,214	1,240	1,307	1,383	1,432	1,482
Arizona	4,947	5,494	6,028	6,615	7,134	7,497	7,777
Arkansas	2,368	2,560	2,734	2,954	3,165	3,327	3,455
California	54,345	60,092	66,168	72,633	77,852	81,501	84,668
Colorado	5,556	6,048	6,681	7,278	7,788	8,171	8,494
Connecticut	8,946	9,814	10,855	11,983	12,686	12,901	13,162
Delaware	783	844	901	961	1,016	1,059	1,096
D.C.	2,193	2,303	2,381	2,526	2,672	2,780	2,884
Florida	14,653	16,093	17,460	18,962	20,301	21,321	22,080
Georgia	7,634	8,245	8,772	9,431	10,000	10,375	10,687
Hawaii	2,534	2,633	2,699	2,841	2,995	3,099	3,211
Idaho	787	852	922	1,011	1,096	1,152	1,199
Illinois	13,208	14,377	15,604	16,931	18,018	18,734	19,330
Indiana	8,339	9,438	10,439	11,341	11,991	12,393	12,742
Iowa	2,599	2,835	3,086	3,319	3,538	3,707	3,838
Kansas	4,467	4,976	5,558	6,111	6,414	6,453	6,511
Kentucky	3,701	3,951	4,172	4,435	4,694	4,883	5,050
Louisiana	6,638	7,000	7,518	8,048	8,549	8,908	9,251
Maine	1,554	1,649	1,783	1,941	2,107	2,232	2,360
Maryland	7,500	8,104	8,664	9,387	10,024	10,504	10,922
Massachusetts	10,291	11,433	12,669	13,987	15,078	15,866	16,580
Michigan	8,802	9,743	10,475	11,227	11,887	12,377	12,750
Minnesota	5,156	5,718	6,322	6,945	7,475	7,864	8,171
Mississippi	3,665	3,940	4,182	4,454	4,736	4,910	5,063
Missouri	8,140	9,012	9,723	10,568	11,260	11,671	11,966
Montana	743	800	864	926	984	1,025	1,060
Nebraska	1,673	1,791	1,918	2,111	2,249	2,335	2,420
Nevada	1,053	1,137	1,222	1,310	1,392	1,448	1,494
New Hampshire	1,565	1,739	1,883	2,075	2,247	2,381	2,492
New Jersey	9,562	10,367	11,185	12,164	12,989	13,598	14,125
New Mexico	2,014	2,164	2,307	2,479	2,641	2,753	2,847
New York	22,044	23,968	26,075	28,437	30,379	31,717	32,878
North Carolina	7,041	7,570	8,063	8,608	9,136	9,531	9,871
North Dakota	753	790	830	894	950	986	1,021
Ohio	13,173	14,555	15,816	17,168	18,198	18,843	19,402
Oklahoma	4,626	4,916	5,239	5,623	5,935	6,113	6,272
Oregon	2,202	2,412	2,614	2,869	3,101	3,261	3,386
Pennsylvania	14,718	16,030	17,374	18,847	20,004	20,766	21,517
Rhode Island	1,385	1,500	1,618	1,750	1,865	1,951	2,023
South Carolina	4,162	4,423	4,646	4,937	5,227	5,446	5,640
South Dakota	656	693	743	825	883	918	952
Tennessee	4,394	4,793	5,159	5,547	5,883	6,143	6,360
Texas	26,978	29,025	31,389	33,869	35,686	36,825	37,895
Utah	2,492	2,722	2,914	3,158	3,357	3,500	3,637
Vermont	847	948	1,060	1,179	1,278	1,351	1,414
Virginia	13,655	14,470	15,060	16,040	17,058	17,821	18,507
Washington	8,361	9,039	9,796	10,660	11,225	11,578	11,860
West Virginia	1,675	1,854	2,056	2,256	2,434	2,566	2,681
Wisconsin	4,482	4,902	5,286	5,665	5,992	6,222	6,420
Wyoming	678	733	780	838	901	934	962
Total U.S.	345,854	377,013	408,556	443,537	472,361	491,926	508,864

Source: The Geographic Distribution of Potential Defense Expenditures,
Economic and Analysis Division, Office of the Director of Program Analysis and
Evaluation, July 1984, p. 46.

stability because contracts can be stopped on short notice when budget swings occur.

Area with large defense industries face similar questions of economic stability. In the past, these regions have undergone violent changes in economic activity as local industries won or lost contracts. However, these swings can be postponed, particularly in times of a massive defense buildup, by the amount of backlog in defense orders. Backlogs occur because the capacity of a defense industry is insufficient to handle the volume of orders. Because there are relatively few major defense contractors, a large defense buildup can cause huge backlogs, and backlogs mean a stable flow of defense orders in the future. For the nine largest defense manufacturers, the backlog at the end of June 1984 was $61.3 billion, up from $53 billion one year earlier.[37] This backlog was already funded by defense appropriation bills, and it represented years of future work, independent of later budget cuts, for the regions in which those nine companies were located.

Recent initiatives by the Department of Defense (nicknamed the Carlucci Initiatives) have been directed at increasing stability in the defense industry as a whole by permitting multiyear contracting and other innovations. Actions of this type, of course, tend to increase the stability of defense-dependent regional economies. These and other aspects of stability in the defense sector will be discussed in Chapter 6.

CONCLUSIONS

The primary purpose of defense spending should never be to promote economic growth and development on either a national or a regional level. Neither should employment be a major concern of defense (or most nondefense) spending—there are far more efficient ways to pursue the nation's economic goals. But because defense spending patterns can be influenced more easily than most other forms of government spending, this vehicle has often been used by Congress and by local leaders to attain regional economic objectives.

Unfortunately, regional economic and employment arguments have obscured the real issue in defense-related employment: the defense sector's absorption of large parts of the nation's engineering and scientific pool. It is this latter phenomenon that most directly affects U.S. industry, and it is also this phenomenon that will have long-term effects on U.S. trade competitiveness and technological leadership. A continuing lack of debate in this area will ensure that the de facto industrial policy of promoting defense-related industries will continue.

Even though some regions have benefited from the injections of federal funds, it is wise to remember the major costs this benefit levies on the

United States: (1) National interests in both the defense and the economic arenas are often subjugated to regional desires; (2) Congress's role as a critic of administration policies has been subverted; (3) The industrial migration from the Frost Belt to the Sun Belt has been accelerated; (4) Weapons, which should be constructed in response to specific needs, are sometimes built for the wrong reasons and in the wrong quantities. From a national perspective, it is not clear that the benefits accruing to various regions compensate for these costs.

NOTES

Epigraphs: Edsall, Thomas B., "Forgotten Issue: How Economic Policy is Shifting Income," *Washington Post*, October 31, 1982, p. F1; Senator D'Amato, reacting to navy plans to station a battleship group in his state, quoted in Weiss, Stanley A., and Morrison, James, "Defense 'Investment' Is Bad Business," *Los Angeles Times*, pt. 4, September 25, 1983, p. 5; Weinberger, "Address to the National Association of Manufacturers," Spring 1982, quoted in Hayes, Thomas C., "Defense Spending—Its Effect on Jobs," *New York Times*, October 16, 1983, p. 5; Ullman, quoted in Ingwerson, Marshall, "Do Arms Dollars Hurt the Economy?," *Christian Science Monitor*, September 11, 1984, p. 3.

1. *An Analysis of President Reagan's Budget Revisions for Fiscal Year 1982*, Congressional Budget Office, March 1981, p. 1.

2. Hiatt, Fred, "Military Construction Spending Benefits Home-Town Projects," *Washington Post*, June 22, 1983, p. 10.

3. "Regional Impacts of Defense Spending," *Defense Economics Research Report* 3, no. 2, Data Resources, Inc., Washington, D.C., February 1983, p. 7.

4. Ibid., pp. 3–4.

5. Weida, William J., Gertcher, Frank, L., et al., *An Economic Evaluation of Variable Housing Allowances*, USAFA Technical Report, December 1982.

6. Chase Econometrics, Conference on the Outlook for the U.S. Economy, Washington, D.C., September 18, 1984.

7. Mulhern, John J., "The Defense Sector: A Source of Strength for Philadelphia's Economy," *Business Review*, The Federal Reserve Bank of Philadelphia, July/August 1981, p. 8.

8. For example, this author recalls a briefing on the B-1 given by an economist for North American Rockwell in Los Angeles in 1971. The Rockwell economist stated that at an assumed multiplier of 3.0 (it was never revealed if this was a GNP or an employment multiplier) the B-1 would create so much employment and generate such large tax revenues that the actual cost to the U.S. government of each aircraft would only be $100,000. (At this point, the audience's patience with the use of such an obviously inflated multiplier was growing a bit thin. It was suggested to the Rockwell economist that as long as he was going to use such an unrealistically high number, perhaps he should raise it to 3.5 and show a profit. The briefing ended rather quickly.)

9. Chase Econometrics, Conference on the Outlook for the U.S. Economy, Washington, D.C., September 18, 1984.

10. Degrasse, Robert W., *Military Expansion, Economic Decline*, M. F. Sharpe, Inc., Armonk, New York, 1983, pp. 1–260.

11. "Defense Spending and Jobs," *Defense Economics Research Report* 2, no. 11, November 1982, pp. 1–4.

12. Conversation regarding the DoD's use of employment statistics held with Dr. David Blond, economist for the secretary of defense, PA&E, November 1983.

13. Brown, George F., Jr., "The Economic Consequences of Defense Spending: Implications for 1984 and Beyond," Testimony Presented to the Task Force on Economic Policy and Growth, Committee on the Budget, U.S. House of Representatives, 1983, p. 3.

14. Silk, Leonard, "Cost-Effective Job Creation," *New York Times*, September 22, 1982, p. D2.

15. Winter, Ralph E., "Defense Dud—So Far, Arms Buildup Creates Few New Jobs," *Wall Street Journal*, March 23, 1983, p. 1.

16. Fine, Stanley, and Weiss, Stanley A., "Yo-Ho-Ho and a Bundle of Bucks?," *New York News*, January 26, 1984, p. 18.

17. Gargan, Edward A., "Army Selects Fort Drum as Home for a New Light Infantry Division," *New York Times*, September 12, 1984, p. 1.

18. "Business Outlook," *Business Week*, December 10, 1984, p. 32.

19. Conversation with David Blond; and "Defense Spending and Jobs," pp. 5–8.

20. Hayes, "Defense Spending," p. 5.

21. "No Reaganomics," *Economist*, February 11, 1984, p. 78.

22. Greenberg, Daniel S., "Science for the Military," *Baltimore Sun*, February 6, 1984, p. 11.

23. "Gulf Cities Vie for Lucrative New Navy Base," *New York Times*, November 25, 1984, p. 27.

24. Silk, Leonard, "Economic Scene—War on Waste a Herculean Job," *New York Times*, December 7, 1984, p. D2.

25. Anderson, James R., *Bankrupting America: The Tax Burden and Expenditures of the Pentagon by Congressional District*, Employment Research Associates, Lansing, Michigan, August 1984.

26. Hayes, Thomas, "Pentagon Spends More in Fewer Districts, Researcher Says," *New York Times*, August 13, 1984, p. 20.

27. Mulhern, "The Defense Sector," p. 11.

28. Ibid., p. 3.

29. Levin, Doran P., "Firms Enriched by Military Buildup Search for Ways to Use The Money," *Wall Street Journal*, January 3, 1984, p. 33.

30. "Defense Dollars, State By State," *U.S. News and World Report*, June 25, 1984, p. 10.

31. Edsall, "Forgotten Issue," p. F4.

32. Alm, Richard, "As Defense Billions Pour Into The Economy," *U.S. News and World Report*, March 12, 1984, pp. 57–58.

33. Weiss "Defense 'Investment' Is Bad Business," and Morrison, p. 5.

34. "Regional Impacts Of Defense Spending," p. 7.

35. *The Geographic Distribution of Potential Defense Expenditures*, Economic and Analysis Division, Office of the Director of Program Analysis and Evaluation, Department of Defense, July 1984, p. viii.

36. Adams, Marc, "U.S. Contracts Hit $6.7 Billion in Area," *Washington Times*, November 2, 1984, p. 5C.

37. Welling, Kathryn M., "No Farewell To Arms," *Barrons*, December 3, 1984, pp. 13–44.

Part 2
The Defense Industry

6
Preparing for War:
The Defense Industrial Base

There is nothing so likely to produce peace as to be well prepared to meet an enemy.
—**George Washington, 1780**

The defense industrial base . . . is as much an element of our military deterrence as our array of weapon systems.
—**Jacques S. Gansler, 1977**

In the event of war or other national emergency, it is highly unlikely that the domestic footwear industry could provide sufficient footwear for the military and civilian population. . . . We won't be able to wait for ships to deliver shoes from Taiwan, or Korea or Brazil or Eastern Europe. . . . Improper footwear can lead to needless casualties and turn sure victory into possible defeat.
—**President, American Footwear Industry, 1984**

INTRODUCTION

The defense industrial base is one part of a mobilization plan that allows the United States to increase quickly its production of defense goods if war should occur. The mobilization plan is comprised of the strategic stockpile of raw materials, the industrial mobilization capacity of the economy (the defense industrial base), the machine tool reserves, and war reserve material (WRM—a stockpile of finished goods).[1]

The volume of research and publication on the defense industrial base might lead one to think that it is the most important area of defense economics. It is not. Instead, it is likely that the defense industrial base receives so much attention because the ease of getting unclassified and open source data in this area has made it one of the simpler subjects for independent scholars to investigate.

In spite of this vast amount of research (and in spite of this chapter), it is probable that, at least in the ordinary sense of the words, the defense industrial base does not exist. Instead, the defense industrial base is an entity that changes size, shape, and composition based on political whim and the various scenarios of conflict being advanced. As such, it is a vehicle altered as necessary to justify trade protectionism, the use of government subsidies for private industries, and other forms of governmental intervention in the free markets.

Thus, one has to remember that one's scenario for future conflict sets the parameters that will determine the characteristics of a particular defense industrial base. For example, a major nuclear exchange, which is over in a matter of hours, puts little importance on the ability to mobilize and produce war goods after the exchange has ended. In contrast, a protracted, conventional war may well be won by the residual productive capacity of the United States. This scenario dependency is complicated by the fact that the government has been unable to come up with any adequate scenario for future conflicts. And this leaves the composition of the defense industrial base open to wide interpretation and political manipulation.

THE CONDITION OF THE EXISTING DEFENSE INDUSTRIES

If one defines the defense industrial base as simply that part of the manufacturing sector currently producing weapons, the condition of defense-related industries is of special interest. The air force investigated various aspects of the health of the defense industrial base in the only comprehensive study completed since the start of the Reagan administration's military buildup. The conclusions of this study (which concentrated on the aerospace sector but also included army and navy programs and the commercial sector[2]) and others are used in the following sections to evaluate productivity, capital investment, subcontractor usage, capacity utilization, and foreign-source dependency of the defense-related industries.

Productivity

Productivity of defense-related industry, measured in dollar value of shipments per employee, improved in the period 1982 through 1984. For example, the Aerospace Industry Association found that productivity in the aerospace sector increased as shown in Table 6.1.

The diversity of products and productivity indicators makes it difficult to measure productivity with a single yardstick. However, the trend toward improvement has been consistent no matter what indicator is

Table 6.1
Industry-Wide Productivity Trends: Value of Shipments per Employee, 1982-1984
(1972 dollars)

Year	Value of Shipments (Billions)	Dollar Value of Shipments per Employee (Total Employment)	Change	Dollar Value of Shipments Per Production Worker	Change
1982	$22.8	$32,300		$65,300	
1983	$24.2	$35,100	+8.7%	$72,900	+10.4%
1984[a]	$24.7	$36,200	+3.1%	$74,800	+ 2.6%

Note: [a]Estimated
Source: Aerospace Industry Association, "Facts and Figures," reported in
Blueprint For Tomorrow, Joint Air Force/Industry Assessment of the Aerospace
Industrial Base, U.S. Air Force, Department of Defense, vol 1,
January 16, 1984, pp. 2-75.

Table 6.2
Major Cost Factors Affecting Productivity in Weapons Production

Process	Personnel	Materials	External Forces
Inadequate material handling systems	Union rules/ inflexibility	Castings Forgings	Government practices Inspection
Lack of management information systems	Turnover Salaries/benefits	Structures Poor quality	Reports Adversarial
Highly technical processes	Support services Maintenance	Late delivery Electronics	relationships Rate changes
Assembly	Engineering	and electro-	Interrupted
Quality assurance/ inspection	Quality control Production control	mechanical components	production runs Uneconomical lot
Test tolerances			sizes
Plant layout			Scheduled delays
Fabrication			Excessive bid
Tooling			negotiation
			Cost of capital
			Unrealistic tolerances and specifications
			Poor specifications
			Customer changes to design

Source: Blueprint for Tomorrow, Joint Air Force/Industry Assessment of the
Aerospace Industrial Base, U.S. Air Force, Department of Defense, vol. 1,
January 16, 1984, pp. 2-80.

chosen. There is general agreement on the major cost factors that affect productivity. These are shown in Table 6.2. Note that it appears that the United States government is a major obstacle to improvement in productivity because of the practices listed in the "External Forces" section.

Capital Investment

After a long period of increase, capital investment in most military production areas decreased during the first half of the 1980s. The primary causes of this decrease appear to be the recession and lowered expectations of commercial sales due to a decrease in civilian demand.

As Figure 6.1 shows, aerospace sector investment is closely correlated with commercial sales. One would expect an increase in military sales

Figure 6.1: Aircraft Sales and Aerospace Industry Capital Investments, 1968–1983 (constant 1972 dollars)

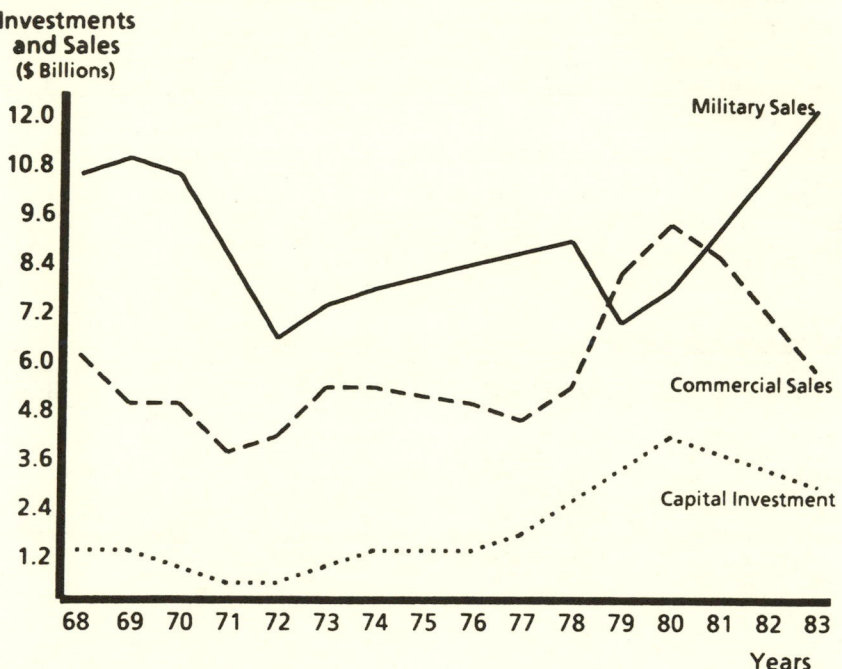

Source: Blueprint for Tomorrow, Joint Air Force/Industry Assessment of the Aerospace Industrial Base, U.S. Air Force, Department of Defense, vol. 1, January 16, 1984, pp. 2–40.

of the magnitude associated with the Reagan buildup to yield a similar, but delayed, increase in investment over the next few years. Investment as a percent of total sales has remained virtually constant at 4.2 percent for the past decade for all types of manufacturing.[3]

Subcontractor Considerations

Of the top fifty sectors in which subcontracting for defense goods occurs, the share of production taken by the Department of Defense's purchases varies from a high of 36.8 percent (in nonferrous forgings) to a low of 6.8 percent (in ammunition—excluding small arms). In only five of these sectors did defense purchases take 30 percent or more of production (nonferrous forgings—36.8 percent, primary nonferrous metals—35.2 percent, semiconductors—33.6 percent, aircraft parts and equipment—30.6 percent, and electronic components—30.6 percent).[4] Although as a general rule, defense business comprises only a small portion of any sector's subcontractor activity, this situation may be much different

for specific industries, particularly in the top five sectors just listed. Table 6.3 shows the direct effect on subcontractors of the recent defense buildup. From this table, it is clear that the subcontractor base has not been overextended by the Reagan defense program. However, evaluating the overall effect of the recent defense buildup on the subcontractor base is difficult because data regarding both the negative effects (business lost due to imports or to purchases that did not occur because money was spent for a defense good instead of for some other nondefense good) and the positive effects (business generated by the increased demand associated with the military buildup) are generally not known by the subcontractors themselves. In addition, a subcontractor from one sector may lose business while a subcontractor from another may gain— all due to the same defense purchase.

Capacity Utilization

Table 6.3 also shows the rates of capacity utilization for both prime and subcontractors in the aerospace industries. These capacity figures are based on three eight-hour shifts per day for a five-day week (a 3×8×5 shift workweek). This type of workweek is normally used for planning high-volume production because it permits the use of the sixth day for overflow work and the seventh day for maintenance, if required. Table 6.3 presents these data in three ways: average capacity used in a week, the range of capacity used across the plants surveyed, and capacity used by the shifts worked. As the table demonstrates, there is a great deal of excess capacity in the aerospace industry.[5] Although this table does not show potential problems for specific products, it is fair to say that in general, capacity in the aerospace industry is not a problem.

Foreign-Source Dependency

Foreign sourcing (the use of imported items in defense goods) is of considerable concern because it affects the ability to sustain weapon production in time of war. As Figure 6.2 demonstrates, offsets (military countertrade—see Chapter 10) are the major reason that foreign-sourced items are used in the aerospace sector. Of these items, only eleven specific cases are *sole* sources; in other words, the foreign source is the only place these goods can be acquired.[6] Foreign sourcing closely corresponds to large offset contracts (Israel and the NATO countries are prominently featured), and Canada, which is a part of the U.S. defense industrial base, is a major supplier.

Considering the number of parts used in modern weapons, the total number of foreign-sourced items is very small. In addition, virtually all of this sourcing takes place in areas such as NATO or Israel where U.S. policy is to support a strong foreign defense base. A more worrisome

Table 6.3
1983 Aerospace Capacity Utilization by Functional Area

	Large Aircraft	Fighter/ Attack	Other Aircraft	Propulsion	Missiles	Subcontractors Avionics	Materials	Structures
Fabrication								
Capacity								
Average %[a]	42	40	26.5	57	43	44.5	33	53
Range of %[b]	10-80	25-66	8-50	31-75	20-66	4-90	11-42	27-81
Shifts[c]	N.A.	1.5	1.0	1.6	1.3	1.43	1.3	1.8
Process/Paint								
Capacity								
Average %[a]	39	45	31.5	64	43	41.9	33	37
Range of %[b]	9-80	25-60	8-70	28-100	20-66	25-60	11-42	12-75
Shifts[c]	N.A.	1.5	1.0	1.2	1.3	1.22	1.3	1.7
Assembly								
Capacity								
Average %[a]	41	40	27	51	43	38.6	33	32
Range of %[b]	8-80	33-80	11-45	28-65	20-66	25-50	11-42	14-70
Shifts[c]	N.A.	1.5	1.0	1.2	1.3	1.2	1.3	1.4
Test & Checkout								
Capacity								
Average %[a]	40	40	26	57	70	58.3	33	41
Range of %[b]	22-80	20-75	11-45	28-65	40-100	40-81	11-42	18-70
Shifts[c]	N.A.	1.8	1.0	2.1	1.91	1.3	1.5

Notes: [a]Average % capacity utilized on a 3x8x5 basis
[b]Range of % capacity utilized on a 3x8x5 basis
[c]Average number of shifts utilized on a 1x8x5 basis

Source: Blueprint For Tomorrow, Joint Air Force/Industry Assessment of the Aerospace Industrial Base, U.S. Air Force, Department of Defense, vol. 1, January 16, 1984, pp. 2-68.

Figure 6.2: Reasons for Foreign-Supplied Aerospace Items, 1983.

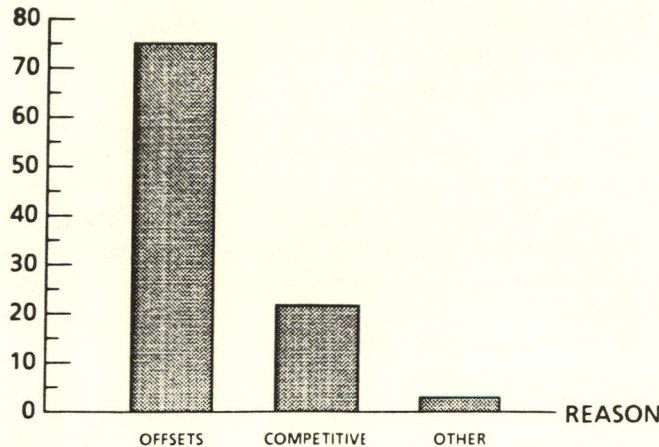

PERCENT OF TOTAL

Source: *Blueprint for Tomorrow, Joint Air Force/Industry Assessment of the Aerospace Industrial Base*, U.S. Air Force, Department of Defense, vol. 1, January 16, 1984, pp. 2–26.

picture of foreign dependence concerns the need to import certain raw materials. But there is a national policy of stockpiling for emergencies and of letting simple supply and demand dominate in normal times.

A similar foreign-source situation is present in army procurements.[7] Again, the NATO countries are, with very few exceptions, the suppliers. There is no indication of the amount of this trade based on offsets, but it would be reasonable to assume that at least as much is based on offset agreements, as was found in the aerospace case. Again, these offset-based agreements are in support of our national policy concerning the NATO countries.

Thus, these data indicate that although offsets have had an effect on the number of foreign-sourced items procured for U.S. weapons, this has been a direct offshoot of a U.S. policy to strengthen the industrial bases of important allies. In addition, if there are any problems caused by this type of sourcing, the remedy is quite simple—stockpile the affected product or raw material.

CONCLUSIONS REGARDING THE INDUSTRIAL BASE

Although we have made no attempt to view the industrial base in the context of the U.S. economy (which experienced excess capacity throughout the period under study), we can draw the following con-

The Defense Industry

clusions about the ability of the industrial base to respond to a surge[8] and to a mobilization:[9]

1. Government-furnished facilities and funding have inhibited long-term productivity.
2. Modernization/capacity investment is more influenced by commercial opportunities than by military programs.
3. The U.S. machine tool industry is in a serious decline.
4. The availability of critical manpower skills is very limited, partially due to the fluctuating demand and instability of the workforce.
5. The industrial base cannot surge in the areas of large aircraft and tactical missiles and cannot sustain a surge in the areas of large aircraft, fighter/attack aircraft, helicopters, and engines.
6. No plan exists for carrying out a surge.
7. The ability to mobilize in a declared national emergency is somewhat better, but initial accelerated production will be limited and the availability of skilled people will be a critical element.
8. There is no comprehensive plan for mobilization.[10]

A review of these problems shows that correcting them is easier said than done. For example, the government's past attempts to provide facilities have resulted in lower productivity—often due to the fact that government facilities and equipment are outdated. The decline in the machine tool industry is due to overseas competition, which could be alleviated by a change in the competitiveness of U.S. industry or by trade protectionism. The low availability of skilled people is due to current U.S. education patterns that favor academic instead of industrial training. Even if this trend were reversed, it would take a generation to have an effect on the labor pool. And the fact that there are no plans for either surge or mobilization reflects the assertion made at the beginning of this chapter that these elements are political in nature and that no politically acceptable scenarios have been developed (or are likely to be developed).[11]

CURRENT ATTEMPTS TO DEAL WITH INDUSTRIAL BASE PROBLEMS

None of the industrial base problems cited in this chapter is new or different from those that have plagued the defense industry in the past. In his book *The Defense Industry*,[12] Gansler thoroughly explored the problems with the industrial base and recommended a number of corrective actions, many of which were later featured in the Carlucci Initiatives, a 1982 effort by then–Deputy Secretary of Defense Frank

Carlucci to strengthen the defense industry. These intiatives, coupled with other actions taken by the Department of Defense in the recent past, have led to the following attempts to deal with the industrial base problem:

Multiyear Procurement

One of the major problems in maintaining a defense industrial base has been the cyclical nature of defense purchases. Spending cycles, created to a large extent by budetary practices that funded weapons programs for one year at a time, caused a "boom or bust" syndrome in the defense industry. This syndrome was not conducive to long-range planning, the maintenance of stable facilities, or consistent investment and modernization. Recent changes have allowed multiyear funding for weapon systems, and similar proposals are now being considered for other types of defense purchases such as spare parts. These changes have had the intended effect of smoothing the cycle of defense purchases, and they appear to have promoted more investment and better planning.

Competition

There is almost no meaningful competition for the production of major weapon systems. This has caused a great deal of inefficiency in the operations of all major defense producers. In some instances, the lack of competitors has even resulted in "blackmail" by sole source contractors who raised prices and adversely affected delivery schedules.[13] Recently, the Department of Defense has made attempts to promote competition. The decision to give parts of the jet engine contract for the F-15 and F-16 both to Pratt and Whitney and to General Electric was cited as evidence that competition was important in military procurement. But competition is meaningful only if noncompetitive producers are allowed to fail. In the Department of Defense, competition seems to mean splitting the contract between two large producers—a condition actually leading to smaller production runs for both producers and to lower efficiency. For example, in the case of the jet engines, the General Electric engine had more thrust and, according to the air force, "was assessed to be lower in overall support costs," had an "outstanding" plan allowing other companies to compete for spare parts contracts, and offered "an excellent warranty."[14] These advantages, coupled with the fact that the Pratt and Whitney engine had a very troubled history, would seem to justify giving the contract to General Electric. However, for defense industrial base reasons among others, Pratt and Whitney was allowed to continue to supply the engine.

In addition, when a major weapon producer is in danger of failing, it is not unusual to see the Department of Defense shift contracts to

that producer to keep it a "viable" part of the defense industrial base. The purchase of the F-105 fighter and the Burroughs mainframe computer are examples of these actions. Meaningful future competition in the procurement of major weapons is likely only in the purchase of smaller components where a number of small competitors are available.

Investing in the Defense Industrial Base

In a direct attempt to institute a five-year peacetime procurement program, provide surge responsiveness, and improve sustainability, the Department of Defense has budgeted sizable spending increases for the defense industrial base. The five-year plan for the years 1985–1989 calls for expenditures of $18 billion for rejuvenating the industrial base, following an initial investment of $2.2 billion in 1984. In fiscal year 1984, $100 million was spent on improving surge capability by accelerating the production of TOW 2 missiles, increasing the Phoenix missile production rate, and reducing the lead time for the Pratt and Whitney F-100 engine.[15] Because of the newness of this effort and because it is proceeding along with a massive defense buildup, it is difficult to determine what the actual effect of this spending has been.

A less direct approach to investment in the industrial base has evolved from the heavy Department of Defense commitment to fund R&D in areas useful to the military. One-tenth of the FY 1985 budget will be used for this purpose—continuing an effort that is so extensive that many claim it constitutes an industrial policy for the United States. This support has resulted in large increases in technology and productivity, both in the defense industrial base and in the economy as a whole.[16] For example, past defense-sponsored research was instrumental in making U.S. industries such as aerospace, computers, scientific instruments, and communications equipment potent international competitors. And the current DoD budget, which contains about one-third of the entire U.S. R&D funding, emphasizes numerically controlled machine tools, automation, software development, flexible manufacturing, and very high speed intregrated circuits, all of which will help shape the composition of tomorrow's exports.[17] Of the many programs involved in building or sustaining the defense industrial base, this effort is clearly one of the most successful.

Protectionism

From an economist's point of view, trade protectionism is an undesirable method of dealing with industrial base problems. However, it is one of the most pervasive political activities associated with building the defense industrial base. From the footwear industry (see quote at the beginning of this chapter) to producers as diverse as those of

motorcycles and dental tools, all have attempted to join the defense industrial base when their industry was threatened by foreign competition.

This situation was exacerbated by the unfavorable trade position experienced by the United States in the mid-1980s. A large number of U.S. firms found themselves in a noncompetitive position—some because of their own problems, others because of the high value of the dollar. The easiest route to protection from external forces was through the defense industrial base, mainly because the base is so ill defined that almost any industry could appear to satisfy the criteria for being a critical defense industry.

Are there legitimate protectionist actions that should be taken to preserve the industrial base? This question is difficult to answer because such actions almost always end up preserving an inefficient industry. The steel industry, for example, has potential defense uses, the preservation of which may merit protectionist actions. However, because of the costs that protectionism levies on the economy (a Washington University study estimated that protectionism costs U.S. consumers over $58 billion per year[18]), it is a rare case where such measures can be justified—particularly because the composition of the defense industrial base is so poorly defined. Such cases would probably occur only where the industry is a sole source of some critical part of defense procurement, and cases such as this would have to be reviewed carefully to determine both why the U.S. industry was being eliminated by foreign competition and whether stockpiling of the foreign-produced goods could satisfy the industrial base requirements better than protectionist measures.

Facilities Management

The United States had a large number of old defense facilities in mothballs, most dating from World War II, which were to be part of a new mobilization or surge effort if the need arose. Over the years, the technology of these plants stayed suspended in time and hence became more obsolete. The result was a stock of old facilities with increasingly limited capabilities, and it became clear that these facilities would soon become worthless unless they were upgraded.

Starting in 1961, the General Services Administration, which had control of these facilities, began to dispose of them by selling the plants to private contractors. By 1982, 114 industrial plants had been sold for a total of $386.8 million. The contractors who purchased the plants had to agree to make the product that the Department of Defense wanted until the facility was no longer needed, and then the firm could put the plant to a more profitable use.[19] Although the benefits to a private contractor of purchasing a plant with thirty- or forty-year-old technology

are often limited, this program has been generally successful in reducing the government's stock of obsolete plants and in restoring some degree of modern technology to the facilities that have been transferred.

Small Business Subsidies

One of the original purposes of small business legislation was to protect the ability of the United States to mobilize small businesses. This legislation gave rise to small business set-aside—the restriction of bidding to only small firms. In FY 1983, the Department of Defense reserved almost 10 percent of its procurement dollars, an amount equal to about $11.7 billion, for small businesses. In addition, small businesses won approximately $11.1 billion in open competition and another $15.6 billion in subcontracts from DoD prime contractors.[20]

It thus appears that the small business sector is in good shape and will be able to contribute significantly to any mobilization or surge effort. This will be important in the future because the small business sector is the only area of the defense industrial base where increased competition can be expected to improve efficiency and reduce costs.

CONCLUSIONS

The defense industrial base will continue to occupy a position of major importance in the defense debate. But the lack of planning for either surge or mobilization, coupled with an absence of useful scenarios to determine the necessary composition of the base, will make most attempts to integrate the defense industrial base into U.S. defense plans difficult at best. The political incentives to keep the current system the way it is probably rule out a number of changes that would promote economic efficiency. The defense industrial base will continue to be thoroughly investigated and endlessly discussed, and all the time this is going on, it will continue to be used for whatever purpose fits the needs of the moment.

NOTES

Epigraphs: Washington, George, Address to Congress, January 1780; Gansler, Jacques S., "Let's Change the Way the Pentagon Does Business," *Harvard Business Review*, May-June 1977, p. 109; American Footwear Industry president quoted in Chanda, Nayan, and Manning, Robert, "Washington Finesses Away Free Trade," *Far Eastern Economic Review*, October 25, 1984, p. 70.

1. Gansler, Jacques S., *The Defense Industry*, MIT Press, Cambridge, Mass., 1981, pp. 111–112.

2. Buck, John T., "The Health and Illness of the U.S. Aerospace Industrial Base Pinpointed in Massive Air Force/Industry Study," *Government Executive*, June 1984, p. 38.

3. *Blueprint For Tomorrow, Joint Air Force/Industry Assessment of the Aerospace Industrial Base*, Department of Defense, U.S. Air Force, vol. 1, January 16, 1984, p. 2-46.

4. *Major Suppliers to the Department of Defense*, Defense Economic Impact Modelling System, PA&E, Department of Defense, April 23, 1984.

5. *Blueprint For Tomorrow*, pp. 2-67 to 2-69.

6. Ibid., pp. 2-28 to 2-29.

7. "U.S. Dependency on Foreign Technology," a memorandum for the deputy commanding general for research, development and acquisition, Department of the Army, December 1, 1982.

8. Expansion of military production in a peacetime environment—without declaration of a national emergency. In this case, a 50 percent increase in production in twelve months was used.

9. Expansion of military production to meet the demands of a wartime situation. Here a 200 percent increase in production over thirty-six months was used.

10. *Blueprint For Tomorrow*, p. 2-48.

11. For example, an attempt during the first Reagan administration to develop a scenario for mobilization became instead a political vehicle for making budget adjustments. It was quickly realized that the size of the stockpiles required for the mobilization (and hence, their cost) would depend on how efficiently resources were used. The entire mobilization scenario was then set up around a free-market system that employed no rationing. This allocative process allowed smaller stockpiles to be justified so the excesses could be sold to help fund the government budget. These decisions were made in spite of complaints by the Department of Defense, citing World War II as example, that rationing would be required in any mobilization.

12. Gansler, *The Defense Industry*.

13. *Conference on Improving National Security by Strengthening the Defense Industrial Base*, Workshop I Findings, Harvard University, May 10–12, 1982, p. 5.

14. Mohr, Charles, "Air Force Divides Jet Engine Order Between Two Rivals," *New York Times*, February 4, 1984, p. 1.

15. Dixon, Clement, "Building The Defense Industrial Base," *Defense, Science & Electronics*, July 1983, p. 25.

16. Schrage, Michael, "Defense Budget Pushes Agenda in High-Tech R&D," *Washington Post*, August 12, 1984, p. F1.

17. Steinberg, Bruce, "The Military Boost to Industry," *Fortune*, April 30, 1984, pp. 42–46.

18. Munger, Michael C., "The High Cost of Protectionism," *Europe*, May/June 1984, pp. 10–11.

19. Struck, Myron, "Pentagon Factory Disposals Running Down," *Washington Post*, November 17, 1984, p. 17.

20. "Opportunities in Federal Procurement," a speech given by a DoD representative before the Council for Labor and Industry, Philadelphia, Pa., January 11, 1984.

7
Efficient Production of Weapon Systems

In order to understand the economic operation of the U.S. defense industry, it is first absolutely essential to recognize that there is no free market at work in this area and that there likely cannot be one because of the dominant role played by the federal government. The combination of a single buyer, a few very large firms in each segment of the industry, and a small number of extremely expensive weapons programs constitutes a unique structure for doing business.

—Jacques S. Gansler

INTRODUCTION

Defense contractors can increase their efficiency and produce weapon systems at relatively lower costs if they are given the right incentives. However, as Gansler pointed out, incentives for efficiency do not prevail in defense industry markets.[1] In this chapter, we explain the conditions that would result in the efficient production of weapon systems. We begin with a discussion of the profit-maximizing behavior of defense contractors and the implications of such behavior within the defense procurement structure. We continue with a discussion of optimal (lowest cost) production rates. Finally, we point out the effects of funding constraints, which often result in higher than necessary weapon system production costs.

To present an in-depth analysis, the discussions in this chapter are highly technical. The reader who has a serious time constraint may choose to skip the details in favor of a general review of the analysis and conclusions.

DEFENSE CONTRACTORS AND PROFITS

As explained in Chapter 1, market forces compel defense firms to attempt to maximize the present value of expected future profits. If the

firm does not select the optimal stream of profits, the existence of suboptimal profits provides an incentive for stockholders to install new managers to rectify profit performance.

Prior to price negotiations with the U.S. government, a defense prime contractor often has a unique product and has some control over price. However, once negotiations are completed, the price of the system is fixed according to the terms of the contract. In practice, fixed-price contracts for complex systems are usually subject to some variance due to uncertainties such as variations in contractor costs, the division between contractor- and government-furnished equipment, allowances for government-proposed modifications, and the variable costs associated with work done on the system by other contractors.

Production runs of major weapon systems (e.g., aircraft, tanks, computers) almost always occur over several years. Thus, the producing firm has an incentive to set a production schedule that will maximize profit over the production run, subject to the constraint that only a given number of systems has been ordered by the buyer. For example, suppose a prime contractor gets an order for sixty new aircraft at a fixed price from the Department of Defense. Suppose also that the contractor has two years to produce all sixty aircraft and deliver them to a particular air force base for final test and acceptance. From the contractor's point of view, how many aircraft should be produced in the first year and how many should be produced in the second year if the objective is to maximize present-value profits?

For this example, dynamic considerations are necessary because for profit maximization, the number of aircraft produced in the first period is not independent of number produced in the subsequent period. This simplified situation will provide some interesting insights into the effects of interest rates, profit-maximizing production runs, and the effects of competition on monopoly pricing. We begin with the interest, or discount rate, which reflects the cost of capital funds to a firm. The interest rate holds the key to the allocation of production over time by bringing into current decisions the revenues and costs associated with future production.

With only one production period, profit maximization occurs at the production level at which the marginal revenue from the last unit produced equals its marginal cost. However, profit maximization for a production run that lasts n periods involves generating an optimal stream of profits (p_i) over time periods $i = 0,1,2, \ldots ,n$. The rate of interest (r) provides the firm guidance as to how to evaluate a profit of $1 currently in comparison with a profit of, let us say, $1.10 one year later. If the firm must pay 10 percent interst annually ($r = 0.1$) for investment funds, then a profit of $1.10 next year has a present value of $1.00. As illustrated by equation (1), it is possible to calculate the present value

of an expected profit stream (p_i) beginning in the current period 0 and terminating at the end of some distant period n in the future.[2] The interest rate may also be indexed (r_i) to indicate different rates for each period *I*.

$$\text{Present-Value Profits} = \sum_{i=0}^{n} \frac{p_i}{(1 + r)^i}. \tag{1}$$

By setting production levels to certain optimal values for each period $i = 0,1,2, \ldots ,n$, the present value of a stream of expected future profits will be maximized. Any other set of production levels will result in a lower present value of expected profits.

MAXIMIZING PRESENT-VALUE PROFITS
FOR A PRODUCTION RUN

Consider the case of a firm that has negotiated a contract to produce and deliver sixty aircraft over a two-year period. To simplify matters, assume that the firm will deliver the aircraft at the end of each year, i.e., it will deliver the aircraft produced during the current year (year 0) at the end of the current year, and it will deliver the aircraft produced during the next year (year 1) at the end of that year, and payment will be obtained upon delivery. Assume for illustrative purposes that marginal cost for period 0 is $MC_0 = -\$5 + \$0.5Q_0$ (millions of dollars), and Q_0 represents the quantity produced in period 0. For period 1, the marginal cost changes to $MC_1 = -\$5 + \$0.4Q_1$ (millions of dollars) due to expected changes in resource prices and production costs (later, we shall show how the lowest production cost might be achieved as a function of the production rate). Finally, suppose that the firm has an allocated fixed cost (overhead) of $500 million in each year of production. Suppose that before the contract is signed, price equals $27 - \$0.25Q_i$ (millions of dollars), for $i = 0,1$. Marginal revenue before the contract is signed is therefore, $27 - \$0.5Q_i$ (millions of dollars), $i = 0$.

If the firm had an unlimited production run, the solution would be very simple: Produce where marginal revenue equals marginal cost in period 0 and where price (marginal revenue) equals marginal cost in period 1. Given profit-maximizing behavior, it is reasonable to assume that price in period 1 will remain constant at the price level that was fixed by contract in period 0, which is $P_0 = \$27 - \$0.25Q_0$. Because price in period 1 and thereafter is a constant, marginal revenue in period 1 and thereafter is equal to price.

If the price has not yet been fixed in period 0, the profit maximizing production for each period would be

Marginal Revenue = Marginal Cost in Period 0,
$$\$27 - \$0.5Q_0 = -\$5 + \$0.5Q_0$$
$$Q_0 = 32 \text{ aircraft}$$
$$\text{Price} = \$19 \text{ million.}$$

Marginal Revenue = Marginal Cost in Period 1,
$$\$19 = -\$5 + \$0.4Q_1$$
$$Q_1 = 60 \text{ aircraft}$$
$$\text{Price} = \$19 \text{ million (determined in period 0).}$$

This would imply selling thirty-two aircraft at the end of period 0 and sixty aircraft at the end of period 1. However, the firm has an order for only sixty aircraft, not ninety-two.

How then should the firm proceed? One solution is to produce and deliver thirty-two aircraft in the current period, leaving twenty-eight to be produced and delivered in the future period. Because profit is the difference between total revenue (price $\times$ quantity) and total production costs (integral of marginal cost plus fixed cost), we have:

$$p_0 = 27Q_0 - 0.25Q_0^2 + 5Q_0 - 0.25Q_0^2 - 500 \text{ (millions of dollars)}$$
$$p_0 = \$12 \text{ million}$$
$$p_1 = 19Q_1 + 5Q_1 - 0.2Q_1^2 - 500 \text{ (millions of dollars)}^2$$
$$p_1 = \$16 \text{ million.}$$

Using an interest rate of 10 percent leads to:

$$\text{Present-Value Profits} = 12 + \frac{15.2}{1.1} \text{ (million dollars)}$$

Present-Value Profits = $25.81 million (Case 1)

Now suppose the firm wants to calculate the opportunity cost of producing one aircraft currently or the same aircraft in period 1. This is easily found by assuming thirty-one aircraft are produced currently and twenty-nine are produced in period 1. Using the same technique explained above and holding price constant at $19 million, we obtain:

$$\text{Present-Value Profit} = 3.75 + \frac{27.8}{1.1} \text{ (million dollars).}$$

Present-Value Profit = $29.02 million (Case 2)

Therefore, the present value of profits can be raised by 29.02 − 25.81 = $3.21 million by shifting one aircraft from production in period 0 to production in period 1, at a constant price of $19 million.

For a more elegant solution, we can take first differences between the present-value equations for Case 1 and Case 2 and obtain:

$$\Delta PV = (MR_0 - MC_0)\ \Delta Q_0 + \frac{1}{(1 + r)}\ (MR_1 - MC_1)\ \Delta Q_1. \qquad (2)$$

where: ΔPV = Change in Present Value
       MR = Marginal Revenue
       MC = Marginal Cost

Substituting the numbers (millions of dollars) for period 0, we obtain:

$(MR_0 - MC_0) = 19 - 5(31) + 0.25(31^2) + 5(32) - 0.25(32^2)$
$(MR_0 - MC_0) = \$8.25$ million.

For period 1, we obtain:

$(MR_1 - MC_1) = 19 + 5(29) - 0.20(29^2) - 5(28) + 0.20(28^2)$
$(MR_1 - MC_1) = \$12.6$ million.

Substituting the numbers into the equation for ΔPV, we obtain:

$$\Delta PV = 8.25\ (-1) + \frac{12.6}{1.1}(1) = \$3.21 \text{ million}$$

Note that marginal cost in period 0 is the change in total cost for period 0 divided by the change in the number of aircraft produced in that period, and fixed costs cancel. Similarly, we can calculate marginal cost for period 1. Marginal revenue equals price in this example, and is therefore constant at $19 million. Because one aircraft is being transferred from the present to the future, ΔQ_0 is (-1) and ΔQ_1 is (1). This difference in sign causes the signs for MC_0 to be opposite from the signs for MC_1.

From the equation for ΔPV, the opportunity cost of not producing one aircraft in the current period is $8.25 million, and the opportunity cost of not producing it in the future period is $11.45 million, discounted to the current period (i.e., 12.6/1.1 = 11.45). As long as the discounted opportunity cost for the future period is higher than the opportunity cost in the current period, it makes sense to defer current production to the future. We can visualize moving aircraft from current to future production until the present-value profit does not increase further, indicating that we have reached the profit-maximizing combination. To put it another way, at the profit-maximizing combination, the loss in present-value profits from reducing current period production will just equal the discounted gain of increasing production in the future period.

However, we have yet to arrive at the profit-maximizing production schedule. The basic principle is that the opportunity cost of producing an aircraft in period 0 must equal the discounted opportunity cost of producing the same aircraft in period 1. As long as the marginal profit is higher in one period than another, it makes sense to move production

to the higher marginal profit period. Thus, a necessary condition for present-value profit maximization is

$$\Delta PV = (MR_0 - MC_0)\,\Delta Q_0 + \frac{1}{(1 + r)}\,(MR_1 - MC_1)\,\Delta Q_1 = 0. \quad (3)$$

The sufficient condition is that the second differences between the present-value equations of Case 1 and Case 2 are less than zero:

$$\frac{\Delta^2 PV}{\Delta Q_i^2} < 0. \quad\quad (4)$$

To solve mathematically for the profit-maximizing production schedule, we utilize the following two facts: (1) the present value of marginal profits for the two periods must be equal; and (2) only sixty aircraft will be produced over the two periods. These two facts yield two equations with two unknowns:

$$(MR_0 - MC_0)\,\Delta Q_0 = \frac{1}{(1 + r)}\,(MR_1 - MC_1)\,\Delta Q_1, \qu\quad (5)$$

and

$$Q_0 + Q_1 = 60. \quad\quad (6)$$

Now suppose price is fixed and the value $27 - 0.25Q_0$ million dollars equals marginal revenue in both periods. Using the equations for marginal cost for the respective periods, we get:

$$(27 - 0.25Q_0 + 5 - 0.5Q_0) = \frac{1}{1.1}\,(27 - 0.25Q_0 + 5 - 0.4Q_1)$$

Substituting $(60 - Q_1)$ for Q_0 and solving, we get:

$Q_0 = 28$, and
$Q_1 = 32$.

To maximize profits over the two-year production run for this example, the firm should produce twenty-eight aircraft in period 0 and thirty-two aircraft in period 1. The price at the optimal output would be $20 million in period 0 $(27 - 0.25Q_0)$. Given a fixed-price contract, the firm will also get $20 million in period 1. With this production schedule, the firm's profits would be:

$P_0 = 27Q_0 - 0.25Q_0^2 + 5Q_0 - 0.25Q_0^2 - 500$ (millions of dollars)
$P_0 = \$4$ million
$P_1 = 20Q_1 + 5Q_1 - 0.20Q_1^2 - 500$ (millions of dollars)
$P_1 = \$95.2$ million.

Present-Value Profit $= 4 + \dfrac{95.2}{1.1}$ (millions of dollars)

Present-Value Profit $= \$90.54$ million,

which is $\$90.54 - \$25.81 = \$64.73$ million greater than producing thirty-two aircraft in period 0 and twenty-eight in period 1 at a price of $19 million per aircraft.

This methodology can be expanded to maximize profits for a production run over n periods if $n - 2$ additional contraints can be found. In practice, the analyst must find relationships among the amounts that can be produced in future periods so that the number of equations available equals the number of unknowns. This is normally done by using engineering estimates for assembly line flow rates and learning-curve analysis for labor inputs.

In general, the equations become:

$$(MR_0 - MC_0)\,\Delta Q_0 = \frac{(MR_1 - MC_1)}{(1 + r)}\,\Delta Q_1 + \frac{(MR_2 - MC_2)}{(1 + r)^2}\,\Delta Q_2,$$

$$\ldots, + \frac{(MR_n - MC_n)}{(1 + R)^n}\,\Delta Q_n, \tag{7}$$

and

$$Q_T = Q_0 + Q_1 + Q_2 + \ldots + Q_n \tag{8}$$

and $n - 2$ contraints.

PRODUCTION SCHEDULE DIFFERENCES
BETWEEN MONOPOLY AND COMPETITIVE MARKETS

Theory states that price will tend to be lower in a competitive market than in a monopolistic market. From the Department of Defense point of view, an important issue is to identify the impact of competition on both price and production schedules. To illustrate the effects of competition, suppose that two or more firms are capable of producing the sixty aircraft in the example. In both periods, price will tend to be bid down to the level of the free-market demand curve. Thus the price in each period would be $27 - 0.25Q_i$, where $i = 0,1$. Also, under competitive conditions, price would tend to equal marginal cost for each period.

Using the previous methodology, we find that:

$$(27 - 0.25Q_0 + 5 - 0.5Q_0) = \frac{1}{1.1}\,(27 - 0.25Q_1 + 5 - 0.4Q_1)$$

Substituting $(60 - Q_1)$ for Q_0 and solving, we get:

$Q_0 = 29$, and
$Q_1 = 31$.

To maximize profits under competitive conditions, the firm would produce one more unit in the current period and one fewer in period 1 compared to the monopoly case. Thus, the buyer tends to get the aircraft sooner when competitive conditions prevail. Solving for profits, we find that:

$P_0 = 27Q_0 - 0.25Q^2_0 + 5Q_0 - 0.25Q^2_0 - 500$ (millions of dollars)
$P_0 = \$7.5$ million
$P_1 = 27Q_1 - 0.25Q^2_1 + 5Q_1 - 0.20Q^2_1 - 500$ (millions of dollars)
$P_1 = \$59.55$ million.

Again using the previous methodology, we find:

Present-Value Profit $= 7.5 + \dfrac{59.55}{1.1}$ (millions of dollars)

Present-Value Profit $= \$61.64$ million.

Compared to the case of monopoly, profits are reduced by $\$90.54 - \$61.64 = \$28.90$ million.

What about costs to the Department of Defense? After all, not all of the reduced profit results in savings to the government because the firm operates at higher costs due to nonoptimal production levels. In the example, the monopoly price was fixed at $20 million per aircraft in both periods. Under competitive conditions, the prices are $19.75 million in the current period and $19.25 million in period 1.

In summary, competition tends to result in more aircraft produced in the earlier period and a lower price in both periods, even with slightly higher marginal costs. The difference, in comparison with the monopoly case, is accounted for by lower profits to the firm under competitive conditions. However, the examples do not tell the whole story. Traditionally, large defense firms "buy in" to an initial production contract by bidding low, sometimes below cost. Why? This occurs because once the firm has the initial contract, the buyer is "locked in" to buying future runs of that product from the firm that is the monopoly producer. Thus, the firm expects to make up its initial loss by obtaining a larger profit margin on future production runs. Learning curves also result in lower future production costs; therefore, the combination of higher future prices and lower future costs improves the long-run profit picture considerably, making up for the initial loss.

Thus, the buyer must consider the possibility that by fostering competition on future production runs, buying in may no longer be feasible

because the firm is unsure about winning future production run contracts. The result is that for the initial production run, the bid price may be higher than the case where the firm has little or no future competition.

EFFICIENT PRODUCTION RATES

Chapter 1 briefly mentioned that changes from an optimal production rate tend to increase the per unit production cost of a weapon system. Several examples were given. At this point, it is appropriate to explain why stretch-outs of production result in per unit cost increases. For weapon systems that involve labor-intensive production, labor costs per unit produced tend to decrease as more units are produced. This is due to the fact that managers and workers learn more efficient ways of doing tasks that are repeated on each unit. The learning effect can be expressed in terms of process time reductions or in terms of increased monthly production rates.[3]

To illustrate, suppose a major aircraft assembly task has a first unit (T_1) labor-hour requirement of 12,000 man-hours. Suppose also that twenty-five people, each working a full eight-hour day, are assigned to this operation and that they learn according to an 80 percent learning factor. For the first unit, 200 man-hours per day can be applied to the 12,000-hour total task. The process time of the first unit is sixty days (calculated by dividing 200 hours per day into 12,000 total task hours). The second unit requires only 9,600 total hours (12,000 hours $\times$ 80 percent). The application of 200 man-hours per day will complete the second unit in forty-eight days. Similarly, the third unit process time is forty-two days, and so on.

For any given task where the applied man-hours per day (based on the assigned quantity of workers and the shift length) is set and the T_1 known, the first unit process time can be calculated and the process time of subsequent units will diminish according to the learning factor. The reduction in the process times of sequential units results in a decline of production flow time and a reduction in production labor costs per unit.

The learning curve is directly applicable only to sequentially produced units. This gives rise to the problem of how to apply the learning curve to parallel production operations. Consider the case in which one particular task is associated with three identical work stations on an assembly line. These three stations are necessary to keep aggregate output in pace with successor and predecessor stations. Unlike a one-station operation, which produces each unit in sequence, each of these three stations involves learning on every third unit of aggregate output. In theory, units 1, 2, and 3 would require the same T_1 quantity of labor

hours: The T_2 labor-hour value would apply to the second unit of output for each station, i.e., units 4, 5, and 6, and so on.

There are several ways of treating the problem of parallel work stations. For example, Boeing Aircraft Company treats parallel production as sequential production. Each unit of output is subjected to learning-curve reduction in labor hours and process time. The assumption is made that parallel stations are not independent: Stations learn from one another by sharing labor-saving ideas and procedural innovations, and hence, parallel production results in improvements sufficient to treat it as sequential production with regard to the learning curve. Thus, Boeing adjusts the b exponent by experience or judgment to account for less learning by each parallel station and treats output as sequential. Other methods are used by other companies.

The learning-curve phenomenon indicates that production rates continue to increase as the number of units produced increases. This is true up to a point. Beyond some production rate, diseconomies begin to occur: Tools and equipment are unavailable for additional units being produced because they are being used elsewhere or workers make mistakes because they are rushed. For these and other reasons, costs begin to rise. Thus, the lowest-cost production rate is termed the optimal production rate. Deviations either above or below this rate will increase the per unit cost of production.

It is worthwhile to note that the profit-maximizing output schedule determined by equations (7) and (8) is almost always consistent with the optimal (lowest-cost) production rate. The key to this consistency lies in the marginal cost function, which appears in equation (7). This function is related to production cost curves, which, in turn, are related to the production rate. Therefore there is no inherent conflict between the production manager who attempts to minimize production costs and the marketer who tries to maximize profits.

However, there is a conflict between efficiency-motivated weapon systems producers and politically motivated budget makers in the government. Given current government-producer relationships, the budget makers usually win, and deviations below the optimal production rate are the norm rather than the exception. Historically, these deviations have been driven by fiscal year funding constraints and the annual "battle of the budget" between Congress and the administration.

GOVERNMENT AND PRODUCTION DECISIONS

The decision process on weapon system production rates begins in the Pentagon. Pentagon planners establish the force structure requirements that a new weapon system is intended to fill. For example, aircraft

requirements include basic wing and squadron structures, the initial operating capability date and the expected attrition rates over the weapon system life cycle. Program planners translate these requirements into a weapon system delivery schedule, which sets the initial production rate. Based on actual and expected congressional and Office of Management and Budget actions, Pentagon programmers adjust the delivery schedule to meet fiscal contraints because yearly delivery quantities must be consistent with available funds. The production rate is adjusted accordingly. Typically, only secondary consideration is given to the production rate as a driver of costs per unit of the system being produced. Thus, efficiency criteria at the weapon system production level are typically overridden by higher level considerations.

The F-15 aircraft program provides an example. In 1968, the Air Force F-15 System Program Office issued to potential contractors a request for proposal (RFP) with instructions to submit a cost proposal for a twenty-per-month aircraft production rate. Program planners developed this rate, based upon force structure and operational date requirements set by the Plans and Requirements Directorate at the Pentagon. However, in the midst of the source selection process, the program office was advised by the Pentagon that a schedule strentch-out was necessary due to funding limitations. A revised schedule of twelve per month was then issued to the potential contractors.[4]

CONCLUSIONS

The defense industry is unique because of the special relationship between a few large firms and a dominant buyer, the federal government. It is clear from the examples given in this chapter that fostering competition among prime contractors for major weapon systems will tend to reduce profits and accelerate delivery schedules of weapons. It is not clear that the government will necessarily benefit in the short term because firms will no longer have an incentive to "buy in" to a production contract. Over the long term however, the government will tend to benefit from competition because the weapon system price will be lower both for the initial contract and for contracts for subsequent production runs.

Up to a point, the learning-curve phenomenon results in progressively lower costs for labor-intensive weapon systems production. After that point, production costs tend to increase due to diseconomies of scale. The production rate that results in the lowest cost is called the optimal production rate. This rate can be calculated for any labor-intensive production process. Indeed, it is standard practice to do this throughout defense industries. Although fiscal funding and other political factors

are relevant in determining a production schedule, it seems logical that budget limitations, rather than being absolutes in themselves, should be evaluated in the context of an optimal (lowest-cost) production rate. The Department of Defense is well aware of the sensitivity of production costs to production rates, but there has been no concerted effort to date by the Pentagon to optimize production rates of new weapon systems.

NOTES

Epigraph: Gansler, J. S., *The Defense Industry,* MIT Press, Cambridge, Mass., 1981.

1. Gansler, J. S., *The Defense Industry,* MIT Press, Cambridge, Mass., 1981. Also see Gansler, J. S., "Let's Change the Way the Pentagon Does Business," *Harvard Business Review* 55 (May-June 1977).

2. Grant, E., Ireson, W., and Leavenworth, R., *Principles of Engineering Economy,* John Wiley and Sons, New York, 1976.

3. *Military Cost Analysis,* Department of Economics, Geography and Management, U.S. Air Force Academy, 1979. Also see McNichols, G., ed., *Cost Analysis,* Operations Research Society of America, November 1984.

4. *Military Cost Analysis.*

8
The Growth of Cost: Efficiency Issues

I have had considerable experience in letting public contracts and I have never yet found a contractor, who, if not watched, would not leave the government holding the bag.

—**Harry S. Truman**

Because of the way we do business, there are not a lot of incentives for contractors to work hard to reduce costs.

—**Air Force Contracting Official, 1985**

INTRODUCTION

Cost growth in weapons has been a serious problem for the past thirty years. This was demonstrated most recently when the adverse publicity surrounding the prices paid by the Pentagon for various items of military equipment was a major factor in bringing the Reagan defense buildup to a standstill. However, total cost growth in a weapon is due to a complex mix of factors, some of which are structural and imbedded in the process of acquiring weapons and some of which are transient and quite dependent on both the type of weapon being built and the environment in which the weapon is being acquired. All these factors must be considered when accounting for the cost of a weapon, and it should come as no surprise that the problems that receive the most publicity (waste, fraud, and abuse) are often the least important contributors to increasing costs. This chapter will deal with the factors that determine the efficiency of defense contractors. The following chapter will then investigate the impact of other factors, such as technology, waste and fraud, and procurement practices, on the growth of cost.

EFFICIENCY AND THE PRODUCTION OF ARMS

A fair amount of literature in the defense area concerns the profitability of the industries that manufacture weapons. Profit is a concern both in making industries viable members of the defense industrial base and in controlling the potential for profiteering, particularly in times of armed conflict. However, profit is not an adequate measure of the performance of defense contractors because profit is merely the result of subtracting total costs from total revenues—it says nothing about the efficiency of the operation generating those costs and revenues. A defense contractor may have low profits because of an inefficient operation, not because the compensation for making weapons is inadequate. Similarly, high profits could indicate an efficient operation, higher compensation, or even overpayment.

In the early 1970s, the air force became concerned about the efficiency of defense production. Several studies, including the 1973 project ACE (Aerospace Cost Experience), revealed many inefficiencies in the defense industries. To improve efficiency, the air force proposed applying work-measurement standards to defense production. This initiative resulted in Regulation 1567, issued in 1975, which required contractors to establish their own work-measurement standards. In 1980 the General Accounting Office reported favorably on this concept, stating that the use of such standards could increase efficiency by 10–30 percent and reduce weapon costs by as much as 5 percent. About 70 percent of air force contracts are now covered by this regulation. The army and navy are working to introduce similar standards into their procurement systems,[1] but the actual effect of having work standards for the defense industries is still undetermined.

THE LACK OF COMPETITION
IN THE DEFENSE INDUSTRY

There are a number of economic reasons for the belief that the defense industry is not efficient. As Gansler has pointed out, the industry is concentrated in a few large firms and has a large amount of vertical integration, high barriers to entry, and a distinct dual economy favoring prime contractors over subcontractors.[2] Each of these factors mitigates against the type of competition that would lead to lower costs. In fact, this concentration is so great that in 1982, only twelve companies accounted for over 50 percent of a procurement budget of roughly $80 billion.[3]

The Defense Department has attempted to introduce more competition into the procurement process by getting small businesses to become

defense contractors. However, real competition is still minimal because there are so few major defense manufacturers in each sector that the DoD cannot maintain the defense industrial base and still allow a large arms maker to fail. Claims by a group representing 14,000 metalworking companies and machine shops that $8 billion could be saved by increasing competition and awarding defense contracts to small businesses have been disputed by the Department of Defense, which estimated that "only" about $5 billion could be saved.[4]

It is difficult for small contractors to bid on military jobs. The data required to submit such a bid are usually available only to the major contractor who originally supplied the item; in fact, private companies have had to sue the military services to get data needed to bid. In 1985 the Department of Defense (in an attempt to stop the flow of unclassified data to the Soviet Union) was considering new rules that would make it even more dificult to get technical data.[5]

WAGES AND HOURS IN DEFENSE PRODUCTION

In addition to a lack of competition, other efficiency problems abound. The internal costs of companies are an example. A 1982 Defense Logistics Agency report showed that the salaries of higher executives at Pratt and Whitney "exceeded the norm for other defense contractors by 40 percent," while the "average salary for some categories of GPD (Government Products Division) employees [also] exceeds the average paid by competitors."[6] In 1984, another report found that the average pay for top executives at twelve large aerospace companies was 42 percent higher than that of executives of similar-sized companies nationwide.[7] The pay of executives is reflected in higher overhead rates on defense contracts. This alone reduces efficiency. But a 1984 study of six of the top ten defense contractors by A. Ernest Fitzgerald found that GPD labor rates, which are direct labor costs, were increased by a factor of seven to twenty before they were billed to the government. Thus, a "standard hour" of labor at Pratt and Whitney, which was valued at $10, was billed to the government at about $195 by the time that overhead and administration (and 13 percent profit) were added. In a similar manner, a $14 rate at Boeing rose to $114, and a $16 rate at Rockwell rose to $141.[8]

With the hourly rate inflated in this manner, the method by which the hours are calculated becomes very critical. Data gathered by the Pentagon in the first quarter of 1984 showed that the "should take" hours initially estimated by a contractor to complete a project were usually exceeded by a large margin by the time the project was finished. Boeing took 188,760 hours to complete reengining work it estimated

would take 78,000 hours, and Rockwell International took 1,224,872 hours to complete work on the B-1 it estimated would take 391,183 hours. Raytheon, Northrop, General Electric, Honeywell, and others had similar records. In no case did any company ever finish a project in fewer than the number of "should take" hours it had estimated.[9]

These problems even affect weapons that have been in production for a considerable amount of time. One expects, theoretically, that as the production of a weapon continues, the cost of that weapon will drop because of learning-curve effects. However, the average flyaway costs of both the F-16 and the F-15 have increased over the life of their production runs. The F-15, which cost $5.5 million in 1970, cost $7.4 million (in 1970 dollars) in 1985. In 1975 dollars, the price of an F-16 rose from $3.9 million in 1980 to $4.8 million in 1984. These increases were based on the amount of labor required to build each airplane. An F-15, which was supposed to take 22,978 hours to build, took 37,193 hours to complete in 1984. An F-16 took 67 percent more work hours to complete than had been planned.[10]

By comparing the "should take" hours to the time actually expended on a project, it is possible to develop a measure of labor efficiency ("should take" time divided by actual time). Using this methodology, the efficiency rate for the ten largest defense contractors was about 30 percent. The contractors noted that the efficiency rate is not a good measure because production runs are small and government specifications are subject to frequent changes. But an official from the National Tooling and Machining Association, which engages in commercial (nongovernment) work, noted that his group's 3,700 members could not afford to be off by more than 10 percent on this type of estimate if they wanted to stay in business.[11]

THE QUALITY OF DEFENSE WORK

Given inefficiencies in the manner in which inputs are assembled to produce weapons, what can be said of the products of these endeavors? Major General Jasper Welch commented succinctly on this problem when he made "the simple observation that if military equipment were built to be reliable enough in the first place, there would be little need for spare parts."[12] Quality has been a continual problem with the entire range of products the Department of Defense acquires.

Part of the quality problem is that government inspectors are so swamped with work that the same contractors who make the weapons are also hired to perform quality checks on the weapons they produce. Other problems have arisen because the huge buildup in defense spending has taxed already overburdened and inefficient producers. Whatever the

reason, Richard D. DeLauer, under secretary of defense for research and engineering during the period 1981 through 1984 claimed that "Since I've been [in the Department of Defense], there have been problems in almost every single major [military weapon] program. Workmanship is lousy. No one is paying any attention to quality control."[13] It is interesting to question how industries typified by such a record could survive in the face of competitors who offered a better product. Clearly, they could not—unless there was little or no competition. Thus, the very conditions that assure an inefficient defense industry also contribute to the low quality of the products that industry produces.

Military Specifications

The low quality of many of the products purchased by the military stands in contrast to the extensive process used to establish the specifications for those goods. This process creates overspecified requirements for run-of-the-mill items used for everyday maintenance and operation and also for many of the items employed in combat or other life-and-death situations.

Much overspecification for common items is the fault of Congress, which has prohibited the military from buying these items off the shelf (from existing commercial sources). Congress believes such purchases would favor goods already established in the commercial market and may adversely affect small and minority businesses that are just starting. As a result, the Department of Defense has 18 pages of specifications for a handkerchief and 24 pages of specifications for men's briefs.[14] These specifications are so complicated and so far removed from common sense that errors (committed through omission or ignorance) reducing the overall quality and usefulness of the good are not infrequent. In fact, just by adding up the pages of specifications required to assemble a military meal (16 pages for sugar cookies, 25 pages for coffee, 20 pages for whipped cream, etc.) one quickly reaches a total that exceeds the 400 pages of specifications necessary to purchase a Boeing 707 jet aircraft.[15]

Obviously, a process requiring such extensive specification for simple items becomes increasingly more complicated as the complexity of the item grows and the need for the item becomes more critical. Thus, the invitation to bid (and the specifications) for an air defense simulator is 436 pages long, requiring a response of about 2,000 pages with the bid. For comparison, a similar French request is only 13 pages long.[16] Not only is there no indication that such a level of specification increases quality, there is also considerable likelihood that the only real function of such a process is to limit competition. With proposals so extensive and complicated, it is virtually certain that only old, established concerns

that have the large staffs necessary to deal with the process can compete. This creates another barrier to entry in the defense market, and, as a result, decreases competition and lowers the efficiency with which defense goods are produced.

SUBSIDIES TO DEFENSE INDUSTRIES

The number of factors that promote the oligopolistic and inefficient structure of the defense industry might be presumed to remove the need for further inducements to stay in the defense business. Whether or not this is true, subsidies, which are another method of guaranteeing inefficiency in the marketplace, are used frequently in the defense industries. For example:

Interest Subsidy. Since 1976 the Department of Defense has paid defense contractors an interest subsidy to compensate the contractor for part of the cost of capital invested in the equipment used to construct weapons. These payments, which cost the government $3 to $5 billion per year, are based on the prevailing Treasury interest rate and cover all the equipment used on a specific contract to make weapons. Investment in new capital goods is not necessary to receive the benefit. A 1982 Air Force Systems Command study found that despite the stated reasons for this subsidy, "our analysis disclosed no reduction in direct labor and no increase in facilities capital in the performance of defense contracts."[17]

Overhead Billing Practices. Unlike normal commercial practices where a good is sold at a price that reflects all costs, defense contractors are allowed to bill the government for a large variety of overhead expenses incurred while the contract was being performed. Although this is meant to compensate for the change and risk inherent in many defense contracts, in practice it tends to encourage less care in initially computing the price of the equipment to be manufactured. Two types of overhead billing constitute particularly valuable subsidies:

1. Payment for Capital Equipment: This is a payment made to the contractor's overhead account for the general tools and machinery used in the production of the weapon being purchased. Although the government pays for these tools, the contractor retains title to them. In some cases, such as the B-1, this payment is given to the contractor "up front" before the start of production.[18]

2. Reimbursement for Independent Research and Development: This payment is also made to the overhead account for independent research carried out by the contractor. Not only does this subsidy give an advantage to existing contractors by financing the research they can use to stay ahead of potential competitors, but the results are often of

questionable use to the military. Although projects in this category are evaluated by reviewers in the Department of Defense, the evaluation forms are concerned only with the capability of the contractors to do the research and with the progress of the study. Neither the actual need for the project nor the projected military benefits from such an endeavor are considered.[19]

Government Ownership of Buildings and Other Facilities. The U.S. government owns many of the factory buildings used by defense contractors to construct weapons. This theoretically ensures that these facilities will be available for use in the defense industrial base, but such ownership also frees capital for defense contractors to use for other purposes.[20]

Department of Defense Purchase of Peculiar Equipment. In addition to the overhead payments made for general tools and equipment, the Department of Defense purchases any peculiar equipment required specifically for the construction of the weapon being produced. This equipment is retained by the U.S. government and leased to the contractor at low rates.[21]

Up-Front Payments and Progress Payments. A military contract generally involves two types of costs: nonrecurring costs (the fixed costs of establishing the production process) and recurring costs (the variable costs involved in producing the weapon). The Department of Defense pays the contractor up front for nonrecurring costs before work has started on the contract. Eighty percent of recurring costs are then reimbursed through progress payments over the life of the contract. Thus, unlike commercial producers, the defense contractor does not have to borrow the money to start a new production process—or pay the interest charges associated with such an arrangement. Instead, the defense contractor receives what is essentially an interest-free loan from the U.S. government to cover the start-up and operation costs.[22]

Government Funding of Large Research and Development Projects. The Department of Defense funds a large number of research and development studies, the results of which are then used by defense contractors in the construction of new weapons. This acts as a subsidy to defense contractors both in terms of their own research and development work (which is supplanted by government-funded programs) and in the area of international sales, where the research and development that made possible the contractor's product has been subsidized by the U.S. government.

Completed-Contract Accounting. Under this method of accounting, defense contractors (and other manufacturers) who engage in lengthy contracts may defer taxes on the income from those contracts until the entire contract is completed. For major defense systems this can mean

tax deferrals of five to ten years. The result has been that most large defense contractors do not pay taxes at all. In fact, for the period 1981–1983, four large defense contractors actually had negative tax rates (General Dynamics: −7.6 percent, Boeing: −17.5 percent, General Electric: −4.3 percent, and Martin Marietta: −19.2 percent).[23] Secretary of Defense Caspar Weinberger noted in 1985 that "the impact [of completed-contract accounting] on public opinion is very unfortunate" and he recommended that the provision be dropped from the tax code.[24] This was done in 1986.

Extraordinary Contractual Relief. This little-known act allows the Department of Defense to give grants to companies that are failing but regarded as essential to national security. Unfortunately, the defense industrial base is so loosely defined (see Chapter 6) that virtually any company can be construed as being essential for national survival. From 1958, when this law took effect, to 1983, the Department of Defense aided more than 7,000 of the 8,059 firms that requested this type of relief. This subsidized federal insurance program for defense contractors has cost the U.S. government about $3 billion over the past twenty-five years.[25] Such a program further destroys any vestige of competition because it makes it virtually impossible for a contractor to fail—even when the firm is noncompetitive and poorly managed.

Foreign Military Sales. In addition to the items just mentioned, when a contractor sells weapons to a foreign customer through a Foreign Military Sales (FMS) agreement managed by the U.S. government, the government assumes all liability for the performance of the contract. If the overseas customer backs out of the agreement, the U.S. government is responsible for purchasing the weapon from the contractor. This results in a risk-free sale for the contractor (unfortunately, this has not been reflected in lower prices for FMS weapons) and a subsidy to the contractor's foreign sales operations.

CONCLUSIONS

The combined effect of the subsidies given to defense contractors is to create an environment isolated from normal competition. In such an environment, efficiency is no longer relevant. Instead, the defense contractor's incentives stem from actions that will enhance the flow of subsidized funds from the U.S. government. These practices encourage large initial investments in new projects, research and development that may not be related to actual requirements, excessive loading of overhead accounts, delaying the completion of contracts, designing production processes requiring unique machinery, and retaining large capital in-

vestments in machinery that may have exceeded its useful life—all practices that limit efficiency and competitiveness.

NOTES

Epigraphs: Truman quote, Miller, Nathan, "Profiteers and Patriots," *Baltimore Sun*, October 30, 1984, p. 9; Air Force Contracting Official, quoted in Gordon, Michael R., "Data on Production Inefficiencies May Spur New Debate on Defense Contracting," *National Journal*, June 1, 1985, pp. 1283–1286.

1. Gordon, "Data on Production Inefficiencies," p. 1284.

2. Gansler, Jacques, *The Defense Industry*, MIT Press, Cambridge, Mass., 1981, p. 54.

3. Cook, David T., "Keeping Pentagon Out of Wild Blue Yonder," *Christian Science Monitor*, December 5, 1983, p. 39.

4. "Potential Cuts Cited in Military Parts Bills," *Washington Post*, October 12, 1984, p. 3.

5. Jacobs, Sanford, "Obtaining Data to Bid on Military Jobs," *Wall Street Journal*, October 15, 1984, p. 35.

6. Mollenhoff, Clark R., "AF Report Shows Salaries at Pratt and Whitney High," *Washington Times*, August 2, 1983, p. 4.

7. Seib, Gerald F., "Defense Firms Pay More to Executives, Report Says," *Wall Street Journal*, October 29, 1984, p. 41.

8. Biddle, Wayne, "New Study Finds Inflated Labor Costs on Weapons," *New York Times*, October 11, 1984, p. 17.

9. Royce, Knut, "Defense Firms Cited for Wasteful Productivity," *Baltimore News American*, June 24, 1984, p. 11.

10. Vickery, Hugh, "Pentagon Probing Increases in Prices of Fighter Planes," *Washington Times*, July 8, 1984, p. 10C.

11. Greenberger, Robert S., "Defense Contractors Exceeded Estimates for Labor on Some Projects, Data Show," *Wall Street Journal*, June 24, 1985, p. 10.

12. Welch, Jasper, "What the Annual Report Does Not Say About Spare Parts," *Armed Forces Journal International*, March 1984, p. 80.

13. "The Pentagon Steps Up Its War On Shoddy Workmanship," *Business Week*, October 15, 1984, pp. 174, 178.

14. Wright, Joseph, "Blocking Federal Efficiency," *Washington Times*, November 27, 1984, p. 1C.

15. Vickery, Hugh, "Would You Believe a 16-page Recipe for Sugar Cookies?," *Washington Times*, July 9, 1985, p. 1.

16. Hiatt, Fred, and Atkinson, Rick, "U.S. a Tough Customer in Foreign Marketplace," *Washington Post*, June 23, 1985, p. A8.

17. Mohr, Charles, "Ban Sought on Incentive to Military Contractors," *New York Times*, January 31, 1985, p. 11.

18. Conversation with Dr. David Blond, OSD/PA&E, June 24, 1985.

19. Department of Defense Form 1855, August 1983, entitled "Independent Research and Development Project Technical Evaluation," contains the following

categories: Objective (of the study), Approach, Resources (adequate or not), and Progress.

20. Conversation with Dr. David Blond, OSD/PA&E, June 24, 1985.

21. Conversation with Dr. David Blond, OSD/PA&E, June 24, 1985.

22. Conversation with Dr. David Blond, OSD/PA&E, June 24, 1985.

23. Carrington, Tim, "Defense Contractors' Emergence as Big Winners in Reagan Tax Plan May Be Political Liability," *Wall Street Journal*, June 18, 1985, p. 64.

24. Rosenbaum, David E., "Weinberger Against Tax Postponing," *New York Times*, June 26, 1985, p. B8.

25. Milligan, Susan, " 'National Emergency' Program Aids Ailing Arms Contractors," *Boston Globe*, July 6, 1985, p. 3.

9
The Growth of Cost: Other Factors

There is no kind of dishonesty into which otherwise good people more easily fall than that of defrauding the government.
—Benjamin Franklin

National support for building military strength has been severely battered by public perception that we pay too much for the goods and services we acquire.
—Verne Orr, 1985

General Dynamics is an honest and reputable company. Our company and its people have been badly maligned by forces beyond our control.
—David S. Lewis, 1985

INTRODUCTION

Growth of defense costs occurs in many ways. Unfortunately, most factors leading to increased costs are not easily understood, and the few that can be readily grasped (and widely publicized) tend to get undue attention. First among these are the "minor sins" of fraud, waste, and abuse. This highly publicized trio actually costs the taxpayer only a fraction of the amount generated by the inefficiencies covered in Chapter 8. Next in the amount of public attention received is the high cost of individual weapons. However, this is only a total figure that does not give any insight into the causes of the costs—causes often stemming from the levels of technology involved. The following pages will discuss the many publicized and the unpublicized determinants of the cost of defense.

THE COST OF MILITARY MANPOWER

The All-Volunteer Force

After the draft was abolished in 1973, the military services struggled to attract new recruits. Many who signed up were substandard in intelligence and education. Indiscipline, poor morale, and low reenlistment rates all hampered military performance. In fact, the only bright spot was the enlistment rate for women—but female recruits comprised only 9 percent of the total accessions.

Observers of this period attributed the military's problems to the fact that military pay lagged behind inflation, the G.I. Bill was curtailed in 1977, and the U.S. economy was healthy enough to maintain low rates of unemployment.[1] The problems of the economy in the late 1970s and early 1980s finally created levels of unemployment that made the all-volunteer force a success.

Because the all-volunteer force did not perform well until unemployment began to increase, one might assume that the wage rates initially established for the force were too low for good economic times. Although this was probably the case, the General Accounting Office found that the all-volunteer force still had markedly increased costs over the draft. The GAO found that "from Fiscal Years 1971 through 1977, annual cost increases attributable to the All-volunteer Force were about $90 million in 1971, $1.5 billion in 1972, $32.0 billion in 1973, $3.3 billion in 1974, $3.4 billion in 1975 $3.3 billion in 1976 . . . and about $3.1 billion in 1977."[2] This, of course, is the fundamental problem with a volunteer force. Even during a period when the rate of remuneration offered was not sufficient to attract the kinds of recruits necessary to maintain the force, it was extremely expensive to operate. This causes one to question what the experience will be in a period of very low unemployment or in a time of potential conflict.

Recruiting

All other issues aside, the single area of recruiting will determine the eventual fate of a volunteer military organization. When fiscal year 1984 ended, the military services had more than 130,000 people on their waiting lists, and recruiting appeared to be well under control. The second part of recruiting, reenlistment, had also risen from 55 percent in 1980 to 67 percent in 1984.[3] To achieve this the services spent significant amounts of money for advertising. In 1984, $155 million was spent, over $33 million for television network time alone. And each service retained its own advertising agency to structure careful campaigns stressing the desired image of the respective branch of the military.[4]

Given the statistics just cited, one only has to be told that 1984 was actually a bad year for recruiting to understand that in recruiting, as in many other areas of military performance, the same statistics can tell many different stories. It was a year of massive and rapid economic recovery. As unemployment dropped, so did the numbers of recruits. Many officials, such as Defense Secretary Caspar Weinberger, claimed that recruitment had been a complete success in 1984 by pointing out that the services met or exceeded their goals for people entering the military. The problem with this argument is that there are two different figures: new enlistment contracts and people actually entering service. Many people who enter service (the statistic cited by those claiming recruiting success) have been allowed to delay reporting for duty for as long as twelve months after signing an enlistment contract. Thus, much of 1984's success was actually attributable to 1983's recruiting.[5]

In 1984, a year of declining unemployment, the army experienced its first recruiting shortfall since 1981—the last previous year of lower unemployment. This loss was greater than the numbers indicate because during 1984 the pool of average or above-average mental category applicants declined by 25 percent. To meet training goals, the army must have 65 percent of recruits in this category. Recruiting success was gained only by drawing on the pool of delayed-entry people—a tactic that cannot be used in subsequent years if the numbers of enlistment contracts remain depressed. The army recognized its difficulties early in the 1984 recruiting cycle and started a program of increased bonuses for reenlistment and for first-time enlistment of quality people—an attempt to increase the rate of pay to a level competitive with civilian jobs.[6]

Thus recruiting, the critical factor in the all-volunteer force, is largely dependent for its success on economic forces that can completely overwhelm even the most extensive marketing efforts by the military. And in the end, money is the deciding factor—and money is, unfortunately, hard to find in times of economic austerity.

The Reserves

The use of reserves is closely linked to the cost of maintaining a military force because the reserves serve as a repository of experience and as a source of reinforcement, all at a fraction of the cost involved in keeping an active duty force. The more experienced and trained the reserve force is, and the better equipped it is, the fewer active duty forces that should be required. And if the reserve is so well trained that it can be called up almost instantaneously, the number of active duty forces can be very small (as in Israel and Switzerland).

Reserves are economical because their pay is low, they have already been trained (usually when on active duty), and most will not retire until they are in their sixties, making the military retirement costs small compared to those of the regular forces. In addition, a reserve force does not involve the day-to-day maintenance and feeding costs of an active duty force. As a result, today's reserves consume only 5.6 percent of the military budget, but they provide nearly half of the combat strength and two-thirds of the support of U.S. forces.[7]

In spite of these benefits, the United States does not compare well with either our allies or our enemies in terms of the reserves we keep. Some representative ratios of active to reserve components are Europe Neutral, 1:8.0; Warsaw Pact (excluding USSR), 1:2.3; Warsaw Pact (with USSR), 1:1.6; USSR, 1:1.4; NATO, 1:1.4; U.S., 1:0.4.[8] Why have both our allies and our enemies come to rely so heavily on the reserves when we have not? The answer is twofold: the size of the cohort of service-eligible youths and the cost of maintaining the force.

The United States did not suffer losses in World War II of the magnitude of those suffered by the European participants. European losses in the 1940s translated into depressed birthrates in the 1960s, 1970s, and 1980s. There were simply not enough people to go around, and it was obvious that in many of these nations a large standing army would directly conflict with the civilian labor requirements of each country's industries. There is also the matter of cost. A standing army consumes resources that could be spent on other programs, and when resources are in short supply, the support of a standing army becomes a much more significant burden.

Neither of these factors was significant enough to cause the United States to pursue seriously a policy of building its reserves after World War II. And for most of that period, it did not have to seek actively reserve resources—reserve strength remained at an acceptable level because service in the reserves was preferable to being drafted. But when the draft ended, so did the easy times for the reserves.

The United States now finds itself in a situation similar to that which has driven other nations to build up reserves and to decrease the size of the standing army. Budget deficits have made the cost considerations of the active duty military a point of major contention, and the size of the cohort of service-age men is shrinking in the United States as it did in Europe. The United States will soon be taking 25 percent of all males, almost 40 percent of all those eligible, and 56 percent of all noncollege eligible males to fill out its armed forces—at a time when the total number of eligible males has decreased by 22 percent from the levels present when the all-volunteer force was established. The reserve forces are capable of accomplishing what no other entity can

do—they can lower the cost of the military establishment and still maintain the quality of the fighting force. However, the United States has no draft to act as a motivator. And without such a motivator, it is unlikely that the reserves will ever be large enough adequately to supplement active forces in an all-out war.

The Inducements

In an effort to make military pay equal to that for comparable civilian jobs, a trend of rising military wages was started in the 1960s. Later, when the all-volunteer force was instituted, it was clear that compensation would have to be further increased to attract volunteers, and pay was raised again. Although it can be argued that military pay never has reached the level associated with comparable civilian jobs (in the late 1970s pay was unable to keep up with inflation, and then in the 1980s the Department of Defense consistently traded pay increases for new weapons), there is no question that other benefits and retirement were never adjusted to reflect the changing levels of military pay. And this raised the issue of whether that lack of adjustment caused military retirement to become too generous for the rates of pay being offered. The military retirement system falls in line with those offered to the Executive Protective Service and to Air Traffic Controllers. However, these are both very generous retirement systems associated with unusual jobs possessing unique demands and stresses (as do some military jobs). It is also true that the military retirement system is far superior to that offered to the civil service. Thus, the fundamental problem is that for the types of military duties that closely parallel the duties of the average civil servant, retirement is too generous (assuming other pay is equal) but for the duties that approximate the danger and stress of the Federal Protective Service or Air Traffic Controllers, retirement is generous but appropriate (again, assuming other compensation is equal).

Because of the special nature of military service, perhaps a better view of this problem is gained by comparing U.S. military retirement with that of the military services of other nations. Although the U.S. military retirement is generally better than that of our allies, the difference is not striking enough to cause a major realignment of the entire retirement system. It is clear, however, that the U.S. system is generous by international standards and is also generous by U.S. government standards.[9]

The cost of the retirement system has tripled since 1975. In fiscal year 1985, the bill will be about $5.8 billion. It will rise to $20 billion in 1988 and $23 billion in 1990. Nine major studies, including five by the Pentagon itself, have recommended major changes in the retirement system such as cutting benefits, delaying payment of full pensions until

age sixty-two or sixty-five, vesting benefits before twenty years of service, and lowering benefits for those retiring at twenty years of service.[10] The military has resisted all cuts and changes, claiming that retirement is deferred compensation, necessary for retention, and important for reenlistment. And because reductions in retirement would have an unknown effect on recruiting and retention, the military has been unwilling to take the risk of altering a system that, by its standards, is working reasonably well.

Because there is no vesting in the retirement system prior to twenty years, many military members will sacrifice a good deal to remain on active duty until that point. But military retirement is only a benefit if it is used, and this means that there is substantial motivation to use it as soon as possible. However, at the twenty-year point of one's career, retirement pay is not substantial enough to support a family or to continue one's life-style.[11] This means that there is a motivation to retire at twenty years, but only those individuals who are readily employable outside the military can afford to retire at this point. And the people who are most employable are, in general, the most competent people. Thus, the retirement system actually tends to encourage the best people to leave the military after twenty years.

In a sense, the military retirement system is used to compensate for bad management. Service members are often subjected to incompetent leaders, bad working conditions, a diabolical personnel system, and an insensitive command structure. They put up with these things because the retirement system is there, waiting to reward those who complete at least twenty years. The current system is necessary because the military organization has found it to its own advantage to make it so. The military might be better off in the long run if externally imposed reductions in the retirement system forced it to begin to manage better its own resources.

TECHNOLOGY AND COST

The crash of a B-1 bomber on August 29, 1984, resulted in a great deal of soul searching over the loss of this technological masterpiece. A remark made during the investigation of that crash by one of the safety consultants nicely summed up the dilemma posed by the expense of high technology weapons. As C.O. Miller put it, "I don't think we can accept any attrition. At 200 million bucks a crack, that's a hell of a resource loss."[12] This expresses the crux of the current problem: Weapons have been designed to incorporate the latest and best technology, but this has resulted in a force composed of fewer weapons of such great expense that they cannot afford to be lost. This is not an ideal

posture for fighting a war, and although it does not typify all aspects of the armed forces, it is common enough to receive closer attention.

The genesis of the technology problem is twofold. First, for the past twenty years the United States has had the opinion that it could not compete with the Soviet Union on the basis of numbers of weapons that would be employed in a war. Not only did the Soviet Union have a different philosophy about arming its fighting units, but also its manpower costs were so low that, for comparable defense budgets, the Soviets had more funds available to buy weapons. (It should be noted that the current approach is distinctly different than that taken by the United States during the Second World War, for which an excellent case can be made that the Germans were the technological leaders.) Second, the moral philosophy of the United States made the types of casualties that might be experienced with more numerous, cheap weapons unacceptable. These factors created the environment leading the United States to invest in high-technology weapons.[13]

The effect on the cost of defense of the shift toward technology was profound. A P-51 Mustang of World War II vintage cost $500,000 in 1983 dollars. The cheapest fighter available in 1983—the F-16—cost twenty-five times as much. In 1983 the army and navy paid ten times more in constant dollars for armored vehicles and ships than they did in World War II. The result has been that fewer and fewer weapons are purchased. Air force fighter strength fell from 4,000 in 1964 to about 2,500 today, and a similar shrinkage has affected the inventories of army and navy equipment.[14]

However, this issue has another side, that of quality. When they are working, modern weapons are so far superior to their earlier counterparts that a single modern system may well be able to defeat the entire number of earlier weapons purchasable with the same amount of money. Readiness, sortie rates, and safety records of the new systems far exceed anything experienced in earlier times.[15] But one must not push this argument too far. First, given the losses expected in combat, there must be a minimum inventory level for a force to maintain its ability to engage in prolonged combat. There are many indications that a majority of members of the military, politicians, and voters felt that the United States had reached that level during the Carter administration, although lacking an actual combat test, all these indications were based on subjective perceptions.

Second, the amount of time and expense required to preserve the U.S. technological edge is increasing so fast that it is doubtful the country can maintain the pace. Figure 9.1 shows the development times encountered as the complexity of the weapons has increased. As development times expand, costs rise. Technological changes in lengthy

Figure 9.1: Development Time for Major Weapon Systems

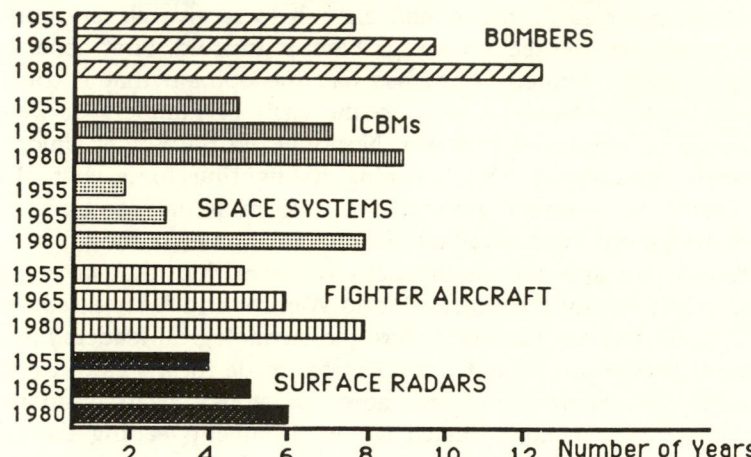

Source: Fossedal, Gregory A., "Reforming the Military Reform Push," *Wall Street Journal*, March 1, 1984, p. 28.

programs often makes redesign of weapons desirable. As a result, redesign costs now occur in 69 percent of the development programs, as opposed to 42 percent of pre-1970 programs. Similarly, technical hang-ups tend to increase, and changed funding and production rates are likely as budgets are altered annually during the development process (changes occurred in 46 percent of the programs prior to 1970 and 66 percent of the programs after that date). Each of these factors plays a major role in increasing cost—the General Accounting Office found that for every year added to the procurement cycle, the final cost of the weapon increased by 25 to 30 percent.[16]

The relationship between technology and increased costs is well known, but there is constant pressure for more exotic weapon technologies. Brown has pointed out that there are four reasons that people are captivated by exotic technologies:[17]

1. Exotic technologies are linked to ambiguous future events where cost estimates, performance estimates, and technological projections can all be believed because there is no hard data to refute them.
2. Exotic technologies offer solutions that are so far in the future that they seem to be permanent fixes for current problems.
3. The use of exotic technologies implies the existence of major strategic problems. Whether or not these problems actually exist, this implication tends to provide justification for using the new technology.

4. The use of exotic technologies is often subject to simplistic and misguided assumptions about technological development. These assumptions tend to downplay the risks associated with the use of such technologies, and they lead one toward the use of a "best case" scenario for weapon development.

In sum, the best way to start and to defend successfully a weapon development program is to employ the most advanced technology available. Unfortunately, this is also the best way to guarantee that the costs associated with that program will be high. Ideally, increased costs would be compared to the increased quality of the weapon developed, and a decision about buying the weapon could be based on economic efficiency. However, the politics of the development process make it impossible to do this type of comparison until the development process is so far downstream that changes are almost impossible. The winners in this game are those who want a wonder weapon that "will do all things for all people and never fail,"[18] but who cannot adequately justify the need for that weapon. The losers are the proponents of simpler, cheaper systems who are never allowed to compare their options on an even footing with those offered by the proponents of exotic technologies.

GENERAL FACTORS IN THE COST OF ARMS

The Contractor's Relationship with the Government and the Rise of Defense Industry Profits

Recent revelations of improper billing and of "proper" billing resulting in inflated prices for weapons have demonstrated an attitude on the part of defense contractors that has damaged both their credibility and that of the entire defense establishment. It is claimed that these actions are technically legal and therefore represent business practices no different from those of any large industry. For example, the chief executives of General Dynamics Corporation and Westinghouse Electric Corporation, defending the high prices they charged for tools, stated that they had "acted ethically and legally in these contracts" in spite of the fact that they would not attempt to defend the contracting procedures that led to the high prices in the first place.[19] This defense does not take into account the subsidized relationship between the government and the defense contractors, and it raises the moral issue of whether any citizen or corporation is obligated to try to rectify government procedures that work to the detriment of the nation, even if those procedures are profitable for the individual or corporation involved.

Figure 9.2: Operating Profit and Imputed Interest for DoD Businesses and General Durable Goods Manufacturing

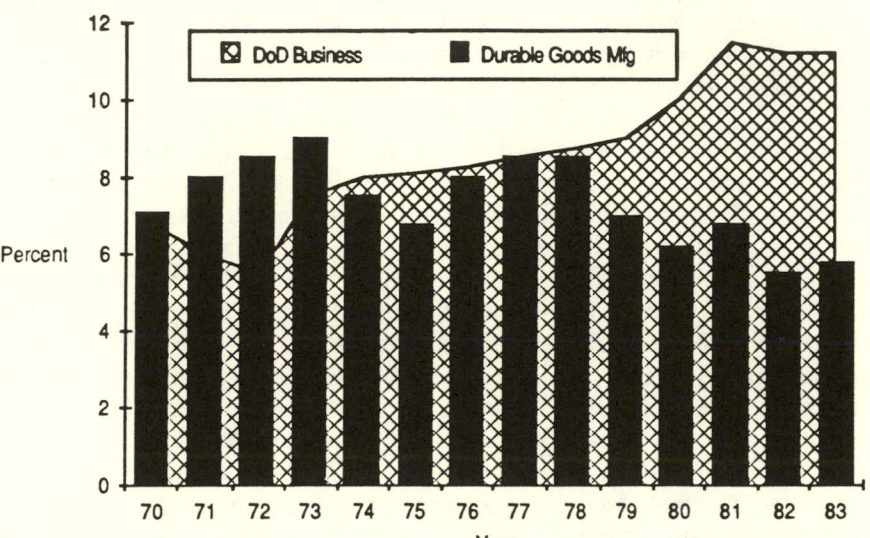

Note: DoD Businesses exclude ships and services, and Durable Goods Manufacturing excludes ESIC 32, 33, and others.

Source: Defense Financial and Investment Review, Department of Defense, June 1985, p. v-31.

The high profits enjoyed by the major defense contractors during the defense buildup of the 1980s indicate that no such obligation is now felt. Through most of the 1970s, the profit experience of defense contractors was mixed when compared to the general experience of all durable goods manufacturers. (See Figure 9.2.) However, since 1978, the defense buildup started by the Carter administration and the more generous subsidies given to defense contractors have dramatically altered the profit situation. Defense contractors have been able to increase steadily their percentage of profit, even during the period of recession in all other business sectors.

These profits are high by anyone's standards, and they are directly reflected in the increased cost of defense. And although they are not the sole determinant of that cost, they adequately demonstrate an approach to billing for weapons that borders on profiteering. As the deputy secretary of defense noted in 1985,

We must correct our problems and restore public confidence in our ability to manage efficiently the acquisition of vitally needed weapon systems,

parts and equipment. . . . Failure to do so risks erosion of public confidence to dangerously low levels—levels where public support can be lost. [Although] the great majority of defense contractors are pristine in their dealings with the Defense Department, [82 percent of the public believes contractors] are ripping off the American taxpayer."[20]

One of the most troublesome aspects of this situation is that it has risen from contractor actions that, although legal, could exist only within the framework of the highly subsidized defense industry. The Department of Defense has been very sensitive to this fact (as the above quote illustrates) and has attempted to minimize the impact of unfavorable information about contractor profits. The most recent example of this occurred when the long-awaited *Defense Financial and Investment Review*, which reported on defense contractor profits through 1983, was embargoed by the Pentagon for two months after the study showed that defense contractors were making almost twice the percentage of profit that their nondefense counterparts enjoyed.

In addition to these legal practices, there is growing concern about less common, illegal activities by the major defense contractors. Defense department audits of the 200 largest suppliers of spare parts to the military found that about half (95) were selling items that were overpriced.[21] Many of these cases involved simple mismanagement, but by May 1985, 45 of the nation's 100 largest defense contractors were under criminal investigation by the Defense Department.[22]

The government's ability to exercise legal recourse against the individuals and companies defrauding the Defense Department has been very ineffective. In October 1985, the Department of Defense's chief investigator, Joseph Sherick, said that his fraud investigators were overmatched by the staffs of major defense contractors who "take us to the cleaners." The Defense Department's record in prosecuting for fraud has also been weak—only eight cases were prosecuted in 1984.[23]

How much these legal and illegal activities have contributed to the high profits enjoyed by defense contractors and the extent to which they have driven up the price of weapons has not been determined. Although illegal activities, no matter how bad, will never account for as much of the cost of weapons as legal practices, it seems clear that the combined effect of both types of activities has increased the price of arms.

The Government's Relationship with Defense Contractors—Problems of Administration

Because the majority of defense contractor practices are legal, it follows that most of the fault for the high costs arising from those practices

must rest with the administrators of the programs and the originators of the rules: that is, the U.S. government. Of the government bodies involved, the Department of Defense bears major responsibility for problems coming from the administration of the weapon programs, and Congress bears the blame for many of the contracting rules that favor defense industries.

Disclosures about the high cost of spare parts and small defense acquisitions revealed the manner in which defense contractors assign overhead costs to those items. Until mid-1984, the common practice was to spread overhead more or less evenly across all acquisitions. Thus, a screwdriver could be allocated an overhead charge as large as that for a major part. In 1984, the air force decided that overhead should be charged according to an item's price—a move that helped reduce some of the grossly inflated prices charged for small items.[24]

Although this step made the costs of small items appear more reasonable, it did absolutely nothing to reduce the amount of overhead charged. Large amounts of overhead were now charged to larger purchases, and the air force paid the same total overhead bill as it would have under the old accounting method. As the following points illustrate, few real reforms actually to lower weapon prices have been implemented:

1. Only 10 percent of items with costs between $1,000 and $5,000 are individually priced. The rest have prices that are accepted as proposed by the defense contractors. Prices are deemed reasonable if they conform to prices charged in the past.[25] Thus, an overcharge in the past leads to an overcharge in the future.
2. Separate services often purchase the same item from the same contractor on different contracts and without conferring with one another to see if a better deal is possible.[26] Since 1984, the uniformed services have been directed by the Department of Defense to begin cooperating on this type of purchase.[27]
3. Defense auditors have fallen so far behind in their jobs that in 1985 auditors in some plants were still working on 1979 contracts.[28]
4. Audits are often waived entirely, and government contracting agents rely instead on data furnished by the contractor about the fairness and reasonableness of proposed prices.[29]
5. Job ratings of the people in charge of buying spare parts have been based on the speed of delivery, not on considerations of economy.[30]
6. Although "cost plus" (a percentage of the estimated cost granted as profit) contracts are being phased out, virtually any expense for production or overhead that the contractor can justify is still

reimbursed by the U.S. government. Although many defense contracts are now fixed-price contracts, these are often rewritten to accommodate "engineering changes" in a way that allows cost increases to occur as in earlier contract types.[31] In addition, contractors are often given several chances to reprice spare parts to recoup any increases in their own expenses.[32]

7. The Department of Defense has a poor record of estimating a cost for new weapons. Franklin C. Spinney, a Defense Department analyst, found that the Pentagon had underestimated the true cost of new weapons for the past thirty years, and he estimated that the cost of the defense buildup of the 1980s may have been underestimated by 30 percent.[33] In another study, the GAO found that the Department of Defense has had a chronic problem of underestimating weapon costs over the past twenty years and that actual spending on ninety-seven weapons over the period 1963 to 1983 increased by an average of 32 percent.[34]

8. Defense contractors who sell spare parts are often hired to tell the military services which spare parts are already in military warehouses and which must be purchased. These reports have often been inaccurate.[35]

Suggestions for Improvement

If real reforms were to be enacted to deal with the high price of weapons, what type of actions should be taken? The suggestions that have been made in this area are few in number and hard to implement:

1. Freeze or cut the defense budget to force the Department of Defense to begin to allocate resources in a more businesslike manner.
2. Close the "revolving door" that makes the relationship between the defense industry and the Department of Defense so incestuous.
3. Get the uniformed services out of the military acquisition business (as a number of foreign countries have done).
4. Force the Department of Defense to permit real competition for defense contracts—this implies that noncompetitive industries would be allowed to fail.
5. Apply meaningful work measurement standards to the tasks performed by the defense industries.
6. Exercise strict control over changes in design of weapons.
7. Make every effort to enhance program stability and to avoid large fluctuations in defense spending.[36]

Figure 9.3: Development, Production, and Maintenance Cost as a Percent of Procurement Expenditures

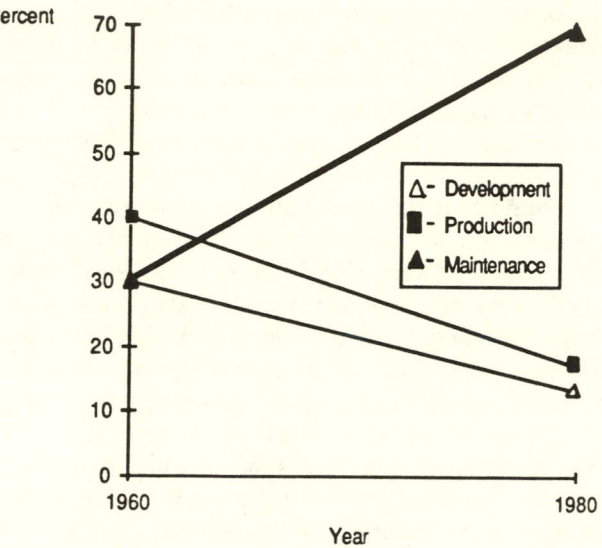

Year

Source: Department of Defense Survey in Biddle, Wayne, "Pushing for Weapons that Work," *New York Times,* July 8, 1984, p. 4F.

DEPARTMENT OF DEFENSE ACTIONS TO LOWER COSTS

Reliability

There is little similarity between the suggestions just listed and actual attempts made by the U.S. government to control defense costs. Government efforts have centered on the problems of weapon system reliability and the tendency of contractors to bill the government for unauthorized expenditures.

Concerning reliability problems, General James P. Mullins, commander of the Air Force Logistics Command, estimated that the quality of the systems the air force bought was so bad that 20 percent of its budget went to repair these weapons. Mullins claimed that over a period of thirty years, these repairs would cost the air force $1.238 trillion.[37] Figure 9.3 shows how maintenance costs have risen from 30 percent to 70 percent of the procurement budget over the twenty-year period from 1960 to 1980. This comparison also makes it clear why concern about the prices charged for spare parts has grown.

Complaints about weapon quality caused increasing demands for warranties on new weapons. In November 1983, Senator Mark Andrews (R–N.Dak.) sponsored a bill requiring that any manufacturer whose weapon failed to meet government performance standards "bear the cost of all work promptly to repair or replace" the defective items.[38] The Department of Defense, which had been forced to accept the warranty law, immediately tried to repeal the provision by inserting language in the 1984 supplemental appropriations bill (and by hiding this repeal provision under the "military construction" budget category, which is governed by friendlier committees in the House and Senate). This attempt failed, but the Pentagon later succeeded in pushing through loopholes to the warranty bill exempting the bulk of defense purchases from warranty requirements.[39] The Department of Defense defended these actions by citing concerns that a warranty requirement would drive up the cost of weapons and stifle innovation. However, because full warranty provisions have been included in contracts for the most advanced communication satellites, for air defense systems purchased by NATO, and for NASA space shuttle orbiters,[40] these concerns appear to have dubious merit.

Overhead Billing

After revelations of improper billing for overhead expenses by several of the nation's largest defense contractors, Secretary of Defense Weinberger announced on March 5, 1985, that no overhead claims would be paid to any Department of Defense contractor unless a high company official certified under penalty of perjury that the claims were legitimate. This ruling raised a storm of protest among defense contractors who initially refused to provide such assurance and who threatened to contest the ruling in court. These industry officials argued that the Weinberger rule required that all overhead expenses directly benefit the government and relate specifically to the contract in question and that most overhead costs were general and could not be specifically allocated to individual contracts.[41]

The ink on the Weinberger pronouncement was not yet dry before Defense Department officials started to modify it. On April 4, 1985, the Defense Department general counsel ruled that the requirement did not alter the contractor's right to pass indirect costs of doing business (such as shareholder's meetings, insurance, and legal expenses) on to the government. On April 5, 1985, the deputy undersecretary for acquisition management ruled that a certification of legitimacy was not required if the Department of Defense had previously agreed to a billing rate for indirect costs.[42] And finally, on April 16, 1985, the Department of Defense issued new rules stating that a contractor must certify claims

only after the end of a fiscal year and only after it has gotten advance payments for nearly all overhead expenses.[43] Thus, the original intent of the ruling has been completely subverted, and any improvement that might come from its implementation is likely to be minimal.

CONCLUSIONS

Chapters 8 and 9 portray a number of serious flaws in the defense establishment. For several reasons, the current military personnel system, which is designed around the all-volunteer force, is in trouble. It is unlikely that the all-volunteer force will last, and its demise will be hastened both by the rapidly shrinking size of the cohort and by any extended period of low unemployment. Plans must be made now to lay the groundwork for the system to replace the all-volunteer force—a system that will have to balance desires to avoid using the draft with the need for sufficient people to fill the armed forces. A short draft to fill the reserves may be necessary, and retention of those people already in the military will become of even greater importance than it is today. This implies fundamental changes in the way the military manages its people as well as changes in incentive systems like retirement, which appear to drive good people out of the military.

The defense procurement and acquisition process is also in trouble. In partial recognition of this, the U.S. Senate approved a resolution on May 22, 1985, establishing a bipartisan commission to look at the whole area of defense procurement. This was followed almost immediately by the designation of a bipartisan presidential commission (the Packard Commission), which dealt with the same subject and which issued its report in 1986. Although the report of the Packard Commission does a good job of discussing the "surface" problems associated with military acquisition, it does not address the fundamental issues causing most of these problems.

Unfortunately, the bipartisan nature of government commissions (and of Congress itself) is better suited to making marginal changes than major reforms. It is therefore likely that the problems in defense procurement have become so serious that they cannot be handled by normal government processes. As is the case in the area of military personnel, major structural changes to the defense procurement system must also be made. If these changes are not made and if necessary reforms are not made in the way the military gets and retains its people, the processes described in this chapter and the preceding one could cripple the U.S. defense effort.

NOTES

Epigraphs: Franklin quoted in Miller, Nathan, "Profiteers and Patriots," *Baltimore Sun,* October 30, 1984, p. 9; both Orr and Lewis quoted in "Quotelines," *USA Today,* April 3, 1985, p. 6.

1. Binkin, Martin, *America's Volunteer Military: Progress and Prospects,* Brookings Institution, Washington, D.C., 1984, pp. 1–63.

2. *Additional Cost of the All-Volunteer Force,* Report to Congress by the Comptroller General of the United States, FPCD-78-11, February 6, 1978, p. ii.

3. Weinberger, Caspar W., "Remarks Before the USO Man of the Year Award Dinner," San Francisco, November 8, 1984.

4. Keller, Bill, "Now It's Not Just 'I want You' but 'You Need Us'," *New York Times,* January 19, 1985, p. 5.

5. Thurston, Scott, "Army Falls Short of Enlistment Goal," *Atlanta Constitution,* November 1, 1984, p. 1.

6. Andrews, Walter, "Drop in Top Recruits Worries Army Brass," *Washington Times,* November 14, 1984, p. 1.

7. Brosman, James W., "Guard on the Front Line of Defense-Cost Fight," *Memphis Commercial Appeal,* February 15, 1984, p. 1.

8. Warner, John W., "Economy Forces Need to Increase Ratio of Reserves to Regulars," *ROA National Security Report,* January 1984, p. 7.

9. Ibid., p. 18.

10. Kelly, Orr, "GI Pensions—Justified or 'An Outrage'," *U.S. News and World Report,* February 18, 1985, p. 36.

11. Military retirement at this time would yield an annual income of about $20,000 for an officer. This rate is calculated at 50 percent of "base" pay, but because military members are paid out of so many different categories, this translates to about 35 percent of gross pay.

12. Vartabedian, Ralph, "B-1 Crash Debate Centers on Possible Design Flaws," *Los Angeles Times,* December 22, 1984, p. 1.

13. For example, see Perry, William J., and Roberts, Cynthia A., "Winning Through Sophistication: How to Meet the Soviet Military Challenge," *Technology Review,* July 1982, pp. 27–35.

14. Conine, Ernest, "Weapons: Quality vs. Quantity," *Los Angeles Times,* August 8, 1983, p. 5B.

15. Houseman, Damian, "The Sirens of Military Reform," *Washington Times,* November 14, 1983, p. 1C.

16. Fossedal, Gregory A., "Reforming the Military Reform Push," *Wall Street Journal,* March 1, 1984, p. 28.

17. Brown, Michael E., "The Strategic Bomber Debate Today," *Orbis* 28, no. 2, Summer 1984, pp. 386–387.

18. Based on a quote from an air force engineer at an Inflation Adjustment Clause symposium held at Wright-Patterson Air Force Base in 1976. The economic ramifications of the search for such a weapon were never discussed.

19. "Defense Firms Cry Fair Play," *Gazette Telegraph,* September 24, 1985, p. A5.

20. "Arms Builders Told Gap in Trust Harms Security," *Gazette Telegraph*, September 27, 1985, p. A11.

21. Andrews, Walter, "Half of Military Parts Overpriced, U.S. Finds," *Washington Times*, September 27, 1984, p. 1.

22. "Why G.E. Became a Pickpocket," *New York Times*, May 16, 1985, Editorial page.

23. "Pentagon Anti-fraud Unit Overmatched, Chief Says," *Gazette Telegraph*, October 2, 1985, p. A4.

24. Kaplan, Fred, "Air Force Answer to High Prices: Hide the Payments," *Boston Globe*, July 6, 1984, p. 31.

25. Ibid.

26. From a March 21, 1985, report by the Defense Department's assistant inspector general, John W. Melchner, and reported in Hiatt, Fred, "Excess Profits: Pentagon's Fault," *Washington Post*, April 21, 1985, p. K5.

27. Seib, Gerald F., "Military Services Ordered to Start Buying Parts Jointly in Big Lots in Wake of Audit," *Wall Street Journal*, June 4, 1984, p. 6.

28. Hiatt, "Excess Profits," p. K5.

29. Ibid.

30. Mohr, Charles, "Critics See Key Flaws in Arms Cost Controls," *New York Times*, May 18, 1985, p. 1.

31. Ibid.

32. Kelly, Orr, "Why Pentagon Pays $44 For a Light Bulb," *U.S. News and World Report*, August 1, 1983, p. 29.

33. Wood, David, "Weapons Cost Estimate Cited As 30% Too Low," *Los Angeles Times*, February 26, 1983, p. 12.

34. Ullman, Owen, "Report Says Pentagon Underestimates Its Costs," *Philadelphia Inquirer*, March 13, 1984, p. 1.

35. Kelly, "Why Pentagon Pays $44," p. 29.

36. Mohr, "Critics See Key Flaws," p. 1.

37. Royce, Knut, "Weapon System Repair Will Cost '$1 Trillion'," *Albany Times-Union*, May 4, 1984, p. 1.

38. "Defense's Sneak Attack on a Warranty Law," *Business Week*, February 20, 1984, p. 30.

39. Carrington, Tim, "Pentagon Frustrates Reform Efforts," *Wall Street Journal*, December 26, 1984, p. 30.

40. Ibid.

41. Carrington, Tim, "Pentagon Softens Rule That Contractors Must Certify Overhead Billings As Proper," *Wall Street Journal*, April 17, 1985, p. 29.

42. Kurtz, Howard, "Pentagon To Change New Rules," *Washington Post*, April 18, 1985, p. 7.

43. Fitzgerald, John, "Pentagon Dilutes Major Reform," *Hartford Courant*, April 17, 1985, p. 1.

10
International Determinants of Defense Costs

Future historians will scratch their heads when asked to contemplate the fact that the United States, with fewer people and less government spending than Western Europe, nevertheless provides most of Europe's nuclear protection, a large chunk of its non-nuclear defenses, and almost all of the men, ships and aircraft which guard the Gulf oil that European industry depends on while Europe provides no reciprocal service for the United States.

—*Economist*, **1984**

Arms sales are foreign policy writ large.

—**Andrew J. Pierre, 1984**

Trade offsets are a key element in the sale of U.S. weapons systems abroad and recent data compiled by the U.S. Department of Defense indicate that around $30 Billion in potential sales of defense equipment is expected to involve offsets for the five-year period from 1983–1988.

—*Defense and Foreign Affairs Daily*, **1984**

INTRODUCTION

The cost of defending the United States is determined by a number of factors that originate outside the borders of this country. Although there is not sufficient space to consider these factors in detail, this chapter presents an overview of several of the most important foreign determinants of U.S. defense costs. One of these, burden sharing, directly affects U.S. defense spending by determining the amount the United States spends on its alliance commitments. Other programs mentioned in this chapter indirectly affect defense costs by determining the costs of transferring arms and aiding our allies. In each case, the program discussed has the potential to lower U.S. defense costs—if it works as planned.

Table 10.1
1984 NATO Troop Strength and Budgets

Country	NATO-Related Troops	NATO Budget (Billions of US$)	Troops/$1000 of Budget
United States	1,238,300	158.6	.0078
Belgium	93,607	1.8	.050
Britain	325,000	23.8	.014
Canada	82,858	6.7	.012
Denmark	31,400	1.2	.026
France	471,350	16.8	.028
West Germany	495,000	17.4	.028
Greece	178,000	2.3	.077
Italy	375,000	8.1	.046
Luxembourg	720	.41.0	.020
Netherlands	103,267	4.2	.024
Norway	36,785	1.7	.022
Portugal	63,500	.547.1	.12
Spain	330,000	3.3	.10
Turkey	602,000	1.6	.38
Iceland	0	Bases only	.00

Source: 1984–1985 Report on World Arms Expenditures, International Institute
for Strategic Studies, London, 1985.

BURDEN SHARING

"Burden sharing" is the generic term for sharing the cost of defending ourselves and our allies from aggression. Most of this defense involves NATO's role in Europe, but burden-sharing issues can arise any time the United States and another country unite against a common threat.

Central to the burden-sharing debate is the view that the U.S. defense budget subsidizes the defense costs of other nations, but one's opinion as to whether the United States bears an unequal burden in defending the free world depends on one's view of defense. It is difficult to measure the effect on the outcome of future military action of differences among countries such as geographic location, amount of industrialization, skill level of the citizens, historical perspective, potential level of contribution not linked to defense spending (ports, roads, rail facilities) and other similar indicators. The difficulty occurs because spending for defense measures input, not output, and can be regarded only as a sign of commitment, not capability. As an example, the figures in Table 10.1 give NATO troop strength and budget figures.

U.S. troop strength in NATO proper was 327,000 in 1984,[1] but Table 10.1 assumes that the total number of troops in the U.S. armed forces committed to the NATO mission is roughly equal to the amount of budget committed—58 percent.[2] Even so, these figures demonstrate that troop strength is inversely proportional to the wealth of NATO countries. Poor countries, like Turkey, Spain, and Portugal, provide soldiers in place of dollars. Richer nations provide more dollars, more technology, and fewer troops. The United States, the richest and the most tech-

nologically advanced of the NATO members, provides the smallest number of troops per dollar and the greatest number of dollars. Should other factors, such as quality of forces or mission be considered? Of course. And this is precisely the reason that considering spending figures alone is meaningless.

In fact, defense spending trends in both Europe and the United States were almost identical until 1981. Why NATO spending stagnated after 1980, in an era of increasing U.S. defense budgets, can be explained in the context of the economic climate in 1981 through 1983. The onset of the global recession in 1981 provided the United States and the NATO European nations with a difficult choice: Should shrinking resources be allocated to social or defense programs? The Reagan administration had a substantial election mandate to allocate resources to defense, and it proceeded to do so. Other NATO members had received no such mandate and, in addition, were more affected by the recession. When the United States pressed the Europeans for defense spending increases to match those in the United States, the result, as expressed by a senior official in the West German defense department, was a feeling that: "We can't be lectured on how to reduce social expenditures in favor of defense spending. We have to win our own elections and maintain social stability. We don't tell the U.S. what's good for Oregon, and they shouldn't tell us what's good for us."[3] Thus, in response to internal pressures, the European NATO members lowered their defense spending increases to roughly 1.5 percent and are forecast to maintain that level through the decade.[4] And although there is little support for the contention that the United States carried more than its share of the NATO burden prior to 1981, the balance may now be changing.

Japanese burden sharing differs from the NATO case in its emphasis on economic factors. At issue is whether Japan has spent enough for self-defense and whether, because the United States has provided most of Japan's protection, Japan's economic development has been greater than it would have been. NATO Europeans are criticized for spending too much for social programs, but the Japanese are criticized for spending too much on capital investment and economic growth and not enough on defense.

The Japanese burden-sharing argument is based on the feeling that if Japan had shouldered an equitable defense burden of 6 percent or more over the past decade, its GNP would be 30 percent lower than today's figure.[5] At the current $12–$15 billion level of spending, Japan will be able to fund only about half of the force improvements called for in its own five-year defense plan. Even full funding of that plan would leave Japan dependent on U.S. naval and air protection in a major crisis. In fact, for Japan actually to assume responsibility for its

own air and naval defense, it would have to spend an average of $25 billion annually for the foreseeable future.[6]

Japan can afford this level of defense spending. With the second largest Western-style economy,[7] it ranks fifth in defense spending in the NATO-Japanese alliance and eighth worldwide. Even when compared with neutral nations, Japan's effort is still very low. Both Sweden and Switzerland spend between 2 and 3 percent of their GNP on defense. Japan spends about 1 percent.[8]

Defense Costs and Burden Sharing

Both Europe's emphasis on social spending at the expense of defense and the subsidization of Japan's economy with U.S. defense funds make burden sharing a potent political issue. In economic terms, this is a cost-benefit question. Does the United States get more from supporting the alliances it has established than it would get by walking out? It is doubtful that the United States can apply much more pressure to NATO than it has in the recent past. It is also doubtful that Japan will respond any more fully to U.S. desires than it already has. If the United States is willing, it can maintain a rough approximation of the status quo with the realization that, in so doing, it may carry more than its share of the defense of NATO and Japan. Or the United States could withdraw and spend its money elsewhere. Such an act presumes that more defense could be purchased elsewhere than is currently provided by NATO and Japan with unequal burden sharing. Because the downside risk of such a move is very high, it is reasonable to assume that the burden-sharing problem will remain unchanged in the future.

DEFENSE COSTS
AND THE INTERNATIONAL ARMS TRADE

Resources are distributed unevenly throughout the world. Some countries have more productive land or labor or capital than others, so it pays for them to specialize in the products that take advantage of their most productive resources. Each nation can specialize according to comparative advantage and trade with other nations for the goods and services that it finds more costly to produce. With specialization and trade, the global amounts of goods and services are greater than if each nation tried to be self-sufficient.

Thus, international trade is based on the law of comparative advantage: Each nation should produce the goods and services that its resources and technologies enable it to produce better and cheaper than other nations. Each nation then trades these products for goods and services that it finds more costly to produce.

For example, the United States currently has a comparative advantage in military aerospace products. In 1983, military aerospace exports included $1.8 billion in deliveries of complete aircraft, $172 million in aircraft engines, $2.5 billion in aircraft and engine parts, and $994 million in guided missiles and rockets. Fighter bombers provided the largest category of complete military aircraft exports. In 1983, the U.S. aerospace industry delivered ninety-three such aircraft valued at $1.4 billion.[9]

International trade in arms, like all foreign trade, affects a nation's income and employment. But this is not the primary reason that such trade is cultivated by arms producers. The main reason that exports of arms are necessary is that no nation except the United States and the Soviet Union has enough demand for arms to permit efficient production runs, and even these two producers find that exports are essential to make most weapons affordable. For this reason, a decision by a country to build an arms industry is (with the possible exception of Japan) also a decision to export arms.

The economic rationale for this position is easy to follow: If the U.S. Department of Defense decides to buy more weapons from abroad than from domestic producers, the U.S. defense industry will earn less income. As a result, it may reduce its research and development and lay off workers, making itself less competitive in the future. In contrast, exports of weapons result in a flow of income that will increase the health of defense industries. If Europeans buy fewer of their own weapons and more U.S. weapons, this fact will have implications for both the short-term health and the long-term viability of U.S. industries.

Domestic economic benefits associated with the arms-export business include lengthening weapon system production runs, which reduces per unit costs for weapons and increases the ability of firms to recoup expenses for research and development. Arms exports also increase the development and maintenance of technological expertise in weapons production and help maintain viable domestic arms industries. Studies by the Congressional Budget Office indicate that domestic economic benefits derived from selling arms abroad, when combined with contracts for services and construction, reduce the actual cost of arms procurement by approximately 7 percent. Assuming a $10 billion foreign sales program, the savings would be about $700 million a year, or 0.2 percent of current defense outlays. Also, Department of Labor estimates suggest that arms sales of $10 billion would generate about 450,000 jobs in the United States.[10]

France and the United Kingdom, with their large defense industries and relatively small military organizations, are often thought to be the nations most dependent on arms exports. However, by some measures

Table 10.2
World Arms Trade, 1970-1982

Year/Nation	Exports as a Percent of GNP	Total Exports (Millions of Dollars)	Military Exports as a percent of Total Exports	Military Exports as a Percent of Total World Military Exports
1970				
United States	4.4	42,700	7.2	53.3
United Kingdom	20.0	1,935	0.4	1.4
France	14.0	1,810	1.1	3.4
Soviet Union	0.4	1,280	12.0	26.1
1975				
United States	7.2	107,600	6.9	38.0
United Kingdom	14.2	4,527	18.0	4.2
France	16.1	3,031	35.8	5.5
Soviet Union	0.7	1,835	33.8	32.0
1980				
United States	8.2	222,600	3.2	23.2
United Kingdom	27.3	12,694	15.8	6.4
France	14.3	7,490	39.4	9.6
Soviet Union	0.1	1,513	72.2	35.7
1983				
United States	6.7	212,300	4.2	26.0
United Kingdom	20.0	10,645	17.8	5.5
France	11.7	7,110	50.6	8.8
Soviet Union	0.2	2,587	39.7	29.9

Source: Statistical Abstract of the United States, 1985, U.S. Government
Printing Office, Washington, D.C., 1985.

they are less dependent than the Soviet Union whose ratio of military to civilian exports was higher in 1970 and 1980 than in any of the other major arms-exporting countries. Table 10.2 shows the division of total arms exports among the major suppliers. Note that for France and the Soviet Union, arms exports have become a significant portion of total exports.

In France, the United Kingdom, and the United States, the aerospace industry is highly dependent on military exports. Representatives of the French and British governments have stated that their aerospace industries must export at least half of their output in order to survive. A number of U.S. firms are also dependent on foreign military sales. For example, in 1975, Bell Helicopter derived about 42 percent of its revenue from foreign sales, Northrop, 34 percent, and Grumman, 26 percent. These figures have changed only slightly over the past ten years.[11]

Arms exports are more important than they appear to be in simple economic terms. For example, the British and French view military exports as necessary for the continued viability of their independent defense production facilities. In the United States, major defense exporters employ large numbers of people, making arms sales abroad an important

issue for congressional representatives from certain districts. These factors are unlikely to change over the next two decades and they will continue to provide strong incentives for high levels of arms exports by major supplier nations.

Recent History of Arms Trade

The flow of arms from one country to another has taken place constantly over the last forty years, and the United States introduced lend-lease even earlier. But in that forty years a number of changes have occurred. From 1945 until the late 1950s, the flow was primarily from the United States and the Soviet Union to European nations, and the character of the flow was dominated by the transfer of surplus equipment, much of it of World War II vintage. During the 1960s, the direction of flow started to shift to nonindustrial Third World areas. Roughly 82 percent of all the arms moving from one country to another now go from industrial nations to Third World nations.[12]

Before the early 1960s, U.S. arms transfers were virtually synonymous with U.S. military assistance because the great majority of military equipment was conveyed in grant (gift) form from U.S. government inventories to recipient nations. After the 1960s, there was a shift from surplus and obsolescent arms toward modern, first-line equipment, and arms transfers increasingly involved systems that had entered the inventories of the major arms-producing nations at the time or shortly before they were offered to other recipients. At the same time, financing the acquisition of weapons changed from simple grants of equipment to sales using a variety of cash grants, concessional credit, or loans. And because of the shift toward first-line, high-tech equipment, the arms that were transferred cost more, and the value of the worldwide arms trade increased accordingly.[13]

By the late 1960s, the grant component of U.S. arms transfers had dropped to about half of the amount transferred, and it remained between a half and two-thirds until a decade later when U.S. arms sales became quite substantial (at least in nominal terms) and grant military assitance declined even more substantially.[14] During this period, France, Great Britain, and Italy all became significant suppliers of weapons. To a lesser extent, smaller nations such as Belgium, Israel, Brazil, Austria, and the two Koreas also began to supply arms, primarily to Third World customers. These smaller suppliers became a very significant factor in the world arms trade, and the arms trade became an increasingly important part of their economies.

The U.S. government believes that arms transfers contribute to foreign policy objectives in a number of important ways. Arms transfers that

strengthen key allies and friends act as building blocks for larger strategic interests of the United States. They help friendly countries cope with internal conflicts or with external threats, and they create an additional force multiplier by increasing standardization and shared military doctrine with the United States. This allows the United States to direct its attention to other, more pressing international security issues without spreading its own forces too thin.[15]

These programs also assist the U.S. ability to project power by facilitating the acquisition and retention of military facilities abroad.[16] In other words, arms transfers are often the payment demanded by countries possessing, by reason of geography or politics, valuable real estate on which the United States would like to have or keep bases. In this role, arms transfers may deviate from some of the objectives in the preceding paragraph. When another country has leverage over the United States by virtue of basing locations (for example, the Philippines, Portugal, Turkey, or Pakistan), the number of arms transferred to that country may correspond only to broader objectives of U.S. strategy.

Over the past thirty years, U.S. arms sales have shifted in response to developments abroad, but two regions of the world have dominated— Europe and the Middle East. Countries in these regions have accounted for perhaps $130 billion, or almost 80 percent of U.S. arms sales, during this period. Asia and the Far East account for another 12 percent. Africa and Latin America, taken together, account for only about $4 billion or about 2.4 percent of the total. Saudi Arabia has been the largest single U.S. customer, buying about $50 billion since 1950, but of that amount some $20 billion is for construction work. Israel is the second largest U.S. customer with approximately $13 billion in arms sales, followed by Iran with about $12 billion (which occurred prior to the overthrow of the Shah). The United Kingdom and the Federal Republic of Germany, NATO allies, have roughly $9 billion in sales agreements each.[17]

Future international arms sales will be severely constrained by the economic condition of the Third World. Concurrently, many factors are also causing the number of arms sellers to increase. The result will inevitably be a major shakeout in the arms market. It is not clear that the large exporters like the United States will come out on top in this process. The rigid, European scenario–determined arms design of the United States, as well as the use of levels of technology far beyond the requirements of Third World customers, may make the United States relatively noncompetitive. The United States does have one major factor on its side: the ability to offer loans and other assistance money to buy its weapons. If this funding ceases, small arms sellers could gain a much larger share of the Third World market.

PAYING FOR WEAPONS: OFFSETS

Structural changes that occurred in the world economy after the late 1970s made it more difficult for many countries to generate the foreign exchange required for major purchases. The expense of new weapon systems and the fact that these systems do not generate future revenues to pay for themselves meant the arms market was hit particularly hard by the economic development. In response, world trade turned increasingly toward countertrade—barter-type transactions resulting in payments to the seller in forms other than cash. Military countertrade is called "offsets."

Offsets are the requirement to purchase products from, or provide other economic incentives to, a country as part of the sale of military or large capital items. Offsets can include:

1. Coproduction or licensed production: producing part of the weapon system in the purchasing country;
2. Buy back: selling back to the Department of Defense or to a defense contractor parts produced in the purchasing country through coproduction or licensing; also called a direct offset because the purchasing country trades back parts to be used in the production of the weapon being purchased;
3. Indirect offset: requiring the U.S. seller to buy or market other products of the purchasing nation not related to the weapon being purchased;
4. Investment: requiring the U.S. seller to invest in, or transfer technology to, the purchasing nation.

Many foreign governments now require offsets of a specified value on each purchase. (For example, Australia required 30 percent of the value of each of its purchases of foreign-produced military goods to be offset by the seller and has recently raised this level to 40 percent. Canada requires 100 percent of the value to be offset.) U.S. concerns about this trend toward increasing offsets center around the following areas:

1. In international trade, offsets can mean a job loss for the United States as arms markets are reoriented due to competition based on offsets instead of on weapon quality and due to trade distortion as new imports are developed to satisfy indirect offsets.

2. If some aspect of offsets is harmful to a specific U.S. industry or to an entire sector of the economy, the U.S. government is not well organized to handle the problem in a coordinated manner. The departments of defense and commerce both try to regulate technology

transfer, the State Department controls licensing and arms export, and the DoD and Congress both control offset use in foreign military sales. However, no one controls the use of everyday offsets in sales agreements.

3. This problem is further complicated by the perspective on offsets maintained by the purchasing countries. Weapons have become so expensive that the major factors in a purchase are now, in order of importance, politics (the purchase may help solve domestic problems or strengthen international alliances), economics (the purchase may solve trade, technology, or employment problems), and, of least importance, the weapon system itself.

The use of offsets is a major element of U.S. policy to improve reliability, sustainability, and "interoperability" of U.S. and allied forces. Cooperative weapon construction programs give alliance members the necessary defense base to provide an equitable share of the alliance defense. As a result, most offsets occur in the NATO region. Concurrent with this, the United States has a policy of requiring production capability for any weapon system it purchases overseas. This is essentially a policy requiring 100 percent offset from its allies to keep the U.S. industrial base capable of supporting all U.S. weapons. The offset policies of U.S. allies have generally been less demanding than this, but the two-way flow of trade stemming in part from these offsets has built a base in foreign nations that is often capable of sustaining the projection of U.S. power.

These benefits must be balanced against the economic consequences of offset deals and against potential industrial base erosion arising from offsets. Although the U.S. government has been careful to monitor the health of the defense industrial base, in 1978 the government decided to leave the economic consequences of offsets in the hands of private enterprise. The major negative effect of this decision may be the loss of subcontractor work through the granting of offsets for overseas production. However, this potential loss must be weighed against the benefits of being able to sell the weapon in the first place (usually not possible without offsets) and against the alliance and foreign policy objectives that offsets fulfill. These latter factors have the potential to lower substantially defense costs.

SECURITY ASSISTANCE: MILITARY AID

The Security Assistance Program has as its purpose the support of foreign governments so that they can fight their own battles without direct U.S. military intervention. However, in 1969 the United States began to substitute loans for grants in security assistance for two reasons. First, the United States was involved in an unpopular war in Vietnam

that was clearly related in the minds of the public to the military assistance program.[18] This relationship hampered later grant assistance funding for all countries and caused the military assistance program to resort increasingly to loans to get required funds.

A second important reason was also related to the Vietnam War. Because of its unpopularity, funding for this war was not allowed to compete with that for social programs. Instead, the government elected to fund both the war and the other programs at levels that revenues could not sustain. The result was increasing inflation, followed by a growing budget deficit—a deficit that was enlarged any time grant or concessional loan funds were used.

One way to appear to reduce government spending (and the deficit) was to use "off-budget" money[19] for security assistance. Therefore, Federal Financing Bank (FFB) funds were lent to most security assistance recipients, and the number of nonconcessional loans expanded. The use of grant funds dropped again after 1973, and the use of loans continued to grow while the effect on the recipients was magnified by a rapid rise in interest rates.[20]

The use of nonconcessional loans was justified in two ways. First, it was thought that the United States could ensure a more responsible approach to weapons acquisition if arms were not "given away" with grants but rather, were "sold" with loans. And second, the 1969 Peterson Commission[21] and others, projecting from early evidence of the encouraging growth rates among the LDCs, actually thought that LDCs would be able to afford the loans and that this would lessen the burden of assistance on the United States.

That these forecasts were wrong is, by now, obvious to all. In addition, the cost of individual weapons has increased greatly over the past few years, resulting in larger loans during a period of rising interest rates— which had to be paid by financially weakened countries. Because off-budget loan allocations are not subject to stringent budgetary restrictions and because countries tend to procure weapons based on perceived needs, not financing, the switch to loans has had no apparent effect on the numbers of arms transferred to the LDCs. As the Commission on Security and Economic Assistance noted in 1983: "Congressional views [were] that limited resources were being diverted to less productive uses and that cost-of-money loans would thus encourage developing nations to reflect more carefully on the real economic costs associated with their defense expenditures. This expectation, however, was not fulfilled."[22]

A number of factors have combined to make the current U.S. security assistance program very different from what it was originally envisioned to be. The current system is structurally unable to design and deliver weapons geared specifically to the needs of the less developed countries.

It has turned many of the most important allies of the United States into debtor nations whose stability is now as threatened by economic problems as it was by the political threat the military assistance sought to counter. And it has become a political grab bag that allocates funds based on the strength of special interest groups instead of on a basis of national need. As a result, the security assistance program serves neither the United States nor its allies very well.

CONCLUSIONS

There are a number of reasons that nations should seek to combine defense efforts. If combined efforts were always possible and successful, the result would be to lower the cost of defense for everyone. But defense, by its very nature, is so political that without the motivation of an active war, full cooperation between any allies is difficult to maintain. In addition, the chance to gain economically through arms sales and the ability to gain politically by shifting defense burdens to another nation create temptations that can not only weaken the economy of the nation assuming the larger defense burden, but that also destroy the trust necessary to make an alliance function. The programs and policies described in this chapter could lead to lower defense costs for the United States, but this outcome is not guaranteed.

NOTES

Epigraphs: Economist, May 18, 1984, quoted in Roth, William V., "Sharing the Burden of European Defenses," *Christian Science Monitor*, December 3, 1984, p. 38; Pierre, quoted in Lewis, Paul, "The Third World Limits Its Arsenals," *New York Times*, March 18, 1984, p. 4F; "U.S.: FMS Trade Offsets Process Considered," *Defense and Foreign Affairs Daily* 13, no. 83, May 2, 1984, p. 1.

1. *Worldwide Manpower Distribution by Geographical Area*, Washington Headquarters Service, Department of Defense, September 30, 1984, p. 4.

2. Total U.S. spending has been used because: (1) research comparable to the 1984 GAO study on the number of U.S. forces committed to NATO does not exist for prior years; (2) the trend will be identical for any constant percent of the total budget; and (3) the total U.S. budget figure is the one cited in the political arguments on this subject.

3. Thurow, Roger, "NATO's Economic Bind Restricts Its Defense Options," *Wall Street Journal*, June 5, 1984, p. 38.

4. Ibid.

5. Adelman, Kenneth L., "Japan's Security Dilemma: An American View," *Survival*, March/April 1981, pp. 72–73.

6. Cordesman, Anthony H., "Japanese Defense: The Election Means Long-Term Dependence on the U.S.," *Armed Forces Journal International*, March 1984, pp. 17–18.

7. At 1980 dollars and exchange rates, the U.S. GDP was $2,998.8 billion, Japan's GDP was $1,273.3 billion, and Germany had the next largest economy with $858.4 billion. The Soviet Union's GDP, although uncertain, is reputed to be about 55 percent of the U.S. figure, or about $1,650 billion.

8. Hempstone, Smith, "Japan's Defense Spending: When Is Enough Enough?," *Washington Times*, March 16, 1984, p. 1C.

9. Total U.S. exports in 1983 amounted to $198 billion. U.S. military aerospace exports therefore amounted to less than 1 percent of total exports. Source: *Statistical Abstract of the United States, 1985*, U.S. Department of Commerce, U.S. Government Printing Office, Washington, D.C., 1985.

10. Capra, James, et al., "The Effect of Foreign Military Sales on the Cost of U.S. Weapons," in *Foreign Military Sales and U.S. Weapons Costs*, Congressional Budget Office, Washington, D.C., May 1976. Also see Cahn, A., Kruzel, J., Dawkins, P., and Huntzinger, J., *Controlling Future Arms Trade*, McGraw-Hill Book Co., New York, 1980.

11. Cahn, et al., *Controlling Future Arms Trade*; also see Standard and Poor's Industry Surveys, *Basic Analysis for the Aerospace Industry*, May 28, 1981.

12. Blaker, James R., "Statement Before the Subcommittee on Foreign Operations," Committee on Appropriations, U.S. House of Representatives, March 28, 1985, p. 9.

13. Ibid. p. 10.

14. Schneider, William, "Statement Before the Subcommittee on Foreign Operations," Committee on Appropriations, U.S. House of Representatives, March 28, 1985, pp. 8–9.

15. Blaker, "Statement Before the Subcommittee," pp. 13–14.

16. Ibid. p. 15.

17. Schneider, "Statement Before the Subcommittee," p. 13.

18. For example, see Halstead, Wayne P., et al., *Security Assistance in Peace and War*, Strategic Studies Institute, U.S. Army War College, ACN 83018, Carlisle Barracks, Penn., pp. 11–14.

19. "Off-budget" funds are usually loans where a paper "asset" (promissory note) is received in return. Because this note takes the place of the asset (money), no budget impact is recorded.

20. For an excellent discussion of the many problems this caused, see Shaw, Harry J., "Debts and Dependency," *Foreign Policy*, Spring 1983, p. 105.

21. The Peterson Commission was the Presidential Task Force on International Development established in 1969. Records are available from the Library of Congress.

22. *A Report to the Secretary of State*, The Commission on Economic and Security Assistance, November 1983, p. 22.

Part 3
The Economics of New Strategies

11
Star Wars: The Political Economy of Strategic Defense

Let me share with you a vision of the future which offers hope. It is that we embark on a program to counter the awesome Soviet missile threat with measures that are defensive. Let us turn to the very strengths in technology that spawned our great industrial base and that have given us the quality of life we have today.

—President Reagan

INTRODUCTION

President Reagan's March 23, 1983, speech was the beginning of an effort to explore technologies that may contribute to a U.S. ballistic missile defense. This new effort, called the "Strategic Defense Initiative" (SDI), may generate new and unique defense concepts, architectures, and systems. If implemented, a ballistic missile defense will substantially alter current U.S. strategic war-fighting capabilities. Although revolutionary strategic systems have been introduced in the past, a ballistic missile defense would be much more expensive than the strategic systems that have preceded it. There are at least three reasons for this: (1) Much of a ballistic missile defense system would have to be deployed in space. (2) The development of such a system pushes the state of the art of many technologies more than ever before. (3) Such a system would be an addition to the existing defense structure. In the near term, it would not replace existing strategic offensive systems.

The debate over whether to proceed with a ballistic missile defense leads to consideration of the future. In brief, the problem is as follows: Given the resource allocations that currently exist for defense, what will happen if, in addition, the United States develops and implements a

totally new system—a system that will compete vigorously with existing defense and nondefense programs for resources.

We begin our discussion of a ballistic missile defense with a summary of the evolution of U.S. strategy since World War II. We continue with a discussion of research and development programs that are being managed by the newly created Strategic Defense Initiative Office (SDIO). Also, we briefly discuss certain economic issues associated with the strategic defense budget. Finally, we outline a possible transition from a reliance on nuclear offense for deterrence to a reliance on strategic defense.[1]

EVOLUTION OF U.S. STRATEGY

Although deterrence has been the objective of nuclear strategy for the past forty years, the strategy itself has undergone considerable evolution. Our discussion does not trace the path of this evolution in detail, but rather it presents two landmarks along the way. First, it presents the strategy of Mutual Assured Destruction (MAD) because many people believe that MAD is U.S. strategy and because MAD gave birth to the ABM treaty. Next, we discuss the current declaratory strategy, that is, the countervailing strategy of the Carter administration as modified by the Reagan administration.

Mutual Assured Destruction, the declaratory policy of the Kennedy and the Johnson administrations, stated that U.S. nuclear weapons should be ready "at any time before, during, or after a Soviet attack to destroy the Soviet Union as a functioning society."[2] This strategy required only that the United States maintain a force of offensive nuclear weapons that satisfied three conditions: (1) The force must be powerful enough to destroy Soviet urban society. (2) The weapons must be inaccurate enough not to threaten Soviet strategic weapons. (3) The weapons must be invulnerable enough to survive a Soviet attack.[3] If these conditions are satisfied and if the Soviets maintain the same type of force, then proponents of MAD argue that the United States has stable deterrence because both U.S. and Soviet cities are at risk. There is stability in a crisis because neither side can remove the risk by striking first, and there is arms race stability because an offensive nuclear weapons buildup, at least of the inaccurate type, cannot place strategic nuclear forces at risk. This philosophy has been identified with minimum deterrence because, if one believes its tenets, very small forces can achieve stability.[4]

However, MAD is not now and never was the basis of U.S. operational policy. Some counterforce targeting was always present in the Strategic Integrated Operations Plan (SIOP).[5] There are several reasons for this. First, destroying the Soviet civilian population for the purpose of

retribution in the event of deterrence failure would be, for the United States, a psychologically difficult and morally abhorrent thing to do. Therefore, there was always a serious question as to whether a U.S. president would actually take such an action, particulary because it would most assuredly result in massive destruction of U.S. populations on subsequent strikes. Additionally, to be effective, a deterrent force must place at risk the highest valued assets in the adversary nation. It is widely believed that contrary to the U.S. policy, Soviet policy does not place the survival of its civilian population but rather the survival of its military and civilian control functions at the top of its priority list. Finally, and perhaps most importantly, for MAD to work, both players must accept it and design their strategic forces accordingly. The Soviets have never shown any inclination to accept the assumptions inherent in MAD. In fact, they have built a nuclear war-fighting capability that is inconsistent with such a philosophy. Because of these reasons, MAD never became the basis of U.S. operational policy either.

The current U.S. countervailing strategy focuses on the need to deter the Soviet leadership from either limited or all-out nuclear attacks. The strategy is to maintain U.S. nuclear forces and command, control, communications, and intelligence assets able to prevent the Soviets from achieving their objectives at any level of conflict or to inflict costs upon them exceeding any of their anticipated gains. Thus, a countervailing strategy requires U.S. forces capable of fighting effectively at each rung on the escalation ladder and of enduring repeated exchanges over an extended period of time.

The countervailing strategy is based on the view that the most effective way to deter Soviet nuclear aggression is by maintaining escalation dominance and by targeting those assets that the Soviet leadership value most. It puts in jeopardy the Politburo's political and military control, Soviet nuclear and conventional military forces, defense industries, and the lives of Soviet leaders.[6]

Deterrence under this strategy is based on the idea that the defender could inflict an unacceptable level of damage on the attacker and that Soviet leaders would be most deterred by the threat of defeat of their war machine, loss of control at home, and U.S. "decapitation" strikes against Soviet leadership. Thus, even if leaders were willing to sacrifice large numbers of their own people in war, they would still have a political and personal stake in seeing that no conflict occurred.[7]

The United States uses the deployment and threat of its nuclear forces to deter a wide spectrum of conflicts. The current strategy for carrying out these multiple responsibilities is still the countervailing strategy of the Carter administration. In contrast to MAD, which gave the president

an "on-off switch," the countervailing strategy provides the national leadership with a range of responses.

In addition, current strategy is to seek extended deterrence of Soviet–Warsaw Pact aggression in Europe by linking such aggression, whether nuclear or nonnuclear, to U.S. strategic nuclear systems. This linkage is accomplished by stationing U.S. nuclear and nonnuclear forces on the European continent. According to advocates, such deployments provide the capability to blunt aggression and credibility that the United States will defend its allies, making clear the importance that the United States places on Europe.[8] Thus, the countervailing strategy tries to deny the Soviet Union victory in Soviet terms and is based on the premise that the Soviet leadership will not initiate a war it is convinced it cannot win. Instead of placing at risk what is of highest value in the United States, the civilian populace, this strategy places at risk what is of highest value of the Soviet leadership, the survival of the state control mechanisms. It also would deny the Soviets a recovery advantage after a nuclear exchange.

Proponents of the current U.S. nuclear strategy and its forerunners point to forty years of relatively peaceful coexistence between the superpowers as evidence of success. In spite of this and in spite of the more sophisticated basis of the countervailing strategy compared to MAD, the current strategy has been seriously questioned in terms of mechanism, capability, credibility, and stability.

Critics claim that the current strategy implements only one mechanism of deterrence, namely, that of punishment. The threat of offensive retaliation does not necessarily deny the enemy its objectives.[9] Critics also question the credibility of current strategy. Even if a U.S. countervailing strategy could inflict unacceptable damage to the Soviet Union, it neglects the problem of self-deterrence: A U.S. president might have inhibitions about unleashing a major nuclear retaliatory strike because the result would be massive casualties among the Soviet population and because the Soviets might unleash further strikes against the U.S. population. This is a particularly serious problem with respect to deterrence against Soviet adventures in Europe.[10]

Moreover, a countervailing strategy, according to its critics, is hampered by technical limitations on the ability of U.S. warheads to dig out hardened Soviet targets. To be able to do so, the United States would have to spend considerable sums of money for offensive weapons improvements. Such funding levels have not been forthcoming from Congress over the past two administrations.[11]

Further, critics point out that Soviet technical advances make first-strike survival of existing U.S. offensive forces less and less likely. These same technical advances raise the possibility of decapitation strikes

against the U.S. national command authorities and command and control communications networks. Thus, even if the country had sufficient surviving forces, it might be difficult to orchestrate a meaningful retaliatory strike.[12]

Finally, the combination of the Soviet preemptive strike preference with the U.S. countervailing strategy is thought to be crisis unstable. In a crisis situation, there would be considerable pressure for the Soviets to go all out with a first strike in order to catch U.S. forces on the ground. Further, the arms-control failure of the past two decades indicates that the juxtaposition of the U.S. countervailing strategy with the Soviet's counterforce strategy creates an unrelenting pressure for continued arms buildup.[13]

PRESSURES FOR STRATEGIC DEFENSE

Dissatisfaction with current U.S. strategy plus other problems have led to a reemergence of the ballistic missile defense debate after a decade of quiescence. Causes of this reemergence include:

1. Discussion of defenses against tactical missiles in Europe, brought about by the change in Soviet forces in the region, has once again focused attention on the merits of defense—the SS-20 dilemma.
2. Allegations about Soviet transgressions have raised the specter of a Soviet breakout from the ABM treaty. The already layered Soviet air and conventional defenses, coupled with even a thin-area ballistic missile defense, could pose a grave threat to East-West stability.
3. Strategic parity has made policymakers more attentive to opportunities at the strategic margin, where even a limited ballistic missile defense could make a difference.
4. The buildup of a Soviet nuclear war-fighting capability has caused U.S. strategists also to consider nuclear war-fighting concepts. Such concepts call for an offensive-defensive balance and identify important roles for less than perfect defenses.
5. The frustrating search for survivable basing modes for the MX missile and the vulnerability of the current Minuteman force have caused U.S. analysts to reconsider ABM alternatives for providing force survivability.
6. Widespread disenchantment with traditional arms control has brought into question the moral basis of the ABM treaty—a treaty that allows destruction of populations and denies the right of self-defense.

7. A lack of even rudimentary defenses leaves the United States vulnerable to accidental launch, devastation by a mad subcommander, and blackmail, coercion, or widespread destruction at the hands of terrorists.[14]

Pressures for a ballistic missile defense would not have caused an official resurgence of interest in the idea if recent advances in technology had not offered the Unitd States the opportunity to develop such a defense and thereby to strengthen deterrence.

LAUNCHING STRATEGIC DEFENSE PROGRAMS

In response to President Reagan's March 23, 1983, speech, the Department of Defense organized a defensive technologies study team comprised of more than fifty top scientists and engineers to assess all feasible ballistic missile defense technologies and to formulate a research program for the most promising ones. This group, which operated formally under a Department of Defense contract through the Institute for Defense Analysis, was chaired by James C. Fletcher of the University of Pittsburgh. In addition to the Fletcher team, parallel study teams addressed the implication of strategic defense for defense policy, strategy, and arms control. One interagency group of experts was led by Franklin C. Miller, director of Strategic Forces Policy for the assistant secretary of defense for International Security Policy; another team of outside experts was led by Department of Defense consultant Dr. Fred S. Hoffman.[15]

By October 1983, these study teams had developed the foundation for the SDI Program. In particular, the Fletcher team mapped out an initial technology development plan that restructured a large number of research programs already carried on the Department of Defense budget. This permitted the launching of the formal SDI program as a $1 billion effort in fiscal year 1984.

The conclusions of the Fletcher team provided a conceptual framework for the structure of ensuing SDI programs as well as an indication of the direction of current major technology development efforts. These conclusions were as follows:

1. Powerful new technologies are becoming available that justify a major effort to develop the technical options to implement a strategic defense.
2. Focused development of technologies for a comprehensive ballistic missile defense will require strong central management.

Figure 11.1: Phases of a Ballistic Missile Flight

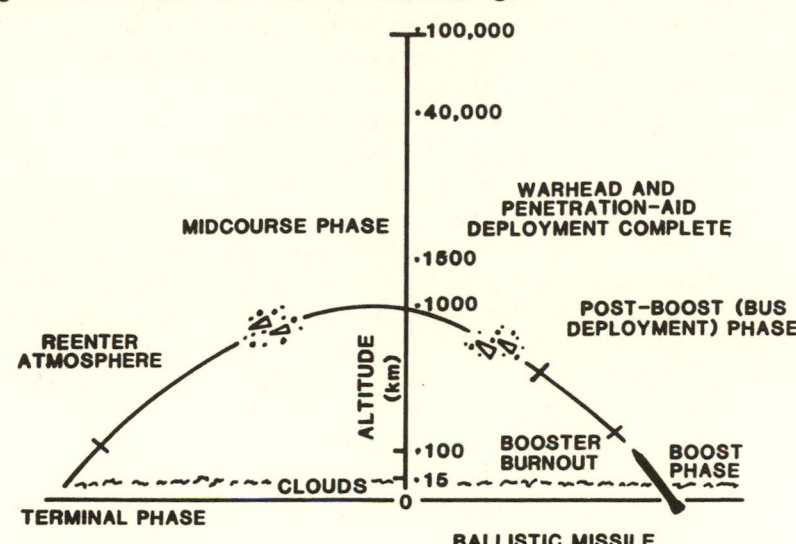

Source: Weinberger, C., *Annual Report to Congress, Fiscal Year 1987*, U.S. Government Printing Office, Washington, D.C., February 5, 1986, p. 288.

3. The most effective systems have multiple layers, or tiers, for the intercept and destruction of incoming enemy ballistic missiles.
4. Survivability of system components is a critical issue whose resolution requires a combination of technologies and tactics that must be worked out.
5. Significant demonstrations of developing technologies for critical ballistic missile defense functions can be performed over the next ten years. These demonstrations will provide visible evidence of progress in developing the technical capabilities required for an effective in-depth defense system.[16]

THE ELEMENTS OF BALLISTIC MISSILE DEFENSE

Ballistic missiles are launched from the earth's surface, rise through the atmosphere into space along a suborbital trajectory, and reenter the atmosphere about a hundred miles from their targets. Ballistic missile defense involves the detection, tracking, engagement, and destruction of ballistic missiles at some point in their trajectory prior to the detonation of their warheads. Trajectory phases are shown in Figure 11.1 In the boost phase, a ballistic missile accelerates up through the atmosphere and into space. The missile moves relatively slowly for a short time

while expending a very large amount of propulsive energy. The infrared radiation associated with the exhaust plume from the burning rocket fuel provides an easily observable phenomenon that can be used to detect and track the missile launch.

Following the boost phase, a postboost vehicle (essentially a third or fourth stage of the missile—also known as a "MIRV bus") separates from the burnt-out booster and may deploy multiple warheads (multiple individually targeted reentry vehicles, or MIRVs) and penetration aids. The latter include reentry vehicle (RV) decoys, chaff, aerosols, electronic jammers, balloons, all designed to confuse the detection-and-tracking systems of the defender. The postboost phase is significant because the process of deploying multiple objects in space from a single missile may increase the number of space objects associated with a single launch by a factor of 100 or more. This complicates the defender's problems in identifying, tracking, and discriminating real warheads from decoys and penetration aids. The problem is particularly important if the defender's system has limited fuel, such as would occur for space-based chemical lasers that would be expected to operate for extended periods during a nuclear exchange. Consequently, "birth-to-death" tracking and track-file maintenance and other efficiency measures are critical.

Once the postboost phase is completed, the "MIRVed" warheads and decoys follow a ballistic trajectory in space. This portion of the flight, known as the midcourse phase, can last up to twenty minutes. This phase provides a relatively long time span for discrimination of real warheads from decoys and for possible warhead intercept and destruction.

Reentry into the atmosphere marks the end of the midcourse phase and the beginning of the terminal phase. Reentry heating usually destroys decoys, which must be made from relatively lightweight materials to avoid taking up valuable space, adding weight, and reducing warhead payload aboard the MIRV bus. Heating also destroys other penetration aids such as chaff and balloons. This process is known technically as "atmospheric strip-out." Atmospheric strip-out eliminates much of the discrimination problem faced by terminal defenses. However, the terminal phase is characterized by extremely compressed decision and engagement "windows," for very little time remains before the warheads reach their targets. Also, certain decoy designs could survive to very low altitudes in order to force a firing and intercept commitment by the terminal defenses.

Finally, although defensive sensors can readily detect and track the extremely hot and energetic reentry vehicles, the defensive weapons allocated to each warhead must have very high velocities to reach the warhead before it detonates above or on its intended target. The geometry and time scale of terminal defense dictate that defensive weapons must

be located near the defended target. Consequently, terminal defense concepts have traditionally focused on defense of relatively localized high-value targets, such as an array of fixed missile-launch silos or selected population centers. Technically, this is referred to as a "point defense," as opposed to a broader "area defense."

The technical requirements and phenomenologies associated with terminal ballistic missile defense have been thoroughly worked out over the past twenty-five years. Some specialists also believe that boost-phase intercept, particularly with satellite-launched, kinetic-kill missiles, is also relatively well defined. They point to the resurgence of interest by the SDI organization in such weapons as a potential option for the near future.[17]

THE SDI BUDGET

By 1985, the Strategic Defense Initiative was moving ahead at a $1 billion annual funding level. This was remarkable in a defense environment that normally includes several years of studies before any major new program can be passed in Congress. The ability to move the program so quickly to that funding level resulted from the fact that much of the technology needed for SDI was already under development. For example, the army had substantial ballistic missile defense programs in surveillance and tracking, interceptor missiles, and terminal defense battle management. The air force and the Defense Advanced Research Projects Agency (DARPA) had several programs under way in directed energy weapons and space surveillance. At least twenty-five separate Department of Defense programs were aggregated and restructured to form the SDI.

Table 11.1 provides an overview of the projected SDI budget. The amounts in the table include the results of the Appropriations Conference Report (98-1159), in which the conferees of the House and Senate reduced the fiscal year 1985 SDI budget from $1.7 to $1.4 billion. The five program categories shown in Table 11.1 account for all currently appropriated or planned SDI funding. The surveillance, acquisition, tracking, and kill assessment category includes research and development programs for detecting, acquiring, and tracking ballistic missiles and discriminating reentry vehicles and decoys over all phases of the ballistic missile trajectory. Directed energy weapons programs include energy lasers and particle beam weapons. Kinetic energy weapons programs include the development of hypervelocity missiles and electromagnetic launch weapons. Systems analysis and battle management programs involve the development of technologies for battle management and command, control, and communications architectures. Finally, SDI support programs include the development of technologies in four key areas:

Table 11.1
Strategic Defense Initiative Projected Budget, 1985 (millions of dollars)

Program Category	Fiscal Years							Estimated 7-Yr. Total
	1984	1985	1986	1987	1988	1989	1990	
Surveillance, acquisition, tracking, and kill assessment	366.5	545.9	1,386.3	1,874.9	2,538	3,065	3,614	13,390
Directed energy weapons	311.3	376.4	965.4	1,195.6	1,435	1,677	1,903	7,864
Kinetic energy weapons	196.8	256.0	859.7	1,238.6	1,480	1,675	1,975	7,681
Systems analysis and battle management	10.0	99.0	243.3	272.5	303	358	445	1,731
SDI support	106.3	112.0	258.2	316.7	400	514	700	2,407
Subtotal	990.9	1,389.3	3,712.9	4,898.3	6,156	7,289	8,637	33,073
SDI program management	0.5	8.0	9.2	10.0	10	10	10	58
Total	991.4	1,397.3	3,722.1	4,908.3	6,166	7,299	8,647	33,131

Source: Bosma, John T. and Whelan, Richard C., Guide to the Strategic Defense Initiative, Pasha Publications, Arlington, Va., 1985. Also see Department of Defense, Report to the Congress on the Strategic Defense Initiative, 1985, and IEEE Spectrum, September 1985, p. 61.

survivability of elements of the defense system; lethality of candidate weapons and vulnerability of hardened targets; the development of space power systems; and the development of space logistic support.

There are other SDI-related programs not listed in the budget on Table 11.1. These include improvements for strategic surveillance and warning systems, upgrades for the NORAD Cheyenne Mountain complex, the development of an air-launched miniature homing vehicle, and the upgrading of orbital support facilities worldwide.[18]

SUPPORT AND CONCERN IN CONGRESS

The immediate task facing SDI officials is to squeeze enough money out of Congress to meet near-term technical goals. The SDI organization wants as much as $11 billion more for its programs over the next five years than those programs had been scheduled to receive from the departments of defense and energy before the SDI was started. In all, the Pentagon is asking for about $26 billion for the SDI from 1985 through 1989. Although this would be less than 2 percent of the total defense budget, the appropriations would consume about 15 percent of the research funds allocated to the Department of Defense.

SDI critics contend that Department of Defense projections may be misleading. The 15 percent figure cited by the Pentagon relates to the total projected research, development, test, and evaluation portion of the defense budget, which includes funds for upgrading defense systems already in place. As for "seed corn" weapons research, the SDI may actually consume about one-third of the total funds by the end of the decade. Thus, the SDI could cut deeply into the research on other new weapons concepts.

It is clear that Congress will not approve all of the $26 billion requested for the SDI. However, it is also apparent that Congress is hesitant to cut or restructure the program drastically. Supporters include Republicans who follow the president's lead, space and military enthusiasts, and Republicans and Democrats who simply see economic benefit to their congressional districts or states. In this regard, the SDI organization has helped its cause by issuing contracts to companies in congressional districts all across the country. It has also won some support from universities that have agreed to work on contracts in such areas as optical computing, advanced materials, and space-based power supplies.

Congress is seeking ways to exert more influence over the SDI program. It already has budget power over each of the five broad categories within which all of the various SDI contracts fall. General James A. Abrahamson, the SDI director, has expressed dissatisfaction with this

situation. When he wants to channel appropriated funds from, let us say, directed energy weapons to kinetic energy weapons, or from one fiscal year to another, he must get congressional approval. A step like this, the SDI director said, "took about eight months to complete last year and was inconsistent with the pace of this program."[19]

Another area of concern in Congress is the lack of precise calculations on the ultimate cost of deploying an SDI system. Estimates vary, depending on the source, from several hundred billion dollars to over one trillion. Those in the best position to make educated guesses—the SDI officials themselves—are reluctant to do so. The official SDI position is that because research is still preliminary and no system has been decided upon, any discussion of cost is premature. In addition, they have said that the cost of such a system would be spread out over many years.

If completed, the SDI system would require enormous annual expenditures just to keep it going and would be a permanent feature in the budget. The American Federation of Scientists has estimated that the addition to the Department of Defense budget would be between $50 billion and $200 billion per fiscal year.

ALLIED ECONOMIC INTEREST

The Reagan administration lobbied hard to gain support for the SDI from its allies, particularly in Europe. It argued that the SDI would enhance existing European defenses against an attack by the Soviet Union. Also, SDI would give participating allies the latest in U.S. high technology.

However, critics argue that U.S.-Soviet ballistic missile defense competition could expose rather than protect U.S. allies. Current U.S. policy postulates that the United States might fire nuclear weapons to stop a conventional Soviet attack on any NATO nation. Europeans fear that if, as the United States has suggested, the Soviet Union has an effective SDI-type system, Warsaw Pact troops could attack Western Europe without fear of retaliation by ballistic nuclear missiles. If the Soviets had even a "light" strategic defense, it could mean the death knell of the whole independent strategic posture of the European nuclear powers, France and Great Britain.

Economic, rather than strategic, considerations make the SDI most tempting to U.S. allies. Companies in Japan, Israel, West Germany, and the Netherlands, among others, have expressed interest in obtaining contracts. In fact, even countries that have officially denounced the program seem to welcome the potential benefits for their domestic economies. For example, the Danish parliament passed a resolution

saying that it opposes deployment and R&D for weapons in outer space. However, as the Danish Washington embassy's first secretary, Carsten Sondergaard, noted: "It's not a law, it's only a resolution. Companies can participate, and some are."[20]

SPIN-OFFS

In the past, research for weapons has spawned valuable nonmilitary technologies. The development of warplanes during World War I helped create commercial aviation. The Manhattan Project gave birth to nuclear power. The construction of U.S. intercontinental missile systems speeded up the development of semiconductors and computers.

Will the SDI, potentially the largest and most ambitious weapons program in history, follow this trend? Proponents stress that the program must stand on its military merits, but if it does succeed, the SDI could generate a variety of nonmilitary inventions, including lasers for atomic microscopy, lightweight materials for cars and planes, computers built of optical components, and low-cost space transportation.

Critics argue that the value of potential SDI spin-offs may be exaggerated. Furthermore, SDI could inhibit rather than inspire commercialization of new technologies. First, at least in the short term, the SDI would siphon off scientific and engineering talent that otherwise would work on civilian projects. As a result, civilian industries would have to pay higher salaries to attract the services of the scientists and engineers that remain in the civilian industry labor pool. Second, by diverting vast amounts of money and manpower into largely classified defense projects, the Department of Defense might hurt rather than help companies that would use for civilian applications the high technologies generated by this research.

THE LONG-TERM COSTS OF STRATEGIC DEFENSE

According to SDI officials, the Strategic Defense Initiative is a broadly based research program designed to determine whether newly emerging technologies could support an effective defense against ballistic missiles. At this time, the actual capabilities of these technologies are not sufficiently defined to provide a sound basis upon which to fashion a likely defense system architecture. Until the Department of Defense has a more complete picture of what an effective ballistic missile defense system might look like, it will not be possible to determine the long-term costs should such a system be fully developed and deployed.

At this point, only the cost of the research program itself—approximately $26 billion over the next five years—is known. This includes

$1.4 billion appropriated in fiscal year 1985; $3.7 billion requested for fiscal year 1986; and $4.9 billion estimated for fiscal year 1987. An additional $16 billion is expected to be spent during fiscal years 1988 and 1989. However, actual expenditures may vary considerably from current estimates, depending on decisions concerning full-scale engineering and deployment, the operations and maintenance of such systems, and political constraints that cannot be predicted at this time.

Cost estimates are available for defensive systems like the retired Safeguard Antiballistic Missile (ABM) test radars, but because these bear little resemblance to potential advanced systems, costs of the older systems are not useful for estimating the costs of future systems. In addition, if the United States were to build a defense system today based on Safeguard and similar technologies, the hardware, production techniques, and costs would likely be substantially different from those incurred over a decade ago.

THE FUTURE OF THE STRATEGIC DEFENSE INITIATIVE

"Star Wars" sets the stage for a general overhaul of U.S. strategic war-fighting capabilities. This assessment suggests a range of alternative futures. First, the Strategic Defense Initiative could result in an array of advanced surveillance and defensive weapons, only to have them terminated abruptly after a few years. This could result from a change in administrations, particularly one that brought in a national security elite unsympathetic to the current concepts of strategic defense. Such a rollback has been advocated by several prominent and active opponents of SDI.[21]

Second, the Strategic Defense Initiative could acquire a "crash" research and development urgency, particularly if the Soviets drop SALT and other arms-control constraints altogether. This could lead to an interest in early deployment of a ballistic missile defense. However, such a rationale for a crash effort seems unlikely, given the past minimal reactions of the United States to Soviet deviations from the original intent of SALT I and II as well as other arms-control agreements. Also, earlier crash defense programs were driven by fears considerably more immediate and visceral than those occasioned by the seemingly legalistic excursions by the Soviets from contemporary arms-control agreements.[22]

Third, strategic defense deployment could be included in a joint U.S.-Soviet agreement to deploy defenses as part of a mutual renunciation of "offensive dominance." This outcome—which was the guiding rationale of the Reagan administration position at the 1985 Geneva arms talks—appears increasingly remote, given the rather strident Soviet opposition. Indeed, the Soviets would lose much of the leverage they

expect to gain with their continued deployment of third, fourth, and fifth generation ICBMs.

Fourth, the Strategic Defense Initiative could continue as a research-only program, with little or no deployment. This status may not be one sought by the present administration, but it could easily result from current congressional attitudes. Should this outcome occur, there would likely be considerable work in surveillance and sensors, but far less in "hard kill" weapons or in related battle management and ballistic missile defense support systems.

Finally, the Strategic Defense Initiative could move into the strategic primacy originally envisioned by President Reagan and his top advisers. However, this would require a bipartisan congressional consensus and an acceptance of the deficiencies of proposed alternative defense concepts over the long term. This consensus has not emerged to date.

If there is any pattern that should be kept in mind when evaluating the future of the Strategic Defense Initiative, it is that the United States has repeatedly embarked on advanced, politically driven research and development programs in defense, only to stop them abruptly before they were completed. This pattern could easily occur with the SDI.

AN OFFENSE TO DEFENSIVE TRANSITION

The ultimate goal of SDI to "render nuclear weapons impotent and obsolete" may never be fully achieved. Even if it is, it will not be attained at once. There would be a transition period as the United States moves from complete reliance on offensive systems for deterrence to a primary reliance on strategic defense.

An important criticism of strategic defense is its asymmetry vis-à-vis the Soviet defenses. The Soviets can protect their highest valued assets with terminal defenses, which can be deployed in the near future. In contrast, the United States needs a complete, multilayered system to protect its highest valued asset, its civilian population. Because of this asymmetry, we agree with Payne and Gray[23] in that the first guiding principle during any offense to defense transition should be that the U.S. should maintain the capability of posing a threat to Soviet highest valued assets at least until the U.S. can protect its own highest valued assets.

Another important element of the critique is that scattered, ineffective defenses on both sides give great advantage to a first strike. This occurs because inadequate defenses would work better against a ragged retaliatory response than they would against a coordinated first strike, thereby creating pressures for a first strike. First-strike advantage, taken together with the argument that the defense of strategic offensive forces would

Table 11.2
A Defense Transition

Phase I (Offense Dominance)	Phase II (Defense Dominance)
1. Damage limitation for deterrence capability enhancement	1. Damage limitation for deterrence credibility enhancement
2. Protect strategic offensive forces	2. Protect population
3. Offense modernization required	3. Offense build-down possible
4. Near-term technologies	4. Far-term technologies
5. Space control deployments	5. Space asset deployments
6. Extended deterrence, protect NATO assets to enhance capability	6. Extended deterrence, protect U.S. population, enhance linkage credibility
7. Deny victory to the enemy by threatening enemy assets	7. Prevent defeat of the U.S. by protecting U.S. assets

Source: Washburn, D., Gertcher, F., The Strategic Defense Initiative: Background, Transition and Strategy Evaluation, RDA-TR-1800072-007, for Air Force Space Command, December 1984.

be stabilizing, but the defense of populations if done without other defenses would be destabilizing, gives rise to the second principle: U.S. deployments should first and foremost seek to enhance U.S. retaliatory capability prior to seeking protection of the U.S. population and the urban industrial base.

Given the U.S. political system, the uncertainties of the international order, and the unknowns of technology, a transition from offense to defense would take many decades and many U.S. political administrations to complete. History provides no reason to assume that consistency of purpose will prevail through such political evolution. Therefore, the third principle should be that each strategy and force structure position during the transition must be able to stand on its own as a potential stopping point.

Finally, as a commonsense matter, the fourth principle must hold throughout the transition: Defensive deployments must add to, or stop an erosion in, U.S. security without decreasing stability.[24]

The preceding principles dictate a certain structure to a defense transition. This structure can be illustrated by dividing the transition into two phases. As indicated in Table 11.2, Phase I begins at the current position of offense dominance and Phase II ends with a defense dominant world. The dividing point occurs when the United States begins seriously to seek population protection. This would occur at a point when the nation has a rough offense-defense balance. However, it should be kept in mind that there is no clear break between stages and that each stage covers an extensive strategic and force posture evolution, perhaps taking decades.

Phase I of the defense transition is a period of offense dominance with increasingly sophisticated defensive deployments. The goal of

defensive deployments during this period is to protect the U.S. strategic offensive forces and to increase the capability aspect of deterrence. There are two driving factors in the choice to defend the strategic offensive forces during Phase I: the enhancement of stability and the application of new technologies. The forces protected would be such as to deny victory to the Soviets by continuing the U.S. capability to strike their military and state control mechanisms. Thus, the strategy during this period is just an extension of the current countervailing strategy. The defenses would increasingly allow the United States to accomplish this objective with fewer and fewer offensive forces because the forces it has would be protected and would therefore be available after a first strike by the Soviets. Of course, the potential decrease in U.S. offensive forces toward the end of this period would have to be balanced against a probable Soviet defensive buildup. This balance or trade-off between offensive and defensive forces could be done in an orderly fashion through arms-control negotiations. Such negotiations would seek to replace offensive capability by defensive capability. However, even in the absence of negotiated agreements, this period of defensive buildup on both sides should be one of increasing stability. Negotiations could make this stability less expensive. In the absence of realistic negotiated agreements that address the current offensive imbalance, it is important for the country to continue its offensive force modernization program in support of the countervailing strategy. Such a buildup would tend to stabilize the transition. Existing Soviet defenses and extensive counterforce capabilities could create a very unfavorable situation if, as is likely, the Soviets also choose to deploy sophisticated defensive systems.

The defensive systems required during Phase I could be developed within the foreseeable future with ground-based terminal and late midcourse weapons systems. However, Phase I would also include the deployment of increasingly sophisticated space assets for surveillance, acquisition, tracking, and perhaps for battle management and command, control, and communications.

As the United States trades offensive for defensive capability, dependence on space systems would grow. It is therefore important to begin to deploy space control assets early in Phase I, and to continue upgrading these assets in anticipation of space-based missile defense systems during Phase II.

In order to alleviate the concerns of U.S. allies over the credibility of extended defense linkage, the United States could begin to deploy similar defenses in Europe to protect European retaliatory capability. At the same time, European countries could be strongly encouraged to build up their conventional defenses in anticipation of Phase II, when

the superpowers would no longer totally rely on the threat of nuclear annihilation for deterrence.

During Phase II, the United States could seek complete protection of its population and prevention of defeat in the event of deterrence failure. The transition from offense to defense dominance would then be complete. The ability to limit damage to the U.S. population and to the urban industrial base would enhance the credibility of deterrence for remaining U.S. offensive forces because the U.S. population could no longer be held hostage after a first strike.

As defenses become increasingly more sophisticated, deep negotiated cuts in both U.S. and Soviet offensive forces become possible because the value of cheating at a low level becomes negligible. Safety from accidental launch and missile attacks by a third nation or terrorist group will also be possible. Safety from such attacks would become increasingly important as more nations attain nuclear capabilities and nuclear deterrence is no longer primarily a U.S.-Soviet affair.

In order to move into Phase II, space ballistic missile defense systems would almost certainly have to be deployed. This would be more viable than it appears today because Phase I would have deployed extensive space control assets that would reduce the risk of attack against ballistic missile defense space platforms. Furthermore, such space assets would provide operational experience with many of the systems required for additional space deployments. Air and cruise missile defenses would also have to become very effective during the latter part of Phase I and into Phase II in order to compensate for expected Soviet reactions in these areas.

CONCLUSIONS

President Reagan's SDI speech gave the development of key strategic defense technologies an initial political push. However, the popular notion that a "star wars" defense against ballistic missiles would negate the threat of assured nuclear destruction does not necessarily follow. According to several prominent scientists, the development of a "leak-proof" ballistic missile defense is not technically feasible, even with substantial improvements in key technologies.[25] Moreover, strong arguments have been made against a leak-proof strategic defense from the political policy and stability points of view.

What then is the proper perspective with regard to strategic defense? To gain objectivity, one must consider many scenarios and likely Soviet responses. For example, one possible Soviet response would be to overpower the U.S. defense by simply building more and better offensive systems. The counterargument is that U.S. defenses would be reliable

and relatively inexpensive to develop, deploy, operate, and maintain. If the Soviets perceive that overpowering U.S. defenses is relatively more expensive than building a strategic defense of their own, then perhaps the SDI purpose will be served. However, such a cost differential between offensive and defensive systems has yet to be proved.

Another U.S. approach would be to develop a ballistic missile defense that protects the national command authorities, strategic offensive forces, and command, control, and communications networks. Such an approach would not attempt to protect the U.S. population per se; it might, however, improve the credibility of U.S. offensive forces and enhance the U.S. deterrence by threatening punishment in case of Soviet attack. Extending strategic defense to U.S. conventional forces and to the urban industrial base would also deny Soviet objectives in the event of war by preventing a U.S. defeat and by easing the country's recovery process should a nuclear exchange occur. Thus, a limited strategic defense, although not leak proof, does have deterrence merit.

Another perspective involves U.S. political realities. Any ballistic missile defense, whether it provides a thin or a leak-proof defense, would be designed, developed, and deployed over several decades. Several political administrations in Washington would necessarily be involved. Political philosophies may change with changing administrations. Consistent with our earlier principle, we suggest that the selected strategy, whatever it may be, include an evolutionary design, development, and deployment schedule. Milestones should be set so that each administration can point to specific accomplishments and can change, enhance, or terminate programs after particular milestones are achieved. This calls for a strategy that remains flexible, involves parallel lines of development, and results in deployment of usable systems consistent with the four-year political cycle.

This chapter concludes with a reminder to the reader that a strategic defense against ballistic missiles does offer some hope that the arsenals of the superpowers can evolve away from offensive nuclear missiles toward a defensive posture that would result in a more stable, less dangerous world. Although alternative strategies, architectures, and systems may be debated, the overall goal of deterrence and peace can be appreciated by all sensible parties.

NOTES

1. For a detailed discussion, see Washburn, D., and Gertcher, F., *The Strategic Defense Initiative: Background, Transition and Strategy Evaluation*, RDA-TR-180072-007, for Air Force Space Command, December 1984.

2. Dyson, Freeman, *Weapons and Hope,* Harper & Row Publishers, New York, p. 240.

3. Builder, C., and Graubard, M., *The International Law of Armed Conflict: Implications for the Concept of Mutual Assured Destruction,* RAND, Santa Monica, Calif., January 1982, pp. 45–46.

4. Ibid., p. 46.

5. Ibid., pp. 45–48.

6. Weinberger, *Annual Report to Congress, Fiscal Year 1984,* p. 18. Also see Builder and Graubard, *The International Law of Armed Conflict,* pp. 45–46.

7. Payne, K., *Laser Weapons in Space: Policy and Doctrine,* A Westview Replica Edition, Boulder, Colo., August 1983.

8. Weinberger, *Annual Report to Congress, Fiscal Year 1984,* pp. 16–18. Also see Brown, H., *Department of Defense Annual Report, Fiscal Year 1982,* U.S. Government Printing Office, Washington, D.C., January 1981, p. 6.

9. Hyland, W. G., *Soviet-American Relations: A New Cold War?,* RAND, Santa Monica, Calif., May 1981, pp. 63–73.

10. Ibid., p. 67. Also see Podhoretz, N., "The Present Danger," *Commentary* 69, no. 3, March 1980, p. 39.

11. Weinberger, *Annual Report to Congress, Fiscal Year 1984,* pp. 51–58.

12. Weinberger, C., *Soviet Military Power,* U.S. Government Printing Office, Washington, D.C., 1984, pp. 27–31.

13. Ibid., pp. 21–22.

14. Carter, A., and Schwartz, D., eds., *Ballistic Missile Defense,* Brookings Institution, Washington, D.C., 1984, pp. 36–37, 46–48. Also see Scowcroft, B., *Report of the President's Commission on Strategic Forces,* Washington, D.C., April 1983.

15. Bosma, John T., and Whelan, Richard C., *Guide to the Strategic Defense Initiative,* Pasha Publications, Inc., Arlington, Va., 1985.

16. These conclusions are paraphrased from a booklet, *The Strategic Defense Initiative,* U.S. Department of Defense, U.S. Government Printing Office, Washington, D.C., April 1984. Also see Bosma and Whelan, *Guide to the Strategic Defense Initiative.*

17. Canan, James, *War in Space,* Harper & Row Publishers, New York, 1982; Carter and Schwartz, *Ballistic Missile Defense;* and numerous Department of Defense technical reports.

18. Weiner, Stephen, "Systems and Technology," in Carter and Schwartz, *Ballistic Missile Defense.*

19. "Star Wars, SDI: The Grand Experiment," *IEEE Spectrum,* September 1985, p. 56.

20. Ibid., p. 61.

21. For examples, see Bethe, H., Garwin, R., Gottfried, K., Kendall, H., "Space Based Ballistic-Missile Defense," *Scientific American,* October 1984. Also see Teller, Edward, "Pros of Strategic Defense," and Sagan, Carl, "Cons of Strategic Defense," *Discover Magazine,* September 1985.

22. Weinberger, *Annual Report to Congress, Fiscal Year 1984.*

23. Payne, K., and Gray, C., "Nuclear Policy and the Defense Transition," *Foreign Affairs,* Spring 1984, pp. 841–842.

24. Washburn and Gertcher, *The Strategic Defense Initiative,* p. 41.

25. Bethe, et al., "Space Based Ballistic-Missile Defense," pp. 39–49.

12
Conclusion:
Finding Better Solutions

THE DEFENSE ENVIRONMENT

This book introduced its study of defense spending by noting that the United States had formulated a series of broad national security objectives to support its foreign policies. Directed primarily against the perceived threat posed by the Soviet Union, these objectives provide the general framework for a defense establishment.

Although these objectives may give guidance in the use of military forces, they are of virtually no help in allocating the resources needed to purchase and maintain these forces. This chapter concludes our discussion of the political economy of defense by noting that the United States lacks a cohesive national strategy to direct the allocation of scarce resources to defense and nondefense uses. This chapter also demonstrates that the conditions created by this lack of strategy are fundamental causes of economic problems in the defense establishment.

The defense of the United States is both an economic and a political problem. From an economic perspective, scarce resources allocated to defense at the national level are not available for nondefense use. Within the Department of Defense, the allocation process can be subjected to economic efficiency criteria—that is, making the choices that result in the highest level of defense, given budget constraints. But at the national level, defense remains more political than economic. This occurs not only because of the political nature of perceived threats, but also because defense spending has significant regional domestic economic effects. For these reasons, actual defense spending and in some cases, detailed decisions on costly weapon systems are determined through political processes that yield results that are often not economically efficient.

Because defense resource allocation is an extremely complex process, and because its politics and economics are so entwined, there is no simple way to assign appropriate resources to defense. Therefore, this

chapter will first identify the defense allocation problems that cannot be solved, given the current structure of both U.S. politics and the defense establishment. It will then provide a framework for analyzing the problems that can be solved, and it will suggest some basic structural changes in the defense establishment.

THINKING ABOUT HALF-QUESTIONS

At the national level, the problems associated with defense usually belong to the class of problems that generates questions such as "Do we have enough of weapon X or of defense expenditure Y?" These questions cannot be answered without referring to a further statement of the problem such as "with respect to a policy of _____ " or "to fulfill the objective of _____ ." This is essentially an exercise in utilitarian thinking. It is goal oriented, but in the area of national defense, clear objectives are often missing (with the possible exception of nuclear deterrence). As a result, quantitative measures, however fashioned, cannot be used to analyze these questions because numbers themselves have no meaning without well-defined objectives. And where defense policy is concerned, numbers often seem to mean very little—the important thing appears to be an assessment of national will or commitment. These factors mean little without capability, but the reverse is also true, as history adequately demonstrates.

The problems generating these half questions can be reduced to problems of defining appropriate objectives and standards of achievement. But political decisionmakers are notoriously hesitant to establish definite objectives and standards against which achievements may be measured. This may be because, in establishing firm standards, they fear that they will show either a lack of understanding of the problems or a preference for a single problem when multiple levels of problems are more likely.

The defense analyst faced with this situation often resolves half questions with respect to a full spectrum of objectives and hopes that the results will not be sensitive to specific objectives. The analyst then lets the decisionmaker choose the most appealing outcomes—in effect, structuring the objectives to fit the solution.

In such situations, economic analysis and well-defined measures become less appropriate as objectives become harder to define. This occurs when any scenario of national action moves progressively into the unknown. Unfortunately, this creates a strategy vacuum in which, because of the lack of firm standards, both everything and nothing can be justified, and adequate economic analysis cannot be performed because no meaningful constraints or objectives exist. The result is a curious world where a strategy for national resource allocation is not possible

without objectives and yet there are perverse incentives that keep decisionmakers from establishing objectives.

IS A STRATEGY FOR ALLOCATING RESOURCES TO DEFENSE POSSIBLE?

There is a view that the United States has a strategy that can be used to determine the levels of resources required for defense. In 1985 Secretary of Defense Weinberger stated that

> If you ask me what is *our* strategy, I would simply say it is to build the *strongest possible deterrent* as quickly and effectively as possible. To be effective, our deterrent must meet two tests: it must *credibly* persuade Soviet leaders that they have no significant exploitable military advantage against our vital interests; and it must minimize the *risk of failure* through any accident, unauthorized use, or miscalculation by the Soviets.[1]

Note first that this statement is open-ended; it implies no constraints to spending. Second, it deals only with the Soviets and does not consider other possible conflicts. Because Secretary Weinberger's statement is open-ended, it cannot be used to allocate scarce resources subject to budget and other constraints. And since it deals only with the direct Soviet threat, it focuses attention on a single, narrow issue and away from other possible conflicts such as surrogate wars. In addition, the issue of direct war with the Soviet Union is essentially irrelevant to other defense strategies because of the relative stability of current nuclear deterrence between the two major powers. That is, the current offensive nuclear structure is aimed at deterrence, not use, and the number of nuclear weapons and delivery systems held by both the United States and the Soviet Union is so far in excess of actual requirements that foreseeable acquisitions or cuts will have relatively minor strategic consequences.

Other strategies, implying other resource allocations, are necessary to deal with more likely conflicts. But in the nonnuclear arena (such as surrogate wars, Third World conflicts) threats to the United States are currently defined, not with respect to a strategy, but instead as a function of both an incremental and a cyclic process. The more the government spends, the more it is able to be "afraid" of, and the more it is afraid of, the more it spends. This mandates that the United States proceed in a reactive mode, and a "strategy" simply to match someone else is no strategy at all.

To plan intelligently for the short run, the United States must have an idea of what it is trying to achieve in the long run. In the defense arena, this presupposes meaningful national objectives. Without objectives, strategy is not possible and neither is optimal resource allocation. This, in turn, implies that current measures of efficiency are meaningless.

However, clearly defined strategies will, by definition, require specific actions to achieve a desired result. As such, each new defense strategy competes with other entrenched reasons for allocating resources— resources that the new strategy will consume. At the present time, it is likely that no national strategy for allocating resources could compete with the other reasons for spending defense money. This is true for several reasons:

- There are many individuals and organizations that benefit from the current way of doing business. Some of these are: (1) the sectors of our economy that rely on the subsidies, support, and technology arising from defense spending; (2) congressional groups that benefit from the impact of defense spending on regional growth and development; (3) military services that can compete more easily for resources if the end use of those resources is not clearly defined; (4) those who profit from public perceptions of how the U.S. defense and spending effort compares with the effort of the Soviet Union.
- The world is uncertain, and a reasonable strategy should recognize this and explicitly account for it. However, any plan sold to Congress is never allowed to express doubt about anything. Uncertainty can be neither recognized nor accounted for.
- Having a strategy implies commitment to a specific course of action. This has the effect of limiting the ability of the political leadership to change direction and therefore is probably asking more than our system is willing to give. In this case, the desirability of having a strategy probably cannot compete with the political rationale for keeping open options and for not disclosing one's course of action.
- There is a valid question of whether U.S. national interests can even be defined—at least with the degree of precision required to formulate meaningful objectives.

As a result of these and other factors, the United States has neither long-term objectives nor strategies to guide resource allocations, and it is unlikely to develop such strategies in the future. Choosing to operate without clear objectives and without the direction of strategies entails a number of economic and political costs.

THE COSTS OF OPERATING WITHOUT A STRATEGY
FOR ALLOCATING RESOURCES TO DEFENSE

The implicit and explicit costs of the lack of strategies are the overhead associated with the current U.S. way of doing business. First, with the standoff between the United States and the Soviet Union in nuclear forces and conventional forces in Europe, much of the action is now in the Third World. And yet, the United States is continually tentative, uncertain, and confused about spending to assist its smaller allies and to build its own nonconventional forces. The lack of either a plan or an objective is obvious. Second, each side now tries for marginal gains; but without clear objectives on the part of the United States. A series of random gains is unlikely to add to anything. And finally, Congress's response to the lack of clear strategies for allocating resources to defense has been to try to regulate weapon use through appropriations.

As a result of all these factors, the United States currently competes with the Soviets and the rest of the world on the input side of the equation, comparing untried weapons, expenditures, and programs, looking for illusive measures of national will, but never comparing actual performance or results to objectives.

THE STRUCTURAL COSTS OF DEFENSE

Added to the factors already discussed are several structural problems that combine with the lack of a strategy to complicate further the allocation process. Each of these problems has an adverse effect on costs:

> The U.S. risk-averse posture as a nation guarantees expensive weapon design and increased costs throughout the defense establishment.
> The perceived requirement to maintain defense industries in times of peace implies contractor subsidies and inefficiencies.
> The appropriations process in Congress depends on political power and responds to short-term rewards. Meaningful strategies depend on long-term objectives. This establishes a conflict between strategy and appropriations that effectively negates long-term planning.

None of these problems has a practical solution achievable in the foreseeable future, and each represents an area of increased costs that must be borne regardless of how other problems in defense allocation are solved.

THE CONSEQUENCES OF NOT ALLOCATING RESOURCES TO ACHIEVE WELL-DEFINED OBJECTIVES

A lack of strategy results in the inefficient allocation of resources, and this produces an increased burden on the economy of the United States. But the United States, as a nation, appears structurally unable to attack the problems that must be solved if it is to have defense objectives and strategies leading to an efficient allocation of resources. If this is the case, and the evidence suggests that it is, the United States is condemned to live with the resulting costs. In such a situation, questioning the amount of the costs without questioning the reasons for the costs will continue to be nonproductive.

Even if it were possible to construct a meaningful strategy for allocating resources to defense, experience has shown that it is impossible to predict the future with enough precision to allow specific, long-range military planning. Thus, uncertainty and the lack of a strategy both create a need for a flexible and diversified economy to support future defense requirements. This leads one to consider the factors affecting the ability of our economy to allocate national resources efficiently and, in turn, focuses attention on the constraints placed on the economic allocation process.

If reasonable constraints to the economic allocation process are used and if the trade-offs inherent in defense spending are made apparent during the annual budget process, it is possible to develop a strategy that will allow the economy of the country to be a major element of defense. If, in contrast, perverse constraints are used to preclude the allocation of resources to defense or to nondefense areas, the result will be a weakened, less flexible economy that supports neither defense nor nondefense requirements.

If the elections of 1980 and 1984 are any indication, this perception was held, in different forms, by a majority of the people in the United States. However, the high levels of defense spending since 1979 have occurred at a time when the U.S. budget problems have multiplied. This has created an atmosphere in which reductions in current military spending rates are likely. But the military finds itself locked into the part of the defense budget—investment in major equipment items—that requires a long-term budgeting commitment. Thus, it may be forced to cut operations and maintenance expenditures. At the same time, the Strategic Defense Initiative may create even more competition for scarce funds—competition that funnels additional money into research and development and leaves even less for readiness.

It is reasonable to assume that, barring an actual war, there will never be an appropriate measure of success for defense spending. It is

also reasonable to assume that defense spending will continue to be justified based on perceptions and to be driven by the factors discussed in this book. Given these considerations, and in light of historical precedent, it is unlikely that a period of growth in defense spending will ever be sustained.[3]

DEFINING THE ISSUES

When weighed against the factors just presented, many questions about defense fall in the category of issues that simply cannot be addressed without fundamental changes in the way the United States plans for defense. Most of these questions fall into three areas. The first is an issue of both social equity and economic efficiency: Considering the objectives of the United States and the competing needs for national resources, are appropriate amounts allocated to defense and to other uses and are these funds allocated efficiently? A second issue concerns the moral, ethical, and rational justification for the maintenance and use of offensive nuclear weapons and/or defensive systems. A third issue concerns the role of the United States and the use of conventional weapons in Third World conflicts.

For the most part, this book deals with allocation and efficiency because these are the issues amenable to economic investigation and solution. The use of offensive nuclear weapons raises issues that are not economic in nature and that should be considered in a moral and political sense. However, offensive nuclear weapons are cheaper than either the conventional arms or the defensive systems that might replace them. This makes the use of economic analysis both appealing and misleading when trade-offs between nuclear arms and conventional weapons are considered.

Given the moral and political considerations dominating the offensive nuclear situation and given the general difficulties in answering most other defense questions, it is appropriate to establish clearly those areas open to economic investigation and solution before posing questions that presuppose that an economic answer could be derived. We believe that the trade-off between nuclear and conventional arms is not an appropriate issue for economic analysis. In addition, the use of defense spending to achieve domestic economic ends is neither efficient nor appropriate—defense spending should only be justified by valid defense requirements. Aside from these two areas, virtually every other facet of defense is fair game for economic analysis if the problems and objectives can be sufficiently defined. For this to occur, the following types of questions must be answered.

CRITICAL QUESTIONS ABOUT DEFENSE

What allocation of national resources between defense and nondefense expenditures should be made? In order to answer this question, the following questions will first have to be addressed: (1) What are the real military threats facing the United States? (2) What international military obligations does the United States have? (3) What are the valid requirements for social spending in the United States? (4) What are the social and military goals of the United States?

How should the United States deal with the requirement for people in the military? Should it draft its resources, try to pay a competitive wage, or use reserve forces? Before these questions can be answered, the following issues must be addressed: (1) What types of people are wanted in the military (young, old, educated, skilled)? (2) What are the roles of women in the military?

What type of industrial base should support the defense sector? This question presumes that the following questions have been answered: (1) What type of war is likely? (2) Should defense industries be privately owned or controlled by the U.S. government? (3) What level of subsidy is appropriate for defense industries? (4) Are subsidized defense industries compatible with the type of free-market economy found in the United States?

Does increased spending for defense automatically mean that the U.S. ability to defend itself will be enhanced? This question can be answered only after the following issues have been addressed: (1) How can cyclic spending patterns for defense be stopped or smoothed? (2) How should operations and maintenance costs be treated when cuts in defense spending are required?

What role should Congress play in the allocation of defense expenditures?

What type of military support for the U.S. allies is appropriate in light of the choices the countries have made regarding military and social spending? What is the appropriate role of military assistance to other countries? This question can be answered only after the following issues are addressed: (1) What are the political and economic effects of military assistance on the country receiving this aid? (2) What are the objectives of the U.S. military aid program?

CONCLUSIONS

These questions are all very difficult to answer. However, only by addressing such difficult questions can the United States hope to solve the fundamental resource allocation problems affecting defense. Ad-

dressing these issues successfully assumes a level of statesmanship on the part of members of Congress, a sense of direction on the part of the administration, and a degree of motivation on the part of industry and the Department of Defense that do not appear to exist at the present time. Unless a crisis acts as a catalyst to spur the kinds of action necessary to redress these problems, it is unlikely that real constructive changes will take place in the defense sector. And this implies that the country will continue to muddle along, suffering the effects of misallocated resources and tolerating a defense sector that operates at levels of effectiveness far below its potential. This, in turn, raises the most critical question of all: Can the United States continue to afford this type of activity on the part of its defense establishment?

The U.S. economy carries within itself the strength required to support its defense interests. But those interests must be funded in such a way that the strength inherent in the economy is preserved. Because the future is so uncertain, efficient central planning for resource allocations is extremely difficult. However, for private goods, a competitive economy will tend to allocate resources in the most efficient manner—if it is not subjected to unrealistic constraints. For defense and other government programs, spending choices should be subjected to efficiency standards based upon long-term national objectives. Hard allocative decisions should be made between defense and nondefense programs, not delayed, abrogated in favor of political gains, or subverted by open-ended assessments of needs or threats. The surest way to facilitate this is to develop clear relationships between government resource allocations and well-defined, long-term government output objectives.

NOTES

1. Weinberger, Caspar W., "What Is Our Defense Strategy?," Remarks to the National Press Club, Washington, D.C., October 9, 1985.

2. "Cap on a Hot Tin Roof," *Time*, February 11, 1985, p. 26.

3. Weinberger, Caspar W., *Annual Report to the Congress, FY 1987*, U.S. Government Printing Office, Washington, D.C., February 1986, p. 315.

Bibliography

Abrahamson, James A., Lt. General, USAF, "The Strategic Defense Initiative," *Defense*, August 1984.

Adams, Bob, "Congressmen Who Can Help Get Helped," *St. Louis Post Dispatch*, April 18, 1983.

Adams, Marc, "U.S. Contracts Hit $6.7 Billion in Area," *Washington Times*, November 2, 1984.

Additional Costs of the All-Volunteer Force, Report to Congress by the Comptroller General of the United States, FPCD-78-11, February 6, 1978.

Adelman, Kenneth L., "Japan's Security Dilemma: An American View," *Survival*, March/April 1981.

Alm, Richard, "As Defense Billions Pour Into the Economy," *U.S. News and World Report*, March 12, 1984.

An Analysis of President Reagan's Budget Revisions for Fiscal Year 1982, Congressional Budget Office, March 1981.

Anderson, James R., *Bankrupting America: The Tax Burden and Expenditures of the Pentagon by Congressional District*, Employment Research Associates, Lansing, Michigan, August 1984.

Andrews, Walter, "Drop in Top Recruits Worries Army Brass," *Washington Times*, November 14, 1984.

———. "Half of Military Parts Overpriced, U.S. Finds," *Washington Times*, September 27, 1984.

"Arms Builders Told Gap in Trust Harms Security," *Gazette Telegraph*, September 27, 1985.

Atlas/State Data Abstract for the United States, FY 1983, Directorate for Information, Washington Headquarters Services, Department of Defense, 1983.

Barry, James, *SDI Arms Control Background Paper*, R&D Associates, prepared for U.S. Air Force Space Command, Colorado Springs, Colorado, August 24, 1984.

Bethe, H., Garwin, R., Gottfried, K., Kendall, H., "Space Based Ballistic-Missile Defense," *Scientific American*, October 1984.

Biddle, Wayne, "New Study Finds Inflated Labor Costs on Weapons," *New York Times*, October 11, 1984.

———. "Pushing For Weapons That Work," *New York Times*, July 8, 1984.

Binkin, Martin, *America's Volunteer Military: Progress and Prospects*, Brookings Institution, Washington, D.C., 1984.

Blaker, James R., "Statement Before the Subcommittee on Foreign Operations," Committee on Appropriations, U.S. House of Representatives, March 28, 1985.

Blueprint For Tomorrow, Joint Air Force/Industry Assessment of the Aerospace Industrial Base, Department of Defense, U.S. Air Force, vol. 1, January 16, 1984.

Bosma, John T., and Whelan, Richard C., *Guide to the Strategic Defense Initiative*, Pasha Publications, Inc., Arlington, Va., 1985.

Brosman, James W., "Guard on the Front Line of Defense-Cost Fight," *Memphis Commercial Appeal*, February 15, 1984.

Brown, George F., Jr., "The Economic Consequences of Defense Spending: Implications for 1984 and Beyond," Testimony Presented to the Task Force on Economic Policy and Growth, Committee on the Budget, U.S. House of Representatives, 1983.

Brown, Harold, *Department of Defense Annual Report: Fiscal Year 1981*, U.S. Government Printing Office, January 1980.

———. *Department of Defense Annual Report: Fiscal Year 1982*, U.S. Government Printing Office, January 1981.

Brown, Michael E., "The Strategic Bomber Debate Today," *Orbis* 28, no. 2, Summer 1984.

Buck, John T., "The Health and Illness of the U.S. Aerospace Industrial Base Pinpointed in Massive Air Force/Industry Study," *Government Executive*, June 1984.

Builder, C., and Graubard, M., *The International Law of Armed Conflict: Implications for the Concept of Mutual Assured Destruction*, RAND, Santa Monica, California, January 1982.

Burgess, Tom, "Readiness an 'Illusive Goal', Analyst Charges," *Navy Times*, February 4, 1985.

Burns, Arthur F., "The Defense Sector: An Evaluation of Its Economic and Social Impact," *The Charles C. Muskowitz Lectures*, no. 8, School of Commerce, New York University, New York University Press, New York, 1968.

"Business Outlook," *Business Week*, December 10, 1984.

"Buying defense—or just weapons?," *Baltimore Sun*, April 22, 1984.

Cahn, A., Kruzel, J., Dawkins, P., and Huntzinger, J., *Controlling Future Arms Trade*, McGraw-Hill Book Co., New York, 1980.

Canan, James, *War In Space*, Harper & Row Publishers, New York, 1982.

"Cap on a Hot Tin Roof," *Time*, February 11, 1985.

Capra, J., et al., "The Effect of Foreign Military Sales on the Cost of U.S. Weapons," in *Foreign Military Sales and U.S. Weapons Costs*, Congressional Budget Office, Washington, D.C., May 1976.

Carrington, Tim, "Defense Contractors' Emergence as Big Winners in Reagan Tax Plan May Be Political Liability," *Wall Street Journal*, June 18, 1985.

———. "Pentagon Frustrates Reform Efforts," *Wall Street Journal*, December 26, 1984.

———. "Pentagon Softens Rule That Contractors Must Certify Overhead Billings As Proper," *Wall Street Journal*, April 17, 1985.

Carter, Ashton B., and Schwartz, David N., eds., *Ballistic Missile Defense*, Brookings Institution, Washington, D.C., 1983.

Chanda, Nayan, and Manning, Robert, "Washington Finesses Away Free Trade," *Far Eastern Economic Review*, October 25, 1984.

Chase Econometrics Conference on the Outlook for the U.S. Economy, Washington, D.C., September 18, 1984.

Cohen, Eliot A., "Constraints on America's Conduct of Small Wars," *International Security* 9, no. 2, Fall 1984.

Comptroller of the Air Force, *An Analysis of Weapon System Contract Cost Growth*, Management Analysis Report 69-10, U.S. Government Printing Office, Washington, D.C., 1969.

Conference on Forecasting the Impact of Defense Expenditures, Data Resources, Inc., Washington, D.C., May 5, 1984.

Conference on Improving National Security by Strengthening the Defense Industrial Base, Workshop I Findings, Harvard University, May 10–12, 1982.

Conine, Ernest, "Weapons: Quality vs. Quantity," *Los Angeles Times*, August 8, 1983.

Cook, David T., "Keeping Pentagon out of Wild Blue Yonder," *Christian Science Monitor*, December 5, 1983.

Cordesman, Anthony H., "Japanese Defense: The Election Means Long-Term Dependence on the U.S.," *Armed Forces Journal International*, March 1984.

———. "Strength Without Strategy, Programs Without Purpose?," *Armed Forces Journal International*, March 1984.

Correll, John T., "Why Spares Are Short," *Air Force Magazine*, September 1983.

Defense Against Ballistic Missiles: An Assessment of Technologies and Policy Implications, U.S. Department of Defense, U.S. Government Printing Office, Washington, D.C., April 1984.

"Defense Budget Seen Becoming Uncontrollable," *Washington Post*, April 4, 1985.

"Defense Department Looks for Double-Digit Growth in 1985," *National Review*, February 4, 1984.

"Defense Dollars, State By State," *U.S. News and World Report*, June 25, 1984.

Defense Financial and Investment Review, Department of Defense, June 1985.

"Defense Firms Cry Fair Play," *Gazette Telegraph*, September 24, 1985.

"Defense Spending and Jobs," *Defense Economics Research Report*, Data Resources, Inc., volume 2, no. 11, November 1982.

"Defense's Sneak Attack on a Warranty Law," *Business Week*, February 20, 1984.

Degrasse, Robert W., *Military Expansion, Economic Decline*, M. F. Sharpe, Inc., Armonk, New York, 1983.

Dewar, Helen, "Aspin Says Deficit's Size Overstated," *Washington Post*, May 14, 1985.

———. "GOP Plan on Defense Payroll Hit," *Washington Post*, April 1, 1985.

Dixon, Clement, "Building the Defense Indusrial Base," *Defense, Science & Electronics*, July 1983.

Doe, Charles, "Analyst Urges Radical Defense Shifts," *Air Force Times*, October 8, 1984.

Dyson, Freeman, *Weapons and Hope*, Harper & Row Publishers, New York, 1984.

Edsall, Thomas B., "Forgotten Issue: How Economic Policy is Shifting Income," *Washington Post*, October 31, 1982.

Fine, Stanley, and Weiss, Stanley A., "Yo-Ho-Ho and a Bundle of Bucks?," *New York News*, January 26, 1984.

"FY 1984 Revised and FY 1985 Budget Estimates Guidance," memo from the comptroller (Program/Budget), Office of the Assistant Secretary of Defense, July 27, 1983.

Fitzgerald, John, "Pentagon Dilutes Major Reform," *Hartford Courant*, April 17, 1985.

Fitzgerald, Randy, "Holding Pentagon Savings Hostage," *Wall Street Journal*, April 4, 1985.

Fossedal, Gregory A., "Reforming the Military Reform Push," *Wall Street Journal*, March 1, 1984.

Ganley, Michael, "DoD Asks 5.9% Real Growth for FY86, but Deficit Threatens Dubious Digits," *Armed Forces Journal International*, March 1985.

Gansler, Jacques S., "Let's Change the Way the Pentagon Does Business," *Harvard Business Review* 55, May-June 1977.

———. *The Defense Industry*, MIT Press, Cambridge, Mass., 1981.

Gargan, Edward A., "Army Selects Fort Drum as Home for a New Light Infantry Division," *New York Times*, September 12, 1984.

The Geographic Distribution of Potential Defense Expenditures, Economic and Analysis Division, Office of the Director of Program Analysis and Evaluation, Department of Defense, July 1984.

Goldwater, Barry, "Let's End Defense's Political Appointees," *Washington Times*, March 22, 1984.

Gordon, Michael R., "Data on Production Inefficiencies May Spur New Debate on Defense Contracting," *National Journal*, June 1, 1985.

Grant, E., Ireson, W., and Leavenworth, R., *Principles of Engineering Economy*, John Wiley and Sons, New York, 1976.

Gray, Colin S., *Nuclear Strategy and Strategic Planning*, Foreign Policy Research Institute, Philadelphia, Pennsylvania, 1984.

Greenberg, Daniel S., "Science for the Military," *Baltimore Sun*, February 6, 1984.

Greenberger, Robert S., "Defense Contractors Exceeded Estimates for Labor on Some Projects, Data Show," *Wall Street Journal*, June 24, 1985.

Greve, Frank, "Is The B-1 A Plane Whose Time Has Come?," *Philadelphia Inquirer*, (Magazine), March 18, 1984.

"Gulf Cities Vie for Lucrative New Navy Base," *New York Times*, November 25, 1984.

Halloran, Richard, "How to Cut the Deficit," *Business Week*, March 26, 1984.

———. "Trimming the Budget: The 7 Places to Look," *New York Times*, April 9, 1984.

Halstead, Wayne P., et al., *Security Assistance in Peace and War*, Strategic Studies Institute, U.S. Army War College, ACN 83018, Carlisle Barracks, Penn., 1983.

Hayes, Thomas C., "Defense Spending—Its Effect on Jobs," *New York Times,* October 16, 1983.

———. "Pentagon Spends More in Fewer Districts, Researcher Says," *New York Times,* August 13, 1984.

Helm, Robert W., "Price Escalation Indices," memo from the comptroller, Office of the Assistant Secretary of Defense, January 14, 1985.

Hempstone, Smith, "Japan's Defense Spending: When is Enough Enough?," *Washington Times,* March 16, 1984.

Hiatt, Fred, "Excess Profits: Pentagon's Fault," *Washington Post,* April 21, 1985.

———. "Military Construction Spending Benefits Home-Town Projects," *Washington Post,* June 22, 1983.

———. "Since Reagan Buildup, Number of Combat-ready Units Is Down," *Washington Post,* March 5, 1984.

———. "Senator Voices Sour Opinion of Air Force Milk Purchase," *Washington Post,* February 1, 1984.

Hiatt, Fred, and Atkinson, Rick, "U.S. a Tough Customer in Foreign Marketplace," *Washington Post,* June 23, 1985.

Hitch, Charles J., and McKean, Roland N., *The Economics of Defense in the Nuclear Age,* Harvard University Press, Cambridge, Mass., 1960.

Hobbs, David, "Ballistic Missile Defense Programmes," *Jane's Defense Weekly,* September 1984.

Hoffman, Fred S., *Ballistic Missile Defenses and U.S. National Security Summary Report,* Washington, D.C., October 1983.

Housman, Damian, "The Sirens of Military Reform," *Washington Times,* November 14, 1983.

"How the Pentagon Spends Its Billions," *Newsweek,* February 11, 1985.

Hyland, W. G., *Soviet-American Relations: A New Cold War?,* RAND, Santa Monica, California, May 1981.

"Independent Research and Development Project Technical Evaluation," Department of Defense Form 1855, August 1983.

Ingwerson, Marshall, "Do Arms Dollars Hurt the Economy?," *Christian Science Monitor,* September 11, 1984.

Jacobs, Sanford, "Obtaining Data to Bid on Military Jobs," *Wall Street Journal,* October 15, 1984.

Jacoby, Edmond, "New PAC To Finance 'Umbrella' Supporters," *Washington Times,* September 30, 1983.

Kanter, Herschel, "Defense Economics: 1776 to 1983," *Armed Forces and Society* 10, no. 3, Spring 1984.

Kaplan, Fred, "Air Force Answer to High Prices: Hide the Payments," *Boston Globe,* July 6, 1984.

Kauffman, William W., "Spending for a Sound Defense: Alternatives to the Reagan Military Budget," *The Committee for National Security,* March 22, 1984.

Keller, Bill, "As Arms Buildup Eases, U.S. Tries to Take Stock," *New York Times,* May 14, 1985.

———. "MX Debate: It's Not Over," *New York Times,* March 30, 1985.

———. "Now It's Not Just 'I Want You' but 'You Need Us'," *New York Times,* January 19, 1985.

————. "Port on Staten I. Is Dropped Out in Budget Plan," *New York Times*, January 18, 1985.

Kelly, Orr, "GI Pensions—Justified or 'An Outrage'," *U.S. News and World Report*, February 18, 1985.

————. "Why Pentagon Pays $44 For A Light Bulb," *U.S. News and World Report*, August 1, 1983.

Kennedy, G., *The Economics of Defense*, Faber and Faber Publishers, London, 1976.

Korb, Lawrence, "Points of Confusion in Forecasting Defense Expenditures," Conference on Forecasting the Impact of Defense Expenditures, Washington, D.C., May 8, 1984.

————. "The Price of Preparedness: The 1978–1982 Defense Program," *AEI Review*, no. 3, June 1977.

Kurtz, Howard, "Pentagon To Change New Rules," *Washington Post*, April 18, 1985.

Kyle, Deborah M., "Congress 'Meddled' With Over Half of DOD's FY84 Budget Line Items," *Armed Forces Journal International*, March 1984.

Layard, P., and Walters, A., *Microeconomic Theory*, McGraw-Hill Book Company, New York, 1978.

Leites, Nathan, *Soviet Style in War*, RAND, Santa Monica, California, 1982.

Lemann, Nicholas, "The Peacetime War," *Atlantic*, October 1984.

Levin, Doran P., "Firms Enriched by Military Buildup Search for Ways to Use the Money," *Wall Street Journal*, January 3, 1984.

Lewis, Paul, "The Third World Limits Its Arsenals," *New York Times*, March 18, 1984.

Lorette, R., "Cost Estimate Growth in Air Force Weapon System Acquisition," unpublished Ph.D. Dissertation, Harvard University, 1967.

"The Lost Squadron," *Detroit News*, June 22, 1983.

Luttwak, Edward N., "Why We Need More 'Waste, Fraud, and Mismanagement' in the Pentagon," *Commentary*, February 1982.

MacFarlane, Robert, assistant for national security affairs, remarks before the Commonwealth Club, San Francisco, California, August 3, 1984.

Major Suppliers to the Department of Defense, Defense Economic Impact Modelling System, PA&E Department of Defense, April 23, 1984.

Mapes, Lynda V., "For PACs It's The Gift, Not The Thought, That Counts," *Wall Street Journal*, November 1, 1984.

McKenna, Joseph, "Ethics and War, a Catholic View," *American Political Science Review*, September 1960.

McNichols, G., ed., *Cost Analysis*, Operations Research Society of America, November 1984.

Melchner, John W., reported in Hiatt, Fred, "Excess Profits: Pentagon's Fault," *Washington Post*, April 21, 1985.

Military Cost Analysis, Department of Economics, Geography and Management, U.S. Air Force Academy, Colorado, 1979.

Miller, Nathan, "Profiteers and Patriots," *Baltimore Sun*, October 30, 1984.

Milligan, Susan, "'National Emergency' Program Aids Ailing Arms Contractors," *Boston Globe*, July 6, 1985.

Millward, R., *Public Expenditure Economics*, McGraw-Hill Book Company, London, 1971.

Mohr, Charles, "Air Force Divides Jet Engine Order Between Two Rivals," *New York Times*, February 4, 1984.

———. "Ban Sought on Incentive to Military Contractors," *New York Times*, January 31, 1985.

———. "Critics See Key Flaws in Arms Cost Controls," *New York Times*, May 18, 1985.

Mollenhoff, Clark R., "AF Report Shows Salaries at Pratt and Whitney High," *Washington Times*, August 2, 1983.

Mossberg, Walter, "Some Congressmen Treat Military Budget as a Source for Patronage," *Wall Street Journal*, April 15, 1983.

Mulhern, John J., "The Defense Sector: A Source of Strength for Philadelphia's Economy" *Business Review*, The Federal Reserve Bank of Philadelphia, July/August 1981.

Munger, Michael C., "The High Cost of Protectionism," *Europe*, May/June 1984.

Musgrave, R., *The Theory of Public Finance*, McGraw-Hill Book Company, New York, 1959.

"NATO Troop Strength," *USA Today*, December 13, 1984.

"New Law Forbids Base Closures," *Gazette Telegraph* (Colorado Springs, Colorado), December 14, 1985.

"No Reaganomics," *Economist*, February 11, 1984.

Nunn, Sam, "It's Not What We Spend on Defense," *Washington Post*, June 4, 1985.

———. "U.S. Military Readiness: Its Measure Is Muddled," *Miami Herald*, August 5, 1984.

O'Brien, William V., *The Conduct of Just and Limited War*, Praeger Publishers, New York, 1981.

Olvey, L. D., Golden, J. R., and Kelly, R. C., *The Economics of National Security*, Avery Publishing Group, Wayne, New Jersey, 1984.

"Opportunities in Federal Procurement," speech given by a Department of Defense representative before the Council for Labor and Industry, Philadelphia, Pa., January 11, 1984.

"PACs of MX Missile Contractors Doubling Campaign Contributions," *Washington Post*, October 14, 1982.

Parry, Robert, "Defense PAC Money Skyrockets," *Washington Post*, April 1, 1985.

Payne, Keith B., *Laser Weapons in Space: Policy and Doctrine*, A Westview Replica Edition, Boulder, Colo., August 1983.

Payne, Keith B., and Gray, C., "Nuclear Policy and the Defense Transition," *Foreign Affairs*, Spring 1984.

"Pentagon Anti-fraud Unit Overmatched, Chief Says," *Gazette Telegraph*, October 2, 1985.

"The Pentagon Steps Up Its War on Shoddy Workmanship," *Business Week*, October 15, 1984.

Perry, William J., and Roberts, Cynthia A., "Winning Through Sophistication: How to Meet the Soviet Military Challenge," *Technology Review*, July 1982.

The Planning, Programming and Budgeting System, Directorate of Programs and Evaluation—AF/PRP, Department of the Air Force, Washington, D.C., December 1983.

Podhoretz, N., "The Present Danger," *Commentary,* 69, no. 3, March 1980.

"Potential Cuts Cited in Military Parts Bills," *Washington Post,* October 12, 1984.

Powers, Bruce F., *Is the United States Prepared for Its Most Likely Conflicts,* P-6592, RAND Corp., Santa Monica, California, February, 1981.

Public Papers of the Presidents of the United States: Dwight D. Eisenhower, 1960–1961, Government Printing Office, Washington, D.C., 1961.

"Quotelines," *USA Today,* April 3, 1985.

Ravenal, Earl C., "Defense Budget: Where is the Bottom Line," *Oakland Tribune,* April 16, 1984.

———. "On Scaling Down Defense Ambitions," *New York Times,* February 16, 1984.

Reagan, Ronald, "Address to the Nation," April 24, 1982.

"Regional Impacts of Defense Spending," *Defense Economics Research Report* 3, no. 2, Data Resources, Inc., Washington, D.C., February 1983.

"Reorganizing the Top Brass at the Pentagon," *Long Island Newsday,* April 29, 1985.

A Report to the Secretary of State, The Commission on Security and Economic Assistance, November 1983.

Rosen, Stephen, "Systems Analysis and the Quest for a Rational Defense," *The Public Interest,* no. 76, Summer 1984.

Rosenbaum, David E., "Weinberger Against Tax Postponing," *New York Times,* June 26, 1985.

Roth, William V., "Sharing the Burden of European Defenses," *Christian Science Monitor,* December 3, 1984.

Rovner, Mark, "We Need a Strong Military, but not Necessarily an Expensive One," *Norfolk Virginia-Pilot,* April 30, 1984.

Royce, Knut, "Defense Firms Cited for Wasteful Productivity," *Baltimore News American,* June 24, 1984.

———. "Weapon System Repair Will Cost '$1 Trillion'," *Albany Times-Union,* May 4, 1984.

Sagan, Carl, "Cons of Strategic Defense," *Discover Magazine,* September 1985.

Schemmer, Benjamin F., "When Reagan Promised You a 600-ship Navy, Why is Lehmen Building You a 700-ship Fleet?," *Armed Forces Journal International,* April 1985.

Schneider, William, "Statement Before the Subcommittee on Foreign Operations," Committee on Appropriations, U.S. House of Representatives, March 28, 1985.

Schrage, Michael, "Defense Budget Pushes Agenda in High-Tech R&D," *Washington Post,* August 12, 1984.

Scowcroft, Brent, *Report of the President's Commission on Strategic Forces,* Washington, D.C., April 1983.

Seib, Gerald F., "Arms Buildup Ordered by Reagan Could be Less Than Meets the Eye," *Wall Street Journal,* October 29, 1984.

———. "Defense Firms Pay More to Executives, Report Says," *Wall Street Journal*, October 29, 1984.

———. "Military Services Ordered to Start Buying Parts Jointly in Big Lots in Wake of Audit," *Wall Street Journal*, June 4, 1984.

"Senator Blames Congress for High Cost of Military," *New York Times*, January 11, 1985.

Shaw, Harry J., "Debts and Dependency," *Foreign Policy*, Spring 1983.

Silk, Leonard, "Cost-Effective Job Creation," *New York Times*, September 22, 1982.

———. "Economic Scene—War on Waste a Herculean Job," *New York Times*, December 7, 1984.

Sloss, Leon, "The Strategist Perspective," *Ballistic Missile Defense*, Carter, A., and Schwartz, D., eds., Brookings Institution, Washington, D.C., April 1983.

Standard and Poor's Industry Surveys, *Basis Analysis for the Aerospace Industry*, May 28, 1981.

"Star Wars, SDI: The Grand Experiment," *IEEE Spectrum*, September 1985.

"Staten Island's Big Payoff," *U.S. News and World Report*, January 28, 1985.

Statistical Abstract of the United States, 1985, U.S. Department of Commerce, U.S. Government Printing Office, Washington, D.C., 1985.

Steinberg, Bruce, "The Military Boost to Industry," *Fortune*, April 30, 1984.

The Strategic Defense Initiative: Defensive Technologies Study, U.S. Department of Defense, U.S. Government Printing Office, Washington, D.C., April 1984.

Struck, Myron, "Pentagon Factory Disposals Running Down," *Washington Post*, November 17, 1984.

Taft, William H. IV, "The Economic Effects of Defense Spending," Forecasting the Impact of Defense Spending, a conference sponsored by the Institute for Defense Analysis, Washington, D.C., May 8, 1984.

Teller, Edward, "Pros of Strategic Defense," *Discover Magazine*, September 1985.

Thompson, Mark, "Military Faulting Congress," *Fort Worth Star-Telegram*, February 24, 1985.

Thurow, Roger, "NATO's Economic Bind Restricts Its Defense Options," *Wall Street Journal*, June 5, 1984.

Thurston, Scott, "Army Falls Short of Enlistment Goal," *Atlanta Constitution*, November 1, 1984.

Tucker, Samuel A., ed., *A Modern Design for Defense Decision: A McNamara-Hitch-Enthoven Anthology*, prepublication edition, Government Printing Office, Washington, D.C., 1966.

"22 U.S. Bases Called Surplus," *New York Times*, March 6, 1985.

Ullman, Owen, "Report Says Pentagon Underestimates Its Costs," *Philadelphia Inquirer*, March 13, 1984.

Ulsamer, Edgar, "Charting a Course for SDI," *Air Force Magazine*, September 1985.

The United States Budget in Brief—FY1985, Office of Management and Budget, Washington, D.C., February 1, 1984.

"U.S. Dependency on Foreign Technology," memorandum for the deputy commanding general for research, development and acquisition, Department of the Army, December 1, 1982.

"U.S.: FMS Trade Offsets Process Considered," *Defense and Foreign Affairs Daily* 13, no. 83, May 2, 1984.

Vartabedian, Ralph, "B-1 Crash Debate Centers on Possible Design Flaws," *Los Angeles Times*, December 22, 1984.

Vessey, John W., chairman of the Joint Chiefs of Staff, address to the 19th Annual International Logistics Symposium, Minneapolis, Minn., August 21, 1984.

Vickery, Hugh, "Pentagon Probing Increases In Prices of Fighter Planes," *Washington Times*, July 8, 1984.

————. "Would You Believe a 16-page Recipe for Sugar Cookies?," *Washington Times*, July 9, 1985.

Warner, John W., "Economy Forces Need to Increase Ration of Reserves to Regulars," *ROA National Security Report*, January 1984.

Washburn, Donald D., and Gertcher, Frank L., *The Strategic Defense Initiative: Background, Transition and Strategy Evaluation*, RDA-TR-1800072-007, for Air Force Space Command, December 1984.

Weicker, Lowell, Jr., "Cap, You're Wrong: Defense Can Be Cut," *Washington Post*, February 28, 1985.

Weida, William J., "Some Fundamental Properties of Governmental Expenditure Patterns—Theory and Evidence Based on Military Expenditures," *Journal of Technology Transfer* 5(2), 1981.

Weida, William J., and Gertcher, Frank L., "Military Weapons Systems and Risk: Theory and Evidence," *International Journal of Social Economics* 13, no. 1, London, 1985.

Weida, William J., Gertcher, Frank L., et al., *An Economic Evaluation of Variable Housing Allowances*, USAFA Technical Report, December 1982.

Weinberger, Caspar W., Department of Defense Annual Reports, Fiscal Years 1981–1986 (various titles), U.S. Government Printing Office, Washington, D.C., 1980–1986.

————. "Remarks Before the USO Man of the Year Award Dinner," San Francisco, November 8, 1984.

————. *Soviet Military Power*, U.S. Department of Defense, U.S. Government Printing Office, Washington, D.C., 1984.

————. "What Is Our Defense Strategy?," Remarks to the National Press Club, Washington, D.C., October 9, 1985.

Weiner, Stephen, "Systems and Technology," *Ballistic Missile Defense*, Carter, A., and Schwartz, D., eds., Brookings Institution, Washington, D.C., 1983.

Weinraub, Bernard, "President Depicts Budget as Chance for a New Course," *New York Times*, February 5, 1985.

Weiss, Stanley A., and Morrison, James, "Defense 'Investment' Is Bad Business," *Los Angeles Times*, pt. 4, September 25, 1983.

Welch, Jasper, "What the Annual Report Does Not Say About Spare Parts," *Armed Forces Journal International*, March 1984.

Welling, Kathryn M., "No Farewell To Arms," *Barrons*, December 3, 1984.

Whence the Threat to Peace?, 3d ed., Moscow Military Publishing House, 1984.

"Why an Army?," *Fortune* 12, no. 3, September 1935.

"Why Congress Won't Freeze Defense Funds," *U.S. News and World Report,* February 11, 1985.

"Why G.E. Became a Pickpocket," *New York Times,* May 16, 1985.

Wilson, George C., "Reagan's Rearmament Plan Meets the Reality of Budget Cuts," *Washington Post National Weekly Edition,* September 30, 1985.

Wilson, George C., and Atkinson, Rick, "U.S. Gambles on Peacetime Military," *Washington Post,* August 19, 1984.

Winter, Ralph E., "Defense Dud—So Far, Arms Buildup Creates Few New Jobs," *Wall Street Journal,* March 23, 1983.

Wood, David, "Weapons Cost Estimate Cited As 30% Too Low," *Los Angeles Times,* February 26, 1983.

Worldwide Manpower Distribution by Geographical Area, Washington Headquarters Service, Department of Defense, September 30, 1984.

Wright, Joseph, "Blocking Federal Efficiency," *Washington Times,* November 27, 1984.

Yegrow, A. et al., *Soviet Military Thought,* no. 3, Moscow, 1983.

Index

WIDENER UNIVERSITY
WOLFGRAM
LIBRARY
CHESTER, PA.